PRAISE FOR *THE RECOVERED LIFE OF ISAAC ANDERSON*

"Sparked by her discovery of a 'mustard yellow all-but discarded brochure' on Isaac Anderson at Lane College, historian Alicia K. Jackson engaged in a near-decade-long quest to recover his extraordinary life as a founding minister of the CME Church, a Reconstruction politician, a school founder, an editor-publisher, a Lane College trustee, and a successful entrepreneur in the post-Emancipation South."
—LOGAN HAMPTON, president, Lane College

"Alicia K. Jackson provides the first biography of minister Isaac Anderson (1834–1906) through impressive research that creatively throws light on shadows and uncertainties in the written record of his life. Isaac Anderson's unique story gives voice to a history often silenced or ignored. After emancipation, Anderson helped lead the new Colored Methodist Episcopal Church, was elected to the Georgia senate, and was a publisher and educator. *The Recovered Life of Isaac Anderson* is an outstanding monograph that illuminates crucial issues in the history of enslavement, the Black church, and Reconstruction."
—JOHN PATRICK DALY, SUNY Brockport

"With the publication of *The Recovered Life of Isaac Anderson*, Alicia K. Jackson sets a new standard for biographies of nineteenth-century African American leaders. Using genealogical and other local records, she pieces together the background story of a mixed-race man born enslaved on the Georgia frontier who becomes, with freedom, one of the first Black elected officials in the state. Readers have Jackson to thank for reclaiming the inspirational story of the remarkable Isaac Anderson."
—GLENN T. ESKEW, Distinguished University Professor, Georgia State University

"*The Recovered Life of Isaac Anderson* is a deeply researched, compelling narrative of Reconstruction-era Black political participation and religious development brought to life through the biography of Colored Methodist

Episcopal minister Rev. Isaac Anderson. Covering the major themes of Black religious and political life after emancipation, including freed people's engagements with the Freedman's Bureau, the establishment of independent Black churches, convict leasing, and Black exodus, this volume revises narratives about the racial politics of the CME Church, while further illuminating the well-established narrative of Black churches as a catalyst for Black political participation and Black politics."

—NICOLE TURNER, assistant professor of religious studies, Yale University

THE RECOVERED LIFE OF ISAAC ANDERSON

THE RECOVERED LIFE OF
ISAAC ANDERSON

Alicia K. Jackson

University Press of Mississippi / Jackson

The University Press of Mississippi is the scholarly publishing agency of the Mississippi Institutions of Higher Learning: Alcorn State University, Delta State University, Jackson State University, Mississippi State University, Mississippi University for Women, Mississippi Valley State University, University of Mississippi, and University of Southern Mississippi.

www.upress.state.ms.us

The University Press of Mississippi is a member of the Association of University Presses.

Frontis photo courtesy of Carolyn B. Cunningham

Copyright © 2021 by University Press of Mississippi
All rights reserved

First printing 2021
∞

Library of Congress Cataloging-in-Publication Data

Names: Jackson, Alicia K., author.
Title: The recovered life of Isaac Anderson / Alicia K. Jackson.
Description: Jackson: University Press of Mississippi, [2021] | Includes bibliographical references and index.
Identifiers: LCCN 2021026158 (print) | LCCN 2021026159 (ebook) | ISBN 978-1-4968-3514-7 (hardback) | ISBN 978-1-4968-3513-0 (trade paperback) | ISBN 978-1-4968-3516-1 (epub) | ISBN 978-1-4968-3515-4 (epub) | ISBN 978-1-4968-3518-5 (pdf) | ISBN 978-1-4968-3517-8 (pdf)
Subjects: LCSH: Anderson, Isaac Harold, 1835–1906. | Anderson, William Jackson, d.1890. | Colored Methodist Episcopal Church—History. | Slaves—United States—Biography. | African Americans—Biography. | African American religious leaders—Biography. | African American politicians—Biography. | African American educators—Biography. | BISAC: HISTORY / African American & Black | SOCIAL SCIENCE / Ethnic Studies / American / African American & Black Studies
Classification: LCC BX8473.A53 J33 2021 (print) | LCC BX8473.A53 (ebook) | DDC 287/.8—dc23
LC record available at https://lccn.loc.gov/2021026158
LC ebook record available at https://lccn.loc.gov/2021026159

British Library Cataloging-in-Publication Data available

One of the hopes of this project is to help shed light on how the pernicious ideology of white supremacy weaponizes language. At times, the author felt it necessary to quote words that would be inappropriate in a spoken context in order to analyze how language functions in that instance. This is in no way an endorsement of the use of such slurs in a non-academic context.

CONTENTS

Acknowledgments IX
Introduction: The Recovered Life of Isaac Anderson. 3
Chapter One: 1868 12
Chapter Two: William Jackson Anderson 26
Chapter Three: Isaac Anderson. 47
Chapter Four: Georgia. 59
Chapter Five: 1870 77
Chapter Six: Exodus 96
Chapter Seven: Promised Land. 114
Chapter Eight: The Colored Methodist Episcopal Church. 130
Epilogue: The Forgetting 147
Notes 154
Index 216

To my grandparents,
who shaped my love for history and whose stories I can finally tell

ACKNOWLEDGMENTS

THIS IS A STORY THAT WAS ALMOST NEVER TOLD, WHETHER BECAUSE OF self-doubt that was reinforced by others or sheer weariness. But for God, it wouldn't have been written. He provided support and encouragement along the way through various people, and among them were Samuel Shepherd and Ted Ownby, both of whom represented the best of the history profession. I can say, without a doubt, that over the years in which this story was written, I would not be where I am today apart from their support. Samuel Shepherd was there for the harrowing calls of frustration and for the joyful personal and professional moments, and I owe much to him and to Julie, his wife, for being pillars of support to me and my family. Ted Ownby, who has unswervingly supported my scholarship, first told my wonderful former editor, Vijay Shah, about my book, and during one of the lowest periods of my career, he bought me dinner, listened to a litany of my struggles for at least an hour, and encouraged me to persevere. Though I have called, texted, and even FaceTimed him accidentally, never once did I feel like I was a bother to him even though he was certainly busy with his own projects and students.

A huge "thank you" also goes to my editor, Emily Bandy, who has been a champion of my book, and to Charles Reagan Wilson, who first introduced me to the study of Southern religion and led me to write about the Colored Methodist Church. He always encouraged my research. Thank you to Nancy Bercaw, a good friend who read early drafts of my manuscript, offering useful feedback and support afterward, and to John M. Giggie, Luke Harlow, Story Matkin-Rawn, and Bonnie Martin, all of whom not only read my work, but also spent time discussing my research and providing helpful suggestions to strengthen my manuscript. Jessica Lepler, Charles Irons, Lillie J. Edwards, Scott Nesbit, Nicole Meyers Turner, and Paul Harvey helped me think through larger issues raised by Isaac Anderson's life, and I thank these consummate historians as well.

I am indebted to the Louisville Institute for graciously awarding me a Grant for Researchers in 2016, which provided the funds to travel throughout the South and conduct research essential to uncovering Isaac Anderson's story. Jeff Hall, vice president of academic affairs at Covenant College, supported me by funding grants to conduct my research, and Paul Morton, my department chair, gave me a course reduction to aid in the publication of my book. Michelle Pickard and Brian Hecker, two of my colleagues, were tenacious in tracking down documents essential to my research, and John Holberg, director of the Covenant library, graciously shared his research skills and expertise in deciphering nineteenth-century cursive writing, which proved invaluable to the project.

Thank you to archivist Wilmetta Jackson at Fort Valley State University for always being willing to help and for embracing my project as if it were her own, and thank you to Jack Wood and Evelyn Keele at the Jackson Public Library for helping me understand Anderson's life after his move to Jackson, Tennessee. Thank you to Kayla Barrett, Steven W. Engerrand, and the wonderful staff at the Georgia Archives; the Madison, Tennessee, county archives; Brian Shelter at Drew University Archives; Brandon C. Wason at Pitts Theological Library; and Bobby Mitchell, of the Marshall County Historical Association. I extend a special thank you to Marilyn Windham, who has encouraged me to keep researching and helped me in every way she could to aid in the publication of this book. Without Marilyn's help, this book would have never been written. Thank you to William Mills who was always willing to direct me to sources and answer questions about life in and around Houston County.

I am grateful to Blanche Johnston, whom I first met years ago. She was gracious enough to tell me about Isaac H. Anderson, her grandfather, and was the first to give me details about him and the relationship he had with his father, William Jackson Anderson. Years after her passing, I would meet other descendants of Anderson who shared with me their stories about a man who shaped their lives decades after his passing. Among them were Joel Anderson, Bert Berry, Louis and Carolyn Cunningham, and Debbie Cannon. Moreover, a book like mine certainly could not have been written without tremendous support from my friends from family. Thank you Diana Cochran and Erika Mosteller for always being willing to encourage my work and self-care especially when the struggles of Isaac Anderson's world were all too familiar to my day-to-day world.

Thank you to my parents, John and Gloria Kaigler, who always encouraged me to strive for my dreams to be a historian, and thank you to my children Olivia, Jack, and Ella, who have been such a bright light in my life! One of my greatest honors is that I am your mother and that you have been with me through this journey, which makes the completion of this book even more meaningful. Learning cemetery etiquette, including not stepping on gravestones as we spent hours in the middle of the July heat trying to find gravesites, dropping your mother off to conduct research at an old prison, sitting in a café drinking hot butter beer, photographing abandoned buildings, swimming in hotel pools, visiting museums, and spending a lot of time at the library are adventures that I hope you will never forget.

Last, to my best friend, editor, and husband, Randolph Jackson Jr., thank you! When we first met, you promised to support me and my work, and you have more than lived up to your promise. You have moved so I could pursue my dream, taken care of the children when I needed to write or conduct research, stayed up virtually all night keeping your promise to edit my work, and have been my biggest supporter, telling your friends, acquaintances, and even people I do not know, about my book. When people recognize you as Reverend Jackson and call me Mrs. Jackson, you are first to make it known that your wife is "Dr. Jackson." We are a team, and I could not have done any of this without your love and support.

THE RECOVERED LIFE OF ISAAC ANDERSON

INTRODUCTION

The Recovered Life of Isaac Anderson

WHETHER TOLD BY MY PATERNAL GRANDPARENTS FROM SOUTH MISSISsippi or my maternal grandparents from South Georgia, stories have always been a part of my life. The stories I heard as a child were of Br'er Rabbit, John the Conqueror, and intermittent episodes from the adventures of my family members as young adults. These stories became a Morse code of sorts signaling everything from who could be trusted to how hardships in life should be handled. As I grew up, these stories matured with me and recentered themselves on subjects like injustice and painful family memories.

My grandparents often told these stories to me in vague generalities, fearing for my safety despite decades of distance from the actual events. These vague generalities or "silences," as defined by Elsa Barkley Brown, are characteristic of the ways in which most Black Americans communicated and operated in the rural South following emancipation, and these "silences" checker studies in African American history for a myriad of reasons, ranging from restrictions of literacy to cross-cultural fear and mistrust. Many significant stories of African American history have been lost or forgotten as a result, and historians bear an honorable burden of uncovering those "silences" when and where they are able.[1] As a historian and a recipient of stories containing many "silences," Isaac Harold Anderson has been my burden since the spring of 2003 and the basis of over a decade of work and research.

My awareness of Isaac Anderson began with a mustard yellow all-butdiscarded brochure that I found while doing research at Lane College in Jackson, Tennessee. His picture on the brochure was that of a light-skinned man with a high forehead, broad nose, and clear eyes. In it, he is wearing a bow tie and white shirt, what could be described as a typical preacher's suit, an expression giving the sense of an impending smile reserved for later use, and a complexion signaling biracial parentage. In nineteenth-century America, he would have been listed in census records as mulatto.

The brochure, put together by his granddaughter, unearthed to me important details of Anderson's life: His date of birth, his service in the Georgia legislature, his eventual move to Jackson, Tennessee, the name of his second wife, the accomplishments of his descendants, and his support for the poor and underprivileged. Two bits of information remained obscure like half-buried relics in the sand: The first was a reference implying a descendance from a William Jackson Anderson; the second, an omission of any reference to his mother. Historians are trained to examine not only details lying in plain sight, but also empty spaces where details should be. In slave narratives and oral histories, former slaves often convey a vague memory or a first name of their mothers, but for Isaac Anderson, nothing of his ancestry existed in the mysterious brochure other than the name of William Jackson Anderson.

Isaac Anderson served as a registrar near Fort Valley, a delegate to the Georgia Constitutional Convention of 1867–1868, a candidate for the state's legislature in 1868, a state Senator, and one of only five Black elected officials in Georgia in 1870. By 1874, he was one of the last two Black officials to serve in the Georgia Senate until Leroy Johnson in 1962. Today, Fort Valley is a notable community and home to Fort Valley State University, one of the oldest historically Black colleges and universities in Georgia, but with such a rich history, most African Americans living there do not recognize his name. He has no plaque or monument, and no notable references in the church that he helped to start and fund.

Silences shroud many of the Black politicians who, following Reconstruction, stayed in the South and whose stories descended into relative obscurity over time as noted by Reconstruction historian Eric Foner in *Freedom's Lawmakers*.[2] A major cause for these shrouds of silence are histories of Reconstruction that have downplayed Black leadership and regarded Black leaders as either radical or inept. W. E. B. DuBois would be the first to challenge these histories in 1935 with his work *Black Reconstruction: An Essay Toward a History of the Part Which Black Folk Played in the Attempt to Reconstruct Democracy in America, 1860–1880*.[3]

Until the last forty years, much of the scholarship exploring Reconstruction has been shaped by William Dunning who attributed many of the failures of Reconstruction to Black leadership and ultimately, to the Black community. The William Dunning school of thought at Columbia University influenced a cadre of doctoral students including C. Mildred Thompson. In *Reconstruction in Georgia: Economic, Social, Political 1865–1872*, Thompson softened some of Dunning's arguments but bemoaned the change in status of Blacks following Emancipation. "When the compulsory methods of slavery disappeared, there was absolutely no power to keep the negro steadily and regularly at work," she wrote. "Everywhere negroes worked more lazily than they did as slaves."[4]

Although scholarship on the role of former slaves' active participation in Reconstruction in Georgia has expanded, many historians still maintained aspects of earlier negative perspectives on Black agency. As Alan Conway wrote in *The Reconstruction of Georgia*, "the Negro as a laborer, was at his most unreliable and irresponsible, quite happy to take a vacation from work at the expense of the Freedmen's' Bureau." Nearly twenty years later in *Black Politicians and Reconstruction in Georgia*, Edmund Drago points to the Black minister as a problematic figure during Reconstruction arguing, "As antebellum preachers, slave and free, [Black ministers] had mastered the art of compromise in order to bring the Gospel message to the slaves ... Translated into politics, this produced a certain conservatism [where] they were acutely aware of the intellectual and material gulf between themselves and native born whites."[5]

Only since the 1990s have large studies investigated the experience and agency of Blacks in Georgia without the filter of Dunning's perspectives. The first major study challenging earlier assumptions about the racial and political acquiescence of Black leaders was Joseph P. Reidy's *From Slavery to Agrarian Capitalism in the Cotton Plantation South: Central Georgia, 1800–1880*. Here, Reidy provided a broader, more in-depth understanding of Reconstruction and the active role that former slaves adopted in grassroots efforts and as leaders in their communities. Susan O'Donovan also shares this perspective of Black agency during this period in *Becoming Free in the Cotton South*.

While many scholars have discounted the history of Black participation in Reconstruction as formulated by Thompson, Conway, and Drago, their perspectives remain prevalent with many who are not conversant with recent historical scholarship. Consequently, their perspectives still dominate the understanding of this period in many commercial and nonacademic publications. Most scholarship about the role of Black Georgians during Reconstruction available to most Georgians is still primarily told through the perspective of Thompson, Conway, and Drago. Their work (252 copies combined) can be found in Georgia's public libraries. In comparison, the state's libraries only have 8 copies of O'Donovan and Reidy's work combined, with nearly half of those only available electronically.[6] The dominance of these ideas in popular thought may offer an explanation for why it was not until 1984 that Robert Benham was elected to the Georgia Supreme Court where he would have been the first African American ever elected to statewide office in Georgia.[7] More recently, the dominance and persistence of these ideas also speaks to the significance of Stacy Abrams's close gubernatorial run against Brian Kemp in 2018 where she almost won election to the highest state office and would have been the first Black woman to do so in the South. Moreover, Abram's continued efforts arguably led to the election of Reverend Raphael Warnock in January 2021, making him only the fifth Black person elected to a statewide office as Georgia's first Black Senator. Abram's efforts are as much a challenge to the discounting of the significance of Black political participation during Reconstruction as they are today.

* * *

Isaac Anderson's story presents a microhistory of a Black minister and politician who struggled against violence and economic deprivation in the rural South during Reconstruction. The narrative that blossomed from a simple, mimeographed brochure is the recovered story of a Black leader's tenuous survival during this period and into the nadir of race relations. Anderson's survival, like that of many Black leaders who remained in the South, required painful acquiescence and a crushing passivity that was needed to navigate biased waters in the South. Yet, survival for Black leaders also required a dangerous impassivity needed to stand against and overcome devastatingly unjust social realities, and these dynamics make Anderson's story an important counterpoint to the Dunning perspective, which still permeates many histories of Reconstruction in Georgia.

The silences that cloaked Anderson created a void that pulled me further into a search to recover his life, and his life became a story bigger than the original brochure, which was simply an acknowledgment of a Black man living in Georgia during Reconstruction and serving his adopted community of Jackson, Tennessee. Like many African American leaders of his time, Anderson was well acquainted with betrayal and disappointment. He left no letters or diary by which others might know him, but threads of his life remain to be uncovered in a smattering of records from the Freedmen's Bureau, columns from his denominational newspaper, documents from municipal courts, and details pieced together from his father's life.

This narrative is a recovery of the lives of both Isaac and William Jackson Anderson, two men who are racially, politically, and culturally polarized yet locked in a tenuous relationship with one another within the context of Reconstruction in the rural South. William Jackson was both Anderson's master and his father, and the story of these two men highlights the power in ideas of race and racial constructs that were insurmountable for Anderson. Although both men had remarkable potential and success, Anderson could never escape the fact that he was a Black man or his decision to be identified as such.

The bond in blood that held the two men together was tested not only by the racial norms of the day but also by their vastly differing political choices. Isaac Anderson was a *radical* Republican, which was a pejorative used by many white Southerners because his political affiliation and his concern for the rights of newly emancipated Blacks classified him as virtually un-American. William Jackson Anderson was a Democrat who supported the Confederacy with his money and his politics. The spring election of 1868 found both men campaigning from Houston County, but for different offices in the Georgia legislature. Though the election was pivotal in their lives, each would experience different outcomes and pressures. The election of 1868 also brought with it the first surge of coordinated Ku Klux Klan violence to emerge in Georgia.

The lives of Isaac and William Jackson Anderson challenge the neat boxes that often characterize relations among former slaves and their masters. During these years, former slaves embraced their freedom and demanded greater economic opportunity, while their former masters responded with violence and legal tactics designed to re-establish a permanent underclass. These realities are represented in the work of Roger Ransom and Richard Sutch's examination of economic measures used by whites to undermine Southern Blacks during Reconstruction, and they are further emphasized in Eric Foner's landmark work, *Reconstruction*. Moreover, in *After Slavery: Race, Labor, and Citizenship in the Reconstruction South*, Bruce E. Baker and Brian Kelly further explore the economic limitations imposed on former slaves by former masters, and they conclude that much scholarship in this area has often resulted in "a steady output of studies emphasizing freedpeople's agency, but little acknowledgement until recently that there were limits to the former slaves' power to remake their world."[8] William Jackson's investments highlight the control of Black labor by the state's railroad and cotton industry and by Georgia's convict lease system which became a statewide source of labor through the work of former slaves. Anderson's narrative gives an understanding of the convict lease system, which he opposed, though ironically, he himself would very likely have been trapped within its legalized slavery if not for his father.[9]

As scholars in the 1990s began to re-evaluate Black leadership during Reconstruction, they simultaneously began to examine the convict lease system in Georgia. Alex Lichtenstein, Matthew Mancini, Douglas A. Blackmon, and Talitha L. LeFlouria have examined the personal stories of Blacks caught in the convict lease system, and Georgia's ranking as the state with the ninth highest incarceration rate in the nation further emphasizes the need to understand this history. In Georgia, three times as many Blacks are incarcerated than are whites, and the convict lease system which began this trend is a story that is essential to Isaac Anderson's experience as both a pastor and a politician.[10]

As the struggle to control the labor of Blacks continued, different perspectives on the role of federal, state, and local government in upholding labor laws developed between Southern whites and newly freed people. Paul A. Cimbala's *Under the Guardianship of the Nation: The Freedmen's Bureau and Reconstruction in Georgia, 1865–1870* demonstrates the hopes and disappointments experienced by Blacks living in Houston County who viewed the Freedmen's Bureau as an extension of the federal government and as enforcers of the rights protected under the Fourteenth Amendment. Many Southern whites extenuated injustice through legal and extralegal methods and curtailed the social and political expression of freed people when they stood in opposition to state and local power structures that were central to Southern white identity. This embracing of Constitutional rights encouraged Anderson and other former slaves to assert their "civil and legal rights" by voting and running for political office during Reconstruction.[11]

Anderson's story is one of how the Black church functioned as a political institution. His political involvement progresses from the antebellum South through the post-Reconstruction Era as former slaves established a power structure within their communities and churches as referenced by Steven Hahn's classic, *Nation Under Our Feet*. It was here that Blacks organized; churches became centers of education and civil engagement as typified throughout Anderson's life.[12] It is no surprise that Black leadership was so closely tied to the church, which was the only space where a Black person could testify against a white person, thus creating a unique albeit limited space for Black ministers to speak to the white power structure.

Anderson's story gives a more complete picture of Black ministers who contended with both intraracial and interracial politics immediately following Emancipation and were politically active within their own communities in ways that were visible and threatening to many Southern whites. In Houston County, political leadership among former slaves began with slave missions sanctioned by whites, and in these missions, Black pastors and lay leaders ministered to slaves who worshipped freely and distinctively as a group. With emancipation, these same men continued as community leaders, using their status as officially recognized clergy to organize their flocks into distinct congregations and their communities into solid political constituencies. Anderson's story brings detail to how Black political organizing coincided with the creation of independent Black churches and their role as a viable means of political organization following Emancipation.

During Reconstruction, the African Methodist Episcopal Church (AME) and African Methodist Episcopal Church, Zion (AME Zion) contended with the Colored Methodist Episcopal Church (CME) for members as many freedmen joined Black-led denominations. Each denomination had a representative involved in Georgia's politics, and these men played a critical role in fostering Black agency during Reconstruction as white Methodists from the North and South competed for influence among Black congregations. AME minister Henry McNeal Turner, AME Zion minister Tunis Campbell Sr., and Anderson, who was a CME minister, all served in the Georgia Constitutional Convention in the winter of 1867–1868. Later, all three would serve in the Georgia legislature: Henry McNeal Turner in the Georgia House; Tunis Campbell Sr. and Isaac Anderson in the Georgia Senate.[13]

Although a number of histories have been written about the CME Church including autobiographies of CME co-founders Lucius Holsey and Isaac Lane, none have examined Anderson's life or his political career, and his narrative challenges the portrayal, dominant with many historians, of the CME Church as a nonpolitical entity in its early years.[14] Uncovering Anderson's ministerial and political involvement builds upon research on Black Methodism by highlighting the relationship between him and Henry McNeal Turner. Recovering his story expands upon research exploring intraracial tensions that developed during Reconstruction as former slaves established their own separate churches.[15] Katherine Dvorak, Reginald Hildebrand, William Montgomery, Christopher Owen, Daniel Stowell, and Clarence Walker have produced work exploring this area and the complexities behind the creation of the CME Church at the dawn of what would become the "Long Civil Rights Movement."[16]

Following Emancipation, Black churches offered former slaves political and social shelter by allowing them freedom of both worship and speech. In their churches, freedpeople could work through the traumas of slavery, the troubles of daily living, and share in a common presence of suffering with silent understanding. They could also verbalize their fear of Klan supporters who employed many of them. The Black church became a safe space, and the Black minister, a great comforter to his congregation. Isaac Anderson's story builds upon research into Black churches established during Reconstruction, and uncovering his life furthers many studies of trauma by exploring how the Black church provided places of spiritual healing for freedpeople from slavery, violence, and the oppression that was part of their daily living.[17] The legacy of such spaces was at the center of much discussion during the Obama administration as scholars debated whether or not the Black Church was dead.[18] During the Trump administration, this discussion resurfaced as a racial divide between evangelicals, and Black Christians raised the question of safe spaces for people of color, yet during Reconstruction, this discussion was central to Anderson's work and the creation of the CME Church.

Beginning in the late twentieth century, Black Americans, and especially Black millennials, began to seek safe spaces and economic opportunities in a reverse migration from the urban North to the South. This new migration is a homecoming of sorts rooted and intertwined in a strange intergenerational link with Anderson's story, the hopes of former slaves after Emancipation, and the experience of freedpeople during Reconstruction.

As Reconstruction waned and freedpeople became exasperated with the barrage of lynchings and violence directed at them, Anderson and other well-known ministers like Henry McNeal Turner and CME co-founder Lucius Holsey encouraged an exodus to safer spaces. Turner called for an exodus to a new "promised land" with his Back to Africa movement, and Holsey eventually called for the creation of an all-Black state in what is today Oklahoma. Black leaders perceived these safer spaces as a "Canaanland" with new opportunities to live free of white control, as highlighted in William Cohen's *At Freedom's Edge,* Ira Berlin's *The Making of African America: Four Great Migrations.* The recovery of Anderson's story enriches the work of these scholars by illuminating the motivation of Blacks from Georgia to find safe spaces in other areas of the South. Rather than traveling west, many opted to move to places like Arkansas and Mississippi, where life was better, for a time. Historians often overlook the story of intrasouthern migration, and a recovery of Anderson's life provides an important lens into understanding why some former slaves stayed in the South while others joined a massive exodus North as typified in Nell Painter's *Exodusters: Black Migration to Kansas after Reconstruction,* and later Isabel Wilkerson's *The Warmth of Other Suns.*[19]

Anderson was instrumental in helping freedpeople leave Georgia for the security of progressive safe havens with significantly large Black communities in northern Mississippi and eastern Arkansas. Eventually under threat to his life, he made his own exodus to Arkansas, which was an initial refuge and incubator for both CME churches and Black leaders like J. H. Blount, the first African American to run for governor in Arkansas. St. Francis County in Eastern Arkansas became home to Black farmers, sharecroppers, and a growing labor movement.[20] Later, Anderson migrated to North Mississippi, where a vibrant Black community and a number of CME churches thrived.

In *Reconstruction in Marshall County Publications of the Reconstruction in Northern Counties of Mississippi,* Ruth Watkins highlights the significant power and influence of Black communities while questioning the ability of

Black leaders during Reconstruction. John W. Kyle in *Reconstruction in Panola County*, and many other histories of Reconstruction in Mississippi follow a similar track that moves from a period of ineptitude for Black leadership to brutal oppression experienced in Black communities at the beginning in the 1890s, the nadir of race relations. Uncovering Anderson's exodus to Mississippi and his experience living there gives a different perspective of these leaders and communities. In *The Negro in Mississippi 1865–1890*, Vernon L. Wharton first began an examination of many of them.[21]

As the turn of the twentieth century approached and hostility grew in Mississippi, many Blacks left the South altogether, migrating to the Midwest and Northeast. Anderson left north Mississippi, migrating to Jackson, Tennessee, which was the location of a large and influential Black community and the birthplace of the CME Church. Yet, his story is rooted in Fort Valley, Georgia, and begins with the election of 1868, where he would make his first major political stand and publicly challenge the political stance of his father, William Jackson Anderson. The next two chapters chart his family's history, his call to ministry, and the role of race in advancing and limiting the opportunities so key to the American experience in the nineteenth century. Chapter 4 delves into Anderson's experience of his community's loss of families, children, and dignity. In chapters 5 and 6, he builds a foundation for the CME Church and simultaneously returns to political office. New opportunities materialize in chapter 7, while disappointment and loss test him in chapter 8 as the nadir of race relations begins in earnest by 1890 and finds Anderson both remaking and embracing his identity as his father's son.

The Recovered Life of Isaac Anderson is a piecing together of lost "silences." By gathering together threads from recovered details of his life, a narrative emerges of unbreakable ties, the search for safe places, and the inescapable role of race in defining how and for whom the American dream is attainable. The search for pieces of his story has often led to a brick wall, where the historical record seems to come to an end, but then an unexpected document is found, or an unexpected contact is made. Genealogists say that these times are when the ancestors want us to find them and the stories they have to tell. It's in these moments that Isaac Anderson's story is very much like the stories I heard growing up, and the narrative of Anderson's life is a vaguely familiar morse code signaling the zeitgeist of Black experience.

> 1865 Civil War Ends—1865 Lincoln Assassinated—
> 1865 Freedmen's Bureau Established

Chapter One

1868

IN JANUARY 1868, JAMES MAURICE THOMPSON, WHO WAS AN ASPIRING engineer, writer, and former Confederate soldier, penned a response in the *Weekly Georgia Intelligencer* to Georgia's Constitutional Convention:

> Shall low-born scum and quondam slaves
> Give laws to those who own the soil?
> No! by our grand-sires' bloody graves,
> No! by our homesteads bought with toil
> Our rights are rooted in our lands,
> Our law is written in the sky,
> Fate flings the fiat from her hands-
> The Whites shall rule the land or die! [1]

To Thompson, Georgia's second federally mandated Constitutional Convention, which included freedmen in the process of revising the state's constitution, was the work of Republican "radicals" who supported the civil and legal rights of former slaves. Thompson and others considered the mandate to be a ploy of white Republican progressives to bring former slaves to power in order to elect even more Republicans. In their eyes, former slaves were considered intellectually and morally incapable of voting, and as Robert L. Dabney, who was a prominent Southern church leader during Reconstruction, explained, "The tenor of the argument concedes, what every man, not a fool, knows to be true: that the negroes, as a body, are now glaringly unfit for the privilege of voting. What makes them unfit? Such things as these . . . a dense ignorance of the rights and duties of citizenship . . . a general moral grade so deplorably low as to permit their being driven or bought like a herd of sheep by the demagogue: a parasitical servility and dependency of nature, which characterizes the race everywhere, and in all ages: an almost total lack of real persevering aspirations: and last, an obstinate set of false traditions, which bind him as a mere serf to a party, which is the born enemy of every righteous interest of our State."[2]

Most Southern whites viewed former slaves as ill-prepared for freedom and political office, and before 1867, their view left most if not all freedpeople in Georgia with no opportunity to vote, serve in office, or elect candidates who supported their concerns. Southern legislators worked to undermine suffrage for Blacks and reinstitute conditions of slavery. They saw former slaves as uninformed, immoral, disinterested in progress, and unmistakable enemies of the state, and the "advice" given to those freedpeople who could vote was clear: "When voting time comes you had best go to your old master and get him to give you a ticket—that is, a little piece of paper—and he will tell you what to do with it."[3] Both freedpeople and former slaves, however, saw suffrage as a solution to the injustice and violence facing them in Georgia and throughout the South.

* * *

In 1865, after Emancipation and the end of the Civil War, efforts to return the South to the Union began under President Andrew Johnson, who focused on quickly restoring the nation. Soon after the end of the war, former Confederates who took an oath of allegiance to the US Constitution received amnesty, and Southern states appointed provisional governors and held constitutional conventions. In Georgia, James Johnson was appointed provisional governor by President Johnson, and the state began its first attempt at Reconstruction, calling a constitutional convention just days later. The all-white convention was held in Milledgeville, the state capital at that time, and by November of that year, white voters ratified the newly written constitution and elected a new legislature and Charles Jenkins as the new governor.

Federal authorities established a massive presence in the state to maintain order and protect the rights of freedpeople and Southern Republicans, and agents from the Freedmen's Bureau were present at Georgia's Constitutional Convention of 1865 to represent the interest of former slaves, yet the convention unofficially excluded Blacks from participation and did not extend or encourage voting franchise for former slaves. Reports of the mistreatment of Blacks continued to stream in to federal authorities in the region, and a year later in 1866, Governor Jenkins and the state legislature, who were ever defiant of President Johnson and federal oversight, rejected early attempts to ratify the Fourteenth Amendment, which grants citizenship and the due process of law to anyone born in the United States.[4]

The nation's congressional elections held in November of 1866 changed the course of Reconstruction as Republicans established a two-thirds majority, gave their party the votes to override any presidential veto, and ended President Andrew Johnson's skewed oversight of the South. Republicans pushed for a more progressive agenda once elected to Congress and, under Congressional Reconstruction, approved a number of bills by the spring and summer of 1867. One established five military districts with military governors and courts empowered to try criminal, civil, and property rights cases, and another barred high-ranking Confederate officials from political participation. That year, Congress required the ratification of the Fourteenth Amendment by states before they could rejoin the Union, which was an important measure since this was required for representation in Congress.

With Congress leading Reconstruction efforts by 1867, the balance of political power began to shift dramatically in the South. The election of white and Black Republicans to state and local positions in the South that year underscored the effect of federal oversight and the voting power of former slaves. In Georgia, opposition to Reconstruction was so intense that the state was subjected to federal oversight for a total of three times (in 1865, 1867, and 1870).

After overriding a presidential veto, Congress passed a third Reconstruction Act in July of 1867 confirming each military governor's power to remove state officials from office. With roughly 15,000 troops stationed in the South, Republicans hoped to expand their party base and combat the violence directed at former slaves and whites who supported the Republican Party. Under the command of former Union General John Pope, Georgia was placed in the third military district alongside Alabama and Florida.[5] Adhering to Congress's mandate, Pope appointed registrars who in turn registered thousands of voters, and he also required that one out of every three registrars be Black. Pope considered it important to register the thousands of freedmen in Georgia to support the legitimacy of the new constitutional process, and his concern was driven by his desire for fair representation, not by any belief in the equality of Blacks with whites. His task was monumental: many white Georgians had faced Northern forces in battle just a year earlier and were hostile to federal oversight and officials from the North who now dictated the details of Reconstruction. Pope succeeded in registering nearly 80 percent of all adult male Georgians in time to vote on whether to hold a new Constitutional Convention and elect delegates to serve in the convention.

Angered by federal intrusion, most whites boycotted the congressionally mandated elections held in Georgia between October and November of 1867. To most white Georgians and Southerners, a newly emancipated Black man was nothing more than a "cuffee" or "big black nigger [who] comes and shuffles off your very fattest hog in his huge paws!"[6] Moreover, many considered the elections to be "the studied intention of the District Commanders to raise radicalism at the expense of the white voters of the South, and to thrust down our throats negro government . . . especially . . . the Convention question."[7] Out of 106,410 total votes, 102,283 were cast in support of the Constitutional Convention due largely to Black voters, and 37 Black delegates, primarily from the black-belt regions of the state, were elected to attend.[8]

White Georgians, angered by the election's results and the upcoming convention, retaliated. As Georgia's provisional governor, Charles Jenkins was overshadowed by the federal oversight of General Pope and reluctantly issued a proclamation calling on white residents to "bow before [God's] throne [when] Subjected to a form of Government, not of their own choosing, nor congenial to their cherished love of liberty, and menaced with social disorder and popular commotion, by the evil machinations of unofficial intruders and agitators."[9] In Milledgeville, many white Georgians refused to provide lodging for the thirty-seven Black delegates to the convention, and in response, General Pope made plans to move the convention's location. Plans had been underway to make Atlanta the state's new capital, so when hostility toward the convention surfaced, Pope sped up the process and moved the event to Atlanta's City Hall, which was near his headquarters and the protection of federal troops.[10]

Residents in the state kept up with the latest developments from the convention in local newspapers where they read daily reports of convention happenings and disturbing news concerning challenges to Southern traditions and perspectives. The arrest of Berry T. Bigby was one such challenge: Bigby, a Jasper County Sheriff, was arrested for failing to apprehend Homer Barnes, a white man accused of murdering Maria Brown, a Black woman who died on Bigby's farm. The *Atlanta Daily Opinion* portrayed Bigby as a man who "always stood high" and had many friends who "regret that anything should have occurred to cause him trouble."[11] Such stories were sprinkled in-and-around reports and commentary about the convention and served to effectively bias its proceedings in the eyes of white Georgians.

The convention lasted from December 9, 1867 until March 11, 1868, and by its conclusion, one hundred, sixty-nine white and thirty-seven Black delegates had extended voting rights to all men, granted married women property rights, and established free public schools and debt relief. Two former slaves joined three white men in representing the twenty-third district which included Houston, Crawford, and Taylor counties: Samuel A. Cobb represented the large Black community in Perry, and Isaac H. Anderson represented the large Black community in Fort Valley.¹² With freedmen having political power for the first time in counties with large Black majorities, fear grew among whites at the prospect of Blacks dominating both local and state government.¹³ Reflecting this sentiment, The *Macon's Weekly Telegraph* published the raucous musings of "Caesar Pumpernickel" of Corn Hollow who though fictitious, represented the former slave with political power to many white Georgians: "Golly, I's free now—I is. Got lots of frenz. All dem white folks in de Norf . . . old Mars, . . . He ain't good as a nigger now . . . He can't hole no offiis. He can't go to der'vention and make de speeches, and help make de laws. All he kin do is ter pay de taxes, . . . I'se got de franchise, I has . . . De franchiseese do make a nigger feel big. Halle-lu-yah!"¹⁴

* * *

Yet, after the convention, Georgia was still a distance away from rejoining the Union. Not only did a new Constitution need to be written and approved with the support of the majority of delegates, but it also had to be approved by Georgia's electorate. A new legislature and governor also had to be chosen, and once in place the new state legislature would need to ratify the Fourteenth Amendment. Over the course of four days in April of 1868, the elections that followed the Constitutional Convention pushed the entire state to the edge of hell. A month after the elections, the *Georgia Weekly Telegraph* would publish these words from an anonymous correspondent: "We want peace, and want, with it, good government, carried on and administered by wisdom, intelligence and virtue—not by ignorance and vice. And hence we say this should be a white man's government, doing at the same time full justice to the colored men."¹⁵

John B. Gordon, a former Confederate officer, and Rufus Bullock contended for Governor, and for most white Georgians, the thought of Bullock as Governor was more than many could stomach. Bullock, who was originally from New York and supported Black suffrage was considered a traitor to his race and accorded with less respect than a "black nigger" in that he was a "nigger from choice."¹⁶ Gordon, however, was known as one of General Robert E. Lee's most trusted officers, and his relationship with Nathan Bedford Forrest, a fellow Confederate General and Ku Klux Klan Grand Wizard, was enduring. Gordon, who grew up roughly thirty miles south of Chattanooga, Tennessee, in the northwest corner of Georgia, was himself the head of the Ku Klux Klan in the state.

That April, Black men publicly ran for office for the first time. Henry McNeal Turner, Samuel A. Cobb, and Isaac H. Anderson had been Black delegates from central Georgia to the Constitutional Convention, and in 1868, they ran for seats in the Georgia legislature.[17] The *Macon's Weekly Telegraph* accused Anderson, who was known as "Big Ike' in the white press, of forcing the votes of Blacks in Houston County: "[Negroes] are getting sick and tired of the tricks that are attempted to be practiced upon them by such men as Big Ike (big in his own estimation) and bad white men who are setting him on in the hope of office and money. Let us have peace . . . Let the races be at peace with themselves and each other . . . That is what all good men, white and Black, should want to strive for."[18]

Earlier, in October of 1867, *The Federal Union* published the editorial conclusion that Black support for Republican candidates was an attempt by the "Cuffee . . . to humble and degrade the white men of the South . . . Those black men who remain at home and attend to their honest business will be respected and treated as neighbors and friends."[19] In April of the following year, Black men not only supported white Republican candidates but also ran for office in Georgia's legislature publicly for the first time, asserting the "civil and legal rights" that they hoped to gain officially when the Fourteenth Amendment, passed by Congress in 1866, would finally be ratified by the state.[20]

The *Georgia Weekly Telegraph* characterized Cobb and "Ike" Anderson as charlatans who "instead of giving [former slaves] their forty acres of land and a mule, or anything else, as promised, had given themselves $9 a day, which the voters do not make for a month of labor."[21] With a veneer of Southern gentility, the newspaper also published the tactics that white leaders used to undermine Black voters in the 1868 elections: "We sought to convince them we were not their enemies but their best friends—that we were dependent on them, and they on us—they on us for employment and homes, and we on them for labor—and that they and we should by all means be friends. We said to them much on this subject, and we think they were impressed by what we said."[22]

The truth was that personal threats of violence pervaded the four days of voting, and because voting was not an Australian or secret ballot, freedmen were keenly aware of the ways that whites throughout the polling stations worked to remind Black voters of what party they should support.[23] The coordination between local whites and federal troops in Houston County promoted systematic intimidation that guaranteed a Democratic victory in the majority Black district. Joel R. Griffin, a self-described lone white Republican in Houston County and a candidate for the county House seat, described the first day of the election on April 20 as chaos. Whites reportedly "went to the polls with the freedmen and saw their votes deposited."[24] Black men gathering to vote at the Perry court observed the sergeant of the federal troops, who was sent to preserve an orderly election, arriving "drunk and talking politics with the colored people [and] advocating for the Democratic side of politics." Griffin was disturbed by the soldiers who mingled with "Colored" voters, expressing "sharp words with them for the way they were voting, [and changing] the ticket they had." He also observed federal troops "carry the Colored [men] into a room where votes were being regularly received . . . even beating them in some instances."[25]

For white Democrats, Griffin became a "radical" and a "blood thirsty, Yankee-hating, confederate scallywag [sic]."[26] In Fort Valley, he was remembered by whites as "a traitor to his race."[27] In commenting on Griffin, the *Georgia Weekly Telegraph* reported after the elections that "many hard, severe things were said of the white Radical . . . who was a candidate for representative with [Cobb and Anderson] . . . He certainly had not been the negro's friend."[28]

Overwhelmed with interference by federal troops, Ben Cobb, who was also serving as the registrar, watched impotently as ballots were manipulated.[29] After his and Anderson's defeat, Griffin protested the results of Houston County's election and filed a complaint with General George G. Meade, the state's military governor at the time. Although Anderson and Cobb were the only Black candidates running to represent Houston County in the state legislature, neither protested the outcome of the election, but they would later join Griffin in petitioning the Georgia legislature to unseat the three representatives elected to the Georgia House in 1868.

In another matter, Griffin also complained to the Freedmen's Bureau regarding Union infantryman Henry Moyatt, who days before the election on April 12, "came in town to give himself up to the Sergeant stating that he had shot a freedman 'in self defence [sic].'" After questioning a witness, the coroner's jury found that the federal soldier was "somewhat under the influence of liquor" when the unnamed freedman was shot.[30]

April of 1868 proved to be a disappointment for many whites in Georgia as the state's new constitution was approved, Rufus Bullock was elected governor (contrary to the previous election results), and thirty-three Black men were elected to the state legislature in a slim Republican victory. Benjamin Hill, who had been elected to the Georgia legislature previously, described the newly revised constitution as a "condemnation of every man, and every member of [Georgia's] society."[31]

On May 1, 1868, the *Georgia Weekly Telegraph* published the following election results from Upson County, where Democrats had triumphed over Republicans. Whites who were considered traitors to their race were overtly noted:

Against the Constitution 765; for the Constitution 738
For Governor—John B. Gordon (Dem.) 735: R. B. Bullock (White Nigger) 728.
For Congress—O.A. Lochrane (Dem) 781; Gove (White Nigger) 713
For States Senate—Geo L. F. Birdsong (Dem) 767; E.J Higbee (White Nigger) 713
For Representative—John C. Drake (Dem) 786; Wm. Gilford (Black Nigger) 713.[32]

On July 4, 1868, Georgia's newly elected legislature met on the nations' birthday as a symbol of the new chapter in the state's history. This symbolism was at first strengthened by the legislature's passage of the Fourteenth Amendment, which granted citizenship to former slaves and stipulated that "no state shall make or enforce any law which shall abridge the privileges or immunities of citizens of the United States; nor shall any state deprive any person of life, liberty, or property, without due process of law; nor deny to any person within its jurisdiction the equal protection of the laws." That September, state legislators violated the amendment by expelling from office every Black leader elected previously in April 1868 on the grounds that the Georgia Constitution did not specify that Blacks could hold public office.[33]

Emboldened by the legislature's actions, white Georgians brutally shot down a gathering of freedpeople along with a handful of whites at a political rally in Camilla only days after the expulsion of the legislators. This event later became known as the Camilla Massacre, and as reports of violence grew, ousted Black Georgia legislators petitioned Congress and found strengthened support among Republicans who, despite losing seats in Congress, were still in the majority and were buoyed by the election of Ulysses S. Grant, the Republican presidential candidate, in November 1868. By January of 1870, Georgia came under federal Reconstruction for a third and final time.

* * *

"One of the most serious problems facing Negroes was the scarcity of competent leaders."[34]

Historians have described the Black delegates to Georgia's Constitutional Convention as "colored men who were easily intimidated by whites" and as men from a "black elite that suffered from misplaced faith in the good intentions of their white opponents." According to this perspective, these men were, historically, victims of circumstances for whom "slavery had not provided any opportunities . . . to develop a capacity for leadership, much less to be familiar with politics."[35]

In addition, scholars of Reconstruction have focused on leaders from outside of Georgia for the simple reason that these men left behind memoirs, diaries, or letters, making their voices more accessible and visible to scholars. Moreover, historians have pointed to the fact that Black leaders in 1868 like Aaron A. Bradley, Tunis G. Campbell Sr., and Henry McNeal Turner were all men from outside the state; consequently, they have concluded that Black indigenous leadership in Georgia was nonexistent; Black men from outside the state were the most vocal in speaking for the rights of Blacks in Georgia.

Yet, the idea that few indigenous Black leaders existed among 3,500 free people of color in Georgia, or among the state's 462,108 slaves in 1860, or among the 545,142 Blacks in the state in 1870, is hard to believe. By maintaining this perspective, scholars have proposed that slavery in Georgia so stripped Blacks of their selfhood and autonomy that no leadership of note ever emerged from within the state and that slavery in Georgia was unique in comparison to slavery perpetuated elsewhere in the American South.[36]

Isaac Harold Anderson, or "Big Ike" as he was known by white critics, was born in Monroe County, Georgia, on March 1, 1835; he was listed in Houston County's census as an illiterate mulatto.[37] His tawny complexion and the mustache framing the corners of his mouth drew attention, but to many, his long hair was his most striking feature.[38] According to his descendants, he was a clerk in his master's cotton business as a young slave; according to other sources, he also worked as a blacksmith, carpenter, and minister in Fort Valley's Slave Mission.[39]

Anderson's development as a leader among former slaves developed through the instruction of white Methodist ministers like Reverend Jasper Cotter, who was the pastor of the Fort Valley Methodist Episcopal Church. He and three other former slaves received instruction from Reverend Cotter, who in 1866 recalled, "We instituted a literary and theological institute for the negroes. These brethren came to my home two or three times a week at night, and we started in the spelling book. Some could read a little."[40]

Anderson's development was also influenced by Rev. James Dunwoody, a white Methodist pastor at Fort Valley's Slave Mission who developed religious instruction to fit what he considered to be the intellectual capacities of Black congregants. His pedagogical focus on "simplicity" and "plainness" resulted from his belief in the innate ignorance of Blacks and an enduring memory of his was the religious devotion that he witnessed in a "man whose name was Dempsey [who] could read, had a bible and testament and hymnbook."[41] Dunwoody's instruction while at the Slave Mission emphasized the teaching of vocabulary and prereading skills; "I would sometimes utter a word which I knew they did not understand but would always explain its meaning," he later recalled.⁴² In the Sunday schools that he organized, Anderson would modify Dunwoody's methods, emphasizing the basic meanings of various religious terms.

Anderson became a founding member of the CME Church and served on its organizing committee. Located primarily in rural portions of the South, this predominantly Black denomination grew out of the Methodist Episcopal Church, South, and also out of the vision of Anderson and other Black religious leaders within the predominantly white Southern Methodist Church who advocated for an independent church free of white oversight and control. During the CME Church's establishment in December 1870, Anderson issued a report to Black Southern Methodists and to white Methodist leaders in which he stated that "the time has come in our history when we believe it will be for the glory of God and the best interest of the Church we represent, that we have a distinct and independent organization."⁴³

Anderson saw the newly formed denomination as "distinct and independent" of the predominantly white Southern Methodist Church from which it came, and he strived for consistency and rigor in the religious instruction of Black Methodists while avoiding the filter of African American inferiority often imposed by white Methodists.⁴⁴ Later, while serving CME churches in North Mississippi, he wrote to Black Methodist ministers in training: " I request all the preachers in the North Miss. Conference that this is the fourth year study to meet me in Byhalia on Dec 10 . . . come prepared to stand written examination. I will expect you all not to fall shorter than 75 per cent on your study."⁴⁵

Anderson's service to the CME Church was a culmination of his previous service while a slave at Fort Valley's Slave Mission where Blacks frequently served as lay leaders. Drawing from his background, he modeled Dunwoody's methods but worked to eliminate the backdrop of paternalism and condescension found under Dunwoody's tutelage. For Black Methodists in Mississippi who desired educational opportunities, his technique and modifications were essential in developing reading skills through June, while also strengthening the commitment to CMEchurches.⁴⁶ He also wanted this consistency and rigor of instruction to extend beyond the Sabbath conventions and into local schools in their surrounding communities. To schools in Hollywood, Mississippi, in the Mississippi Delta, he wrote, "The convention could and ought to do much in the way of building up the school in the District . . . schools in the District [have] no uniformity in learning the school exercises . . . for want of which the schools [are] dying."⁴⁷

* * *

Anderson's motivation to win a seat in Georgia's Constitutional Convention in 1867 and his run for office in the state's legislature the following year was a consequence of his ministerial leadership in Fort Valley's Slave Mission and in CME Churches throughout the region. While most white ministers in the South limited their leadership to their local churches, Black ministers were natural leaders in their communities. During Reconstruction, the bulk of Black officeholders were ministers, and among the sixty-eight Black men who served in Georgia's Constitutional Convention and legislature afterwards, twenty-nine were ministers.[48]

Anderson was selected to be registrar in Taylor County and then won a seat as a delegate at Georgia's Constitutional Convention. General Pope, the state's military governor, required that at least one member of each three-member board of Registrars be Black. Pope named only the white registrars, most of whom were initially against secession or moderately Unionist; Black registrars were chosen by local white leaders who considered them "intelligent and of high moral character," or in actuality loyal to the wishes of whites, and trustworthy.[49] Anderson was perceived as an acceptable choice; he had strong ties to the white community and was instructed by Rev. William Cotter of the Fort Valley Methodist Church.

Additionally, he had a strong connection to his former master, and as Rev. Cotter remembers, Anderson "always went to his former master for advice."[50] Because of his enduring relationship with his former master, Anderson was able to buy land from him for $700.00 in December of 1867; by 1870, the land was worth $1,000.00. During the Constitutional Convention in 1867, the only resolution that Anderson introduced was a resolution providing relief to slave owners for the loss of property; the resolution never came to a full vote.[51]

Anderson's election to the Constitutional Convention in 1867 was no surprise, and white leaders would inevitably have perceived him as a Black Republican radical. In Fort Valley, he was a visible fixture in both the Black and white communities. To Republicans, however, the close ties between Anderson and white leaders in Fort Valley caused concern, and Joel R. Griffin, who practiced law in Macon and owned an 800-acre plantation with twenty-four slaves in Houston County, was one such Republican.[52] He is best remembered in the historical record outside of Georgia for his effort, along with several Black men from Fort Valley, to reinter corpses at the infamous Confederate prison of Andersonville and build a fence for the cemetery there.[53]

From Joel Griffin's perspective, Anderson's purchase of land from his former master placed him squarely under the control of Democratic leaders.

Griffin, who had also run for a seat at the Constitutional Convention, petitioned to have him removed from the delegation, and on January 15, 1868, the convention's Committee on Privileges and Elections declared Anderson ineligible, claiming that he had violated General Pope's order "that no Registrar, who is a candidate for election as a delegate to the Convention shall serve as Judge of the election in any county he seeks to represent."[54]

As a registrar in Taylor County, Anderson had in essence counted the votes that allowed for his own election. The committee then resolved that "J. R. Griffin having received the next highest number of votes cast . . . is hereby entitled to a seat upon the floor."[55] The matter was then referred to General George Meade, the former commander of the Army of the Potomac and Georgia's new military general, replacing Pope. Meade took no further action; he most likely was concerned that a domino effect would occur by declaring Anderson ineligible and the slight Republican majority in the convention would disappear. In fact, sixteen delegates to the convention had also served as registrars.[56]

Griffin's fear of Anderson's loyalty was unfounded. Earlier, his commitment was clearly proven by his role as a leader of the Grant Club in Houston County, which was established to help Ulysses Grant in his run for the presidency that year. By January of 1868, Grant Clubs had sprung up throughout Georgia, and Anderson, Samuel Cobb, Isaac L. Primus, and George Ormond, were leaders of the newly formed organization in Houston County. Because these groups encouraged political participation from Blacks, Anderson and Cobb "daily [feared] for their lives, and the clubs offered them a measure of protection."[57]

Local whites routinely interrupted Grant Club meetings in Houston County. In nearby Schley County in the community of Sumter, Georgia, "large bodies of men were riding about the country at night . . . They and their horses were covered with large white sheets, so you could not tell them or their horses. They gave out word that they would whip every radical in the country that intended to vote for Grant, and did whip all they could get hold of." One witness reported, "I saw them pass my house one night, and I should think there were thirty or forty of them—I took my blanket and gun and ran to the woods and lay out all night. Nearly all the Radicals in the neighborhood lay in the woods every night."[58] Henry McNeal Turner, in corresponding with the Republican committee, called Houston and surrounding counties a "hell-charged section of the state." He also commended Anderson's efforts, reporting, "At Fort Valley, Rev. Isaac Anderson is doing good work."[59]

Both Anderson and his former master ran for election in Georgia's legislature in 1868, which was a unique phenomenon in the history of

Isaac Harold Anderson. Courtesy of Carolyn B. Cunningham.

Reconstruction. Isaac Anderson ran for a House seat as a Republican, and William Jackson Anderson campaigned for a seat in the Senate as a Democrat. Both men ran to represent the same county, and while the Democratic Party in Houston County had originally selected General Eli Warren for the Senate, conservative leaders shifted their support to William Jackson, a wealthy businessman and pillar of Fort Valley, less than a week before the election.

While Anderson's former master won in the Senate, Anderson lost his run for a House seat. Bent, but not broken, he retreated from the role of politician and once again embraced his call as a minister, tilling the spiritual fields of Houston County, nurturing his people, strengthening his fledgling school, and establishing his churches. Two years later, in 1870, he would accept his call as both a politician and minister and gain a remarkable victory for Republicans in Houston County even while Democrats throughout Georgia regained control of the state's government.

The foundation for Isaac Anderson's spiritual and political leadership would have been absent if not for William Jackson Anderson, his former master. As a young slave, Anderson clerked for William Jackson Anderson in his cotton business, bought land from him, and even worked on the Southwestern Railroad where William Jackson Anderson was a founder and major stockholder. The two men were so close that Isaac Anderson reportedly loaned William Jackson Anderson money when he needed it.[60] But, William Jackson Anderson was more than just an inspiration and benefactor to his former slave; he was also Anderson's father.

1825 Treaty of Indian Springs—
1836 Second Creek War—1837 Great Panic

Chapter Two

WILLIAM JACKSON ANDERSON

FOR WILLIAM JACKSON ANDERSON, THE ELECTION OF 1868 MOST LIKELY brought worries about the future of his business interests and his standing in Fort Valley. William Jackson prided himself on being a self-made man from humble beginnings, and if Republicans gained control of Georgia and the reconstruction of the South were mishandled, railroads would never be rebuilt, cotton would never get to market, and Fort Valley's economy would never return to what it once was. Although southwest Georgia escaped much of the destruction that disfigured the rest of the state, things had become dire: labor shortages increased as former slaves, often supported by the Freedmen's Bureau, refused to work for the wages offered them, and the federal government, with its military districts and troops, undermined the South's economy.

The exact details that drove his decision making are hidden by time, but at some point, William Jackson moved from fearing the realities of life under radical Republican rule to considering how he might prosper, not with the Republicans, but *as a Democratic Georgia state senator*. His run for the state senate in 1868 was a last-minute decision. He was not listed as an alternate at the outset of the election, and General Eli Warren, the valorous leader of Houston County, was the candidate backed by the local Democratic Party.[1] Warren was a well-seasoned supporter of the Confederacy, but in the spring of 1868, his familiarity and support of secession worked against him as General Meade, Georgia's military governor, issued a notice that anyone who held office "under the authority of the State of Georgia while the State was in hostility to the United States . . . [was] consequently ineligible [for office]."[2] With less than a week before the election, Democratic leaders in

Houston County withdrew Warren's nomination and scrambled for a new candidate. They found their man in William Jackson Anderson.

Earlier in his life, the Depression of 1837 had brought him to near destruction, and the experience of the unexpected coupled with the fear of loss was familiar to him. At fifty-three, William Jackson accepted the Democratic nomination in 1868 convinced that the life he had rebuilt out of ruin would disappear if Republican "radicals" had their way. His migration to central Georgia and Fort Valley, simply a hamlet in those days, had allowed him to remake himself and build connections with the people of Houston County. He had bought and sold Barlow knives for their children, plows for their farms, and slaves for their plantations. In doing so, he had become a merchant prince of Fort Valley, earning the title of "colonel" without ever holding a commission. His younger brother and business partner, Brigadier General Charles David Anderson, had commanded the Beauregard Volunteers, but William Jackson had supported the South not with a weapon, but with the wealth to support men who fought for the Confederacy.

William Jackson's foray into politics would be an extraordinary addition to a life that began when he was a boy on the verge of manhood, surviving in the wilderness of New Alabama. While in the home of William Robert and Anna, his parents, success and wealth seemed a distant dream, so he left his family in Indian Springs for the frontiers and life among the Creek Indians.

In 1800, Georgia was divided into two starkly different regions: the low country, a long settled plantation region along the Georgia coast known for its "genteel" manner, and the frontiers of central Georgia, where people from all segments of society, including well-established families, migrated, hoping to expand the plantation system.[3] William Jackson's parents migrated to Stone Mountain, Georgia, with several slaves and three slave children under the age of ten.[4] Uncles and aunts of the Anderson family also settled in Georgia, moving into newly acquired Creek land dispersed via the Georgia land lottery of 1827.

Later, the family relocated to Indian Springs after the First Treaty of Indian Springs, which the Creeks signed in 1821, thereby ceding much of their land to white farmers and settlers. Indian Springs, located in Butts County, was known for its camp meetings, which drew ministers and Georgians from a number of denominations, especially the Methodist Church. Upon settling in Indian Springs, William Robert and Anna worked to establish the foundations of a new life, dedicating themselves to cultivating their land and raising their children and delighting themselves in showing hospitality to visiting ministers of various denominations. The Andersons were noted for their piety, and according to William Jackson's obituary, their home was "ever opened to and a favorite house with God's ministers of all denominations."[5] Anna Coker, a pious woman and devoted Baptist, gave her children "early training and wise counsel," and William Jackson attributed to her "whatever of good there was in him."[6]

As recorded in his obituary, William Jackson's parents were "good livers," but they were not wealthy: "He knew very little of the luxuries and had very few of the opportunities that are enjoyed by children of the present day."[7] As the sixth of twelve children, the realities of farming land that produced little was a strain that dulled a person's drive for success and most probably softened any reluctance that William Robert and Anna had to let him go.[8]

At fourteen, either by his own resolve or by family foresight, William Jackson left his respectable home in central Georgia and the mother he cherished and descended into the westward frontiers to clerk for a Mr. Jackson.[9] As a child, he had seen firsthand the wealth that Indian traders could acquire, and as a frontiersman, he channeled the motivations of his great uncle, Robert Anderson, who, according to family lore, spent two years making his fortune as a trader in Cherokee country. Robert eventually settled down on 2,100 acres in what is today Anderson County, South Carolina, named after him in honor of his military service in the Revolutionary War.[10]

At fourteen, William Jackson's journey into the wilderness was not uncommon to youths and men of the country's early national period. In *Democracy in America*, Alexis De Tocqueville observed that "as soon as the young American begins to approach man's estate, the reins of his filial obedience are daily slackened. Master of his thought, he soon becomes responsible for his own behavior. In America there is in truth no adolescence. At the close of boyhood, he is a man and begins to trace out his own path."[11] William Jackson left home at a time when a man's "path to adulthood was far less clearly delineated and much more irregular, haphazard and episodic."[12] Few whites existed around him as he ventured deep into Creek territory, but the frontier promised a fortune. Years later he spoke proudly, both in his obituary and in family histories, of his ability to live among Native Americans. His adaptability spoke to his successful transition from boy to frontiersman.

In 1829, New Alabama was still part of Creek territory and a powder keg of different people existing tensely together. Three years had passed since the Treaty of Washington, which returned to the Creek Nation land wrongfully taken at the Second Treaty of Indian Springs in 1825. This territory in New Alabama was all that remained of Creek land in the South, and though all Creek land was cherished, the land in New Alabama was sacred as it was central to their identity as a nation, their ancestral homeland, and the place from "which [they] were born [and wished] to rest beside [their] fathers."[13]

As a result, those who were vanquished from Georgia swelled the Creek Nation in Alabama and the territory in New Alabama.

In the frontier of New Alabama, William Jackson's newfound lifestyle, with its wild influences and practices that were anything but respectable most likely brought him near to "perdition," but he could not deny the lucrative opportunities available to a trader living in the frontiers of Indian Country.[14] Like his great uncle, he set out to build a fortune trading with Native Americans and amassing wealth on trade routes between New Alabama and Houston County as did James Abington Everett, a founding father of Fort Valley who would eventually become one of his benefactors.[15]

William Jackson's frontier lifestyle necessarily moved him beyond the social expectations imposed by his pious and upright parents and into the "grog shops," cheap saloons, and frontier towns like Sodom, located near Columbus, Georgia, and known as Phenix City, Alabama, today. Here, according to historian John Ellisor, whites lived "side by side with Natives and blacks and formed a democratic yet violent and boisterous union that respectables found appalling."[16] Communities in New Alabama such as Tallassee, Tuskegee, and Jacksonville were comprised of settlers who rested their financial hope on crop production or trade. Two main groups of whites settled in and around the Creek Nation: "Respectables" who longed to reconstitute customs, value systems, and social institutions from the world they had left, and "frontier roughs" who hoped to "escape the constraints of so-called civilized society and establish 'contraculture' communities more amenable to their own desires."[17] Here, according to historian Elliot J. Gorn, "the frontier town or crossroads tavern brought males together in surrogate brotherhoods, where rough men paid little difference to the civilizing role of women and the moral uplift of the domestic family."[18]

Many white men, including roughs, migrated from the Carolinas and Georgia to New Alabama hoping to marry Creek women. Creek society was matrilineal, and ownership of land was matriarchal, yet land rights were patrilineal among Europeans and therefore fell into the hands of male heads of households.[19] Other settlers opened up "grog shops," where white saloon owners could saddle Creek patrons with debt and then acquire their land reserves as payment.

William Jackson's arrival coincided not only with the white settlers' vision of becoming rich by acquiring Creek land, but also with the importation of slaves into the region. With the sanction of the international slave trade in 1807, aspiring planters and yeoman farmers purchased slaves via slave routes that cut across north and central Alabama from Georgia, South Carolina, and states in the upper South like Virginia and Maryland. In 1830, Blacks made up more than 26 percent of the population of Pike County in south central Alabama, but by 1840, in the newly created Barbour County, which encompassed land that had formerly been part of Pike County, the Black population swelled to 46 percent through the growing acquisition of slaves in what would become known as the Alabama Black Belt.[20]

Upon arriving in New Alabama, William Jackson "boarded with an Indian family and learned their language, observed their customs, imitated their habits, and enjoyed their recreations including the art of wrestling. He quickly became a skilled frontier wrestler and reputedly could "throw down with ease the strongest men."[21] Wrestling, a common facet of frontier life, epitomized the most basic attribute of early nineteenth-century manhood: Brute strength. The rules for the sport varied by location, and matches were championed by local men from "various communities [who] strutted, bragged, and issued challenges, which were surely and quickly accepted."[22] At other times, wrestling was used to settle disputes, begin "rough-and-tumble" brawls, or end no-holds-barred fights with "frontier men [who] fought like bears, punching, kicking, biting, and gouging." Here, "rough-and-tumble matches allowed backcountry men to shout their equality at each other. And eye-gouging fights also dispelled any stigma of servility."[23] Wrestling became closely associated with the wild American frontiersmen like Davy Crockett, who fought Indians, wrestled mountain lions, and was popularized in the 1830's as the "Lion of the West." The reality of the rough and tumble life in the New Alabama would forever mark William Jackson Anderson as he would carry a lasting memento, a crippled arm as a reminder. The barbarous tactics employed by frontier wrestlers eventually led a number of states to outlaw boxing and wrestling.

At some point in his life as a trader and frontiersman, William Jackson met the woman who would bear Isaac Anderson. According to the records of the Constitutional Convention of 1867–68, Anderson was born in Monroe County, Georgia, the gateway to Macon located just east of New Alabama. According to the 1900 census, his mother's birthplace is listed as South Carolina, and William Jackson may have known her through his travels along trade routes connecting New Alabama and the Georgia frontier counties of Butts and Monroe, or possibly during sporadic trips home to visit family living in nearby Butts.[24] If Anderson's mother had been among his grandparents' slaves, she was one of the handful of nameless women of childbearing age listed in the slave census of the area. She also could have been enslaved elsewhere on the frontier that was Monroe County, Georgia, but the fact that Anderson knew the birthplace of his mother but did not mention her name to his family later in his life may indicate that his memory of her was somewhat veiled. She remains one of the many "silences" in the recovering of his story.

In the late 1820s and early 30s, tensions increased between the Creek still living in east Alabama and white settlers, and by 1836, William Jackson found himself on the front line of what would become known as the Second Creek War. In 1836, Isaac Anderson was barely one year old when William Jackson, who was then twenty-one, left New Alabama, escaping the violence that surged between whites and the Creek. According to his obituary, "the store he kept was plundered by hostile Indians and the man who took his place was murdered."[25]

After six years spent in the frontier of New Alabama, William Jackson Anderson stood in the middle of the Second Creek War, crippled in one arm, his business disrupted, and his paths to wealth blocked. His duties in eastern Alabama had connected to places in Georgia, including Monroe and Bibb County, and as a clerk, he had been required to travel back and forth between Georgia and Alabama, plying a maze of trade routes that by the 1830s were stage lines that extended from Indian Springs to Macon. The route had also included a stop in the town of Forsyth and connected to a "two horse stage" line that reached Columbus and William Jackson's frontier home in New Alabama.[26] With the war beginning, he turned to Macon, Georgia, hoping to expand his fortune and reinvent himself as a successful businessman.

Macon, which was first established as a fort in 1806 by Benjamin Hawkins, hosted a steady stream of families from the Carolinas by 1819. The town's location established it as a trading center for those in central Georgia's farthest frontier city, and its economic development first began with trading routes that later became roads transporting cotton to the Ocmulgee River and to major port cities of Savannah or Darien. To transport goods back to Macon, slaves typically used flatboats to pole their way up the river, which was a laborious and dangerous job, and the arrival of steamboats in 1833 on the Ocmulgee River marked a significant milestone only surpassed by the development of the railroad a few years later.

With the nearby river trade and expanding economic growth to surrounding towns like Fort Valley, Perry, and Hawkinsville, settlers moved into the fertile land, ready and eager to grow cotton. Between 1820 and 1830, the white population from the six counties surrounding Macon grew dramatically to well over 30,000, and the Black population increased to 25,000, or 43 percent of the population. At the same time, cotton production increased with the influx of slave labor, and in 1828, cotton trade in the city reached 45,000 bales valued at 3,000,000 dollars. By 1832 trade nearly doubled to 80,813 bales, and Macon serving as a clearing house for one-third of the state's cotton production. Its location on the Ocmulgee and nearby Flint River not only made it a gateway to the frontiers of central Georgia, Alabama, Mississippi, and Texas, but a central town for trade.[27] Merchants and traders, hoping to make their fortunes in cotton, and later corn, created an economic engine which fostered massive economic growth in Georgia. Every aspect of Macon's economy depended on "king cotton," and the city became a vital location for its distribution.

Macon was also the main gateway for the sale of slaves into central Georgia, and this exchange fueled the massive economic transformation that turned the state's frontier into part of the black belt that stretched from Georgia through central Alabama. Slaves were therefore the backbone of a developing agricultural and economic system.[28] During a visit in 1861, *London Times* journalist William Howard Russell described Macon as having "constant supplies of Virginia negroes on slave for hire. [Slaving] establishments were surrounded by high walls enclosing slave-pens or large rooms, in which the slaves were kept for inspection."[29]

The majority of these slaves were transported by traders and speculators in slave caravans or "coffles." Women and children were tied together with ropes, and men on occasion were shackled with iron collars if traders feared their escape. At night, slaves, especially men, commonly had their feet shackled, and those in coffles walked Georgia's trade routes as frequently as trucks travel its interstates today. Slaves of every stage of life, including children, commonly walked from the tobacco markets of the upper South to the burgeoning cotton markets of the Deep South, and in both places, they were an essential commodity as "one negro was needed for every three acres and these would yield cotton of the value of $240–$260." Male slaves in their prime, around thirty years of age, were sold in Virginia with its oversupply of slaves, for $300, and then brought to the Deep South and sold for $800 to $1200. Consequently, coffles became quite common.[30]

According to E. A. Pollard, a well-known journalist from Richmond, Virginia, Macon was known as a major slave market.[31] Slaves were crucial to Macon's agricultural and economic development, often laboring on the river transporting Georgia's chief crop, cotton, to markets. Macon had the third largest Black population of any city or town in Georgia, and the state also had more railroad track than any other in the South before the Civil War. Slaves were also used to construct and maintain the state's growing railroad system, which effectively solidified the tie between railroad companies, commerce, and slave labor.

Macon, with its ideal location, supplied slaves to anyone willing to travel to the city, and by the mid-1800s, it became known as "Georgia's Central

City" and an epicenter of agricultural production with two of the state's oldest railroads, the Central and the Macon & Western, running through it.[32] Merchants and landowners could also purchase slaves in nearby Houston County, some of which were brought from slave markets in Virginia.

With his arrival in Macon, William Jackson joined the city's growing population, which increased to 3,947 by 1840 with a majority white population of 2,296.[33] As other settlers and wealthier planters from the Georgia coast settled in Macon, leaders worked to remake the city into a place of refinement and wealth. In 1823, their efforts fostered the *Macon Telegraph*, which quickly became a regional paper. Other endeavors included the establishment of the Georgia Female College, which was supported by Mulberry Street Methodist Church and renamed Wesleyan College in 1836.

In Macon, William Jackson may have reacquired a measure of his former piety. His mother's influence, buried by his frontier lifestyle with its wild influences and practices, possibly resurfaced in his soul when, after six years spent in the frontier of New Alabama, he turned to Macon hoping to make his fortune and reinvent himself. In Macon, he became "identified with the people of God," joining the Mulberry Street Methodist Church.[34] The Methodist Society had planted their flagship church on Mulberry Street in 1826, and the first minister to serve there was ordained by Francis Asbury, the father of American Methodism.

As revivalism swept through growing towns along the frontier, cotton boomed and churches proved essential in building religious, social, and economic networks.[35] George Jewett, a member of the Mulberry Street Church, was known as a "careful, conscientious merchant who had a place for midday prayer in his warehouse." Jewett, who served as a church steward, eventually hired William Jackson, who attended the church with him, as a clerk in his store.[36] George Jewett & Co. sold sugar, coffee, molasses, and other dry goods, as well as manufactured items from New York and Boston. He also was a cotton commissioner and sold, stored, and insured cotton that was shipped to Savannah, Charleston, and New York.[37] In many cases, Jewett functioned as a personal banker to planters, and according to historian Harold Woodman, cotton commissioners or factors as they were sometimes called, "held the planters funds or made funds available through credit and . . . disbursed them as ordered. Instructions verbal or written or in the form of a draft drawn on the factor, allowed the planters to pay the bills from merchants, slave traders and physicians, overseers' wages, taxes and other expenses and to procure cash."[38] Consequently, many cotton commissioners would also serve as de facto low-level slave traders, buying and selling slaves acquired from other markets.

William Jackson would one day transition from clerk to merchant, and then to commissioner, and his training under Jewett would prove to be invaluable with suppliers like Robert Jaffery & Company of New York who would eventually furnish goods for his own business venture. However, he learned more than clerking from Jewett. Since Jewett was also the president of the Ocmulgee Bank, which was chartered at the same time as his arrival in Macon, he also learned the art of banking and gained the ability to tap into lucrative cotton markets.

In 1837, a year after leaving the frontier of New Alabama, William Jackson established the credit necessary to open his own mercantile business, Wm. J. Anderson & Co., on the corner of Cherry Street and Cotton Avenue in what is today known as downtown Macon, blocks away from the Ocmulgee River.[39] A year later, he was listed, along with Jewett, as a stockholder of the Ocmulgee Bank with fifty shares of stock. To establish his company, he would have needed a total of $20,000 in stock and trade for merchandise that included both staple and fancy dry goods like crockery ware, china, glass, and saddles. Unfortunately, William Jackson established his business just as the boom that drew him to Macon went bust.

The Panic of 1837 spread across the nation, reaching well beyond central Georgia and devastating agricultural markets and banks. Cotton prices dropped dramatically from record highs of eighteen cents a pound in 1836 to barely five cents a pound between 1839 and 1845.[40] The effects of the depression that ensued lasted for fifteen years, and many farmers and merchants in Macon were unable to pay their debts as inflation surged and spending slowed. A massive number of bankruptcies occurred in the city between 1838 and the early 1840s, and many banks in Macon refused to loan money, while banks in cities like Augusta and Savannah refused to take currency from banks in Macon.[41]

Despite the growing economic disaster, William Jackson still had enough money in 1839 to pay his road and poll taxes. He may have weathered the Panic of 1837 for a short time through loans from Robert Collins, an investor in the Ocmulgee Bank and held 584 shares along with his wife, Eliza, who held 440 shares. Born in North Carolina, Collins was a physician, attorney, author, financier, and a founding board member of the Georgia Female College.[42] Living between Charleston, South Carolina, and Macon, Georgia, Collins operated as a factor and cotton commissioner in both cities and co-owned a business with a J. F. Cleveland known as Collins and Cleveland.[43] By 1839, with the rapid influx of settlers into Central Georgia, he and Cleveland provided a valuable link between the lucrative trading center of Charleston and the Georgia frontier.

Collins was also a skilled slave trader.[44] In 1853, he released his second edition of *Essay on the Treatment and Management of Slaves*, published by Eastman Press, a Boston-based publishing house. The fact that the manual was in its second edition and was being published in Boston spoke to the broad appeal of his work and expertise in the management of slaves. In his manual, Collins directed new slave owners on how to construct homes, explaining that "[slave] houses should be placed if possible under the shade of native forest . . . about two feet above ground so that the air can pass freely under them." In the section on the feeding of slaves, he instructed that "provisions are given out on some designated night of each week; and for families the allowance is put together, but to single hands it is given to each separately . . . The bread is baked daily in loaves by a woman who is kept for that duty." [45] Undoubtedly, his manual served as a helpful guide for those investing in slaves on the frontiers of central Georgia.

Ellen Craft, one of Collins's slaves and a Black half-sister of his wife, was given to him as a wedding present. In 1848, Craft and her husband, William, made a daring escape North with Ellen posing as a Southern gentleman and her husband as her body servant. In 1850, after the passage of the Fugitive Slave Act, Collins sent bounty hunters North to recover his family's property and also petitioned then President Millard Fillmore who ordered their return to the South and servitude, but Ellen and William were able to escape to England.[46]

By the time of his death on April 8, 1861, Collins owned 102 slaves, along with over 1100 acres of land in Macon, nearly 5,400 acres of land in a "joint account," and nearly 24,000 acres of pine and swamp land all valued at 438,000.[47] The following day, the *Southern Federal Union* brimmed with news of a growing standoff between federal troops and confederate troops at Fort Sumter, and in a brief column, the paper reported, "It is well known to all that Dr. Collins has been in failing health for more than a year, and for the last six month, has been obliged to retire from active business, and his friend have been deeply pained to see him wasting away, day by day, with an incurable disorder."[48]

In 1840, things had worsened for William Jackson, and he was unable to pay his taxes for that year. The following year, Congress passed the Bankruptcy Act of 1841, which allowed for voluntary bankruptcy, extended bankruptcy to individuals rather than just merchants and bankers, and those facing bankruptcy were permitted to directly petition courts for a discharge from their debts. According to the law, "To obtain such a release, petitioners had to surrender all their assets to a court-appointed assignee, who would liquidate the assets and distribute the proceeds proportionately among creditors"[49]

Debtors could also avoid a formal bankruptcy by negotiating a private settlement with creditors and were also allowed to keep three hundred dollars in personal property after their goods were sold off.

In 1841, the bankrupt William Jackson settled his debt with Robert Jaffery & Company, but the courts ruled against him in the case of Robert Collins and the Bank of Charleston. According to court records, he appears to have negotiated with Collins to buy out his debt from the Ocmulgee Bank and the Jewett & Burch firm. Afterward, he left Macon "not only poor . . . but heavily in debt."[50] Learning of new opportunities in the Georgia frontier, he moved west while still owing two hundred dollars to debtors, and according to his obituary, "he paid up the balance of his Macon indebtedness" after arriving in Fort Valley.[51] Court documents, however, seem to indicate that his debt was possibly more substantial than remembered by his family. In January of 1847, he reached an agreement to pay Robert Collins a fraction of his remaining loan and was released from all liability to Collins and any outstanding debt connected to the Ocmulgee Bank, Jewett & Burch, and any creditors connected to Jewett. Graves, Woods & Co., a mercantile and Cotton Commission firm out of Macon, endorsed his payment of $1,552 dollars to Collins and his creditors.[52]

Although records detailing exactly how William Jackson procured the funding to establish his business in Macon remain uncovered, he may have used money earned while working among the Creek, or he may have used slaves as collateral, which was a common practice throughout the South and a plausible solution to his later financial troubles as court records and advertisements for the auctioning of property and slaves suggest.

In September 1844, the *Georgia Messenger* advertised the liquidation of property to satisfy debt attributed to Jewett & Burch, the Ocmulgee Bank, and Wm. J. Anderson & Co. Later in November of 1846, the *Georgia Telegraph* advertised the liquidation of a number of slaves "levied as property of Robert Collins" to satisfy debt attributed to several parties, one of which was Jewett & Burch, the same company to which William Jackson owed money.[53] The postponed Bibb County Sheriff's auction was announced in the *Georgia Telegraph* three months before William Jackson reached an agreement with Collins and was released from all liability to him, Jewett & Burch, and the Ocmulgee Bank.

Collins had proven helpful to those investing in slaves on the frontiers of Central Georgia, and he also had worked extensively with Charles Collins who was well known in Macon as a slave trader.[54] By 1840, both men were involved in providing loans to individuals like Benjamin Trapp, who used his two slaves—Natt, who was nineteen, and Ned who was twenty—as collateral for a loan. In another venture, the two men provided financing for A. G. Smith and Company which used nearly seventy-five slaves ranging from very small children to adults as collateral for its loan.[55]

The use of slaves as collateral was a thinly veiled reality discerned through advertisements for 'Virginia Negroes for Sale" and rewards for runaway slaves that were often buried in pages next to bank reports and stock sales in newspapers like the *Georgia Messenger*, and the *Georgia Telegraph* published in Macon, or the *Chronicle and Sentinel* published in Augusta.[56] As property, slaves were often used to purchase land, supplies, and more slaves needed for farming, and since few if any banks existed in the frontier, many Southerners used human collateral for financing. Slave mortgages were so lucrative that they comprised a majority of bank holdings in what Jessica M. Lepler calls, "property banks."[57] The fluidity of funding for which slaves were used spurred economic development on the frontiers of Georgia and throughout much of the South in the late 1830s. This rationale may explain why William Jackson believed that the boom of 1830 would continue in Macon and that he would be able to quickly pay back anything that he owed if he did indeed mortgage Isaac Anderson.

When a loan could not be repaid, collateral would be collected and often sold in a public slave auction. As one historian, Bonnie Martin, explains, "Local planters, small farmers, and ordinary craftsmen mortgaged their slaves and other property to each other, and raised large amounts of capital locally."[58] Slaves could be seized and sold in a publicly announced auction of the bankrupt person's property, and in some cases, the sale might be averted if an agreement between the parties involved were reached. Creditors would advertise a large slave auction where more buyers could be convened, and slaves were usually identified only by age, gender, and skin color.

In February of 1847, the thirty-two-year-old William Jackson signed a marriage contract with nineteen-year-old Rebecca Caroline Hollinshead. Rebecca was the youngest sister of the Reverend William H. Hollinshead, a doctor and occasional Methodist minister from Fort Valley who was known as "one of the strongest pillars" of the Fort Valley Methodist Church.[59] Like William Jackson's family, the Hollinsheads hailed from South Carolina and migrated to central Georgia. In 1840, Rebecca's father, William Hollinshead, owned a sizeable plantation in Macon County with forty-two slaves. When he died in 1842, his daughter stood to inherit a portion of his estate.[60]

William Jackson's marriage contract with Rebecca, known as a "life estate," intentionally protected her from liability to his past or future debt, especially since her future husband owed money to very powerful creditors. Unlike the more common coverture laws, which gave husbands full control over the property of their wives, the contract between Rebecca and William Jackson maintained her interest in the property that she brought into the marriage. Moreover, should she die, control over her property would pass to her children and not to her husband. The contract, however, did allow her property, by mutual agreement, "to be appropriated to the mutual support, convenience and comfort of himself and Rebecca Caroline."[61]

William Jackson, however, was not only indebted to Robert Collins, but also to Ker Boyce, who was the president of the Bank of Charleston and arguably the wealthiest man in the South before his death in 1854.[62] The life estate contract between him and Rebecca was most likely of little value to creditors since they could never claim the property covered under it, yet William Jackson's marriage would have given him roots in Fort Valley and a business network upon which to build. Moreover, if he had used slaves as collateral to secure funding from Robert Collins, he may have been able to convince the financier to hold off on the auctioning of his property until his marriage into the Hollinshead family. If Isaac Anderson had been one of the slaves used as collateral, his stepmother's wealth would secure his return to his father and also explain why decades later, Anderson kept a picture of both his father and his stepmother, Rebecca Caroline, with him.[63]

Records indicating that Rebecca Caroline knew about the circumstances of Isaac's birth have never been uncovered, but William Jackson's son would have been born well before her marriage to him. Moreover, situations such as these would have been acceptable, especially of men living in the Georgia frontier. Restricting male sexual activity before marriage was considered antithetical to nature for many in the Antebellum South, and "sleeping with a woman was an informal rite of virilization" according to Bertram Wyatt-Brown, author of *Southern Honor: Ethics and Behavior in the Old South*. Wyatt-Brown writes that for many Southern white men of this period, "the obvious way was to pursue a black partner. If the initial efforts were clumsy, or brutal no one would object, in view of the woman's race and status."[64]

In his dissertation, *Masters and Slaves, Planters and Freedmen: The Transition from Slavery to Freedom in Central Georgia*, Joseph P. Reidy writes, "Sons of planters, factors [or cotton commissioners], and professionals moved without stigma among several vocations, and daughters made economic ties stronger through marriage. Professional and mercantile classes buttressed the planter elite without the least thought of challenging its economic and political power."[65] William Jackson's marriage to Rebecca Hollinshead opened new opportunities in the cotton frontier for a man hoping to remake himself, and his arrival in Fort Valley occurred just as the hamlet was growing into a town.[66]

* * *

Fort Valley in 1847 was full of possibilities, and wealthy men like John Abington Everett were filled with ambition to make the most of those possibilities. Everett, who was arguably the wealthiest man in central Georgia, led efforts to virtually guarantee the town's success by securing the Southwestern Railroad from Perry, Fort Valley's competitor in the southeastern part of Houston County.[67] He and business leaders in Fort Valley understood the boom-and-bust cycles common in the nineteenth century and most recently typified in the 1837 Panic, and in William Jackson Anderson, they saw a product of those cycles who was familiar with cotton and banking, two things essential to the financial growth of central Georgia.

William Jackson could not only establish a mercantile business stocked with quality manufactured goods, but he had the benefit of being from a pious family that was well respected in their community and in Butts County. Soon after arriving in Fort Valley broke and penniless, he joined the Old Pond Methodist Church, which later became the Fort Valley Methodist Church, and "was kindly received and assisted by the best citizens of the town."[68] Like in Macon, where he had joined the Mulberry Street Church, his membership at the Old Pond Church allowed him to interact with well-connected and prominent people such as Everett and William H. Hollinshead, his future brother-in-law.

William Jackson's decision to join the Methodist Church in Fort Valley and eventually serve as a leader and Sunday School Superintendent spoke to his resolve to remake himself following his years in Creek Country and his financial ruin in Macon. In Fort Valley, he was able to bring his skills as a businessman to bear in a frontier town on the verge of a boom, and with the promise of new residents and a new railroad, Fort Valley was set to establish itself as a major center of wealth as a top five producer of cotton in the state helping to solidify Georgia as a major exporter of cotton in the South by the 1850s.[69]

* * *

By 1854, The *Southern Business Directory and General Commercial Advertiser* listed Fort Valley as having a population of eight hundred, and Anderson, Wm. J & Co. as one of only three general merchants.[70] William Jackson's company was vital in a town with no banks, and his services were invaluable in providing funds for supplies and storage for cotton. Farmers and plantation owners needed his services, and he built his success on buying "cotton throughout the plantation area of Middle and Southwest Georgia."[71]

By 1856, he was listed as an agent for a foreign bank, and by 1858, he was an agent for the People's Bank of Charleston.[72] As he had in Macon, William Jackson progressed from cotton merchant to commissioner, or factor, in Fort

Valley, and consequently, he became vital to the small community with its large cotton production and local planters who needed access to bigger marketplaces. His mercantile services went from selling bat guano as fertilizer to purchasing cotton from plantation owners and yeoman farmers throughout the region and warehousing it to be sold at a greater value in the future. With his acumen in accessing vital credit and his ties with foreign banks and the Peoples Bank of Charleston, he became powerful in Fort Valley and Central Georgia, and by 1860, he personally held real estate valued at $13,000 and assets totaling more than $33,000.

In 1850, the Houston County Slave Census listed a fourteen-year-old male mulatto as the property of William Jackson Anderson.[73] While he personally owned thirty-seven slaves, his business, Wm. J. Anderson & Co., listed ownership of only three slaves, valued at a total of $1400.[74] His business's ownership of slaves may indicate that he operated as a low-level slave trader at times, acquiring slaves from larger markets in Columbus or Macon. As a cotton commissioner, or factor, he regularly interacted with slave traders on behalf of local planters.[75] According to Robert H. Gudmestad, a historian, the interstate slave trade was a "vital component of the southern economy" by 1820, and major slave-holding firms like Franklin and Armfield as well as smaller scale slave traders and speculators transported their cargo to various slave markets in Natchez, Mississippi, or Chattanooga, Tennessee.[76] As one former slave remembers, Fort Valley was a place where "negroes were bought and sold like horses."[77]

Businessmen who occasionally engaged in the slave trade were commonly listed as general agents, brokers, or commission merchants. In *Slave-Trading in the Old South*, Frederic Bancroft writes, "commission merchants nearly everywhere made it a part of their business to buy and sell slaves for others for a definite purpose ... [They] did not go about the country buying or selling slaves, nor were they often seen with the slaves they handled, and they were not even thought of as slave-traders."[78] Moreover, in *Carry Me Back: The Domestic Slave Trade in American Life*, Steven Deyle explains that Southern businessmen who operated in this manner "saw themselves primarily as farmers, planters or merchants who supplemented their income by trading slaves. Others, such as commission brokers and auctioneers who specialized in their type of property, usually referred to themselves by their general occupation."[79]

Acquiring the skills of a regional and international bank agent was a result of his time in Macon, and the services of men like William Jackson, who was an agent for a foreign bank and for the People's Bank of Charleston, was essential to the expansion of commerce in Houston County, including its slave trade.[80] Moreover, Wm. J. Anderson & Co.'s ownership of three slaves most likely meant that he rented slaves out and did not always report the income gained from their work. Bancroft explains that "slave-hiring" was "a restricted kind of slave trading," and these slaves were often considered dependable and trustworthy, having skills such as blacksmithing or carpentry that enhanced their value.[81] Historian Jonathan D. Martin highlights how hiring out slaves reinforced the slave trade by making it more elastic as the southern economy supported the needs of those who wanted slave labor but could not purchase a slave outright. It also reinforced the slave system by bolstering the idea of slaves as assets to be rented out much as one would a plow or a saw. Hiring out slaves encouraged slave owners to view their slaves as what Calvin Schermerhorn terms, "prime commodities", and not just paternalistically. In the case of Isaac Anderson, his family remembers him working as a clerk for William Jackson, although Eric Foner and Joseph P. Reidy identify him as a carpenter.[82]

By 1853, Fort Valley saw the completion of the Southwestern Railroad, which later became part of the Central Railroad. William Jackson held stock in the Southwestern Railroad, which, as a business, owned twelve slaves before it was eventually absorbed into the Central line. The line also may have been part of the internal slave trade as railroads were increasingly available throughout the South but especially in Georgia by the 1850s.[83] During this period, the cotton boom in Houston County in fueled rapid growth in the white population, but this growth was outmatched by the surge in the county's Black population, which was fueled by the slave market in Macon. In 1830, whites totaled 5,161, and Blacks totaled 2,194 of the county's population, but by 1860, the number of whites had dipped to 4,828, and the number of Blacks had grown by nearly five times to 10,755.

The perception and fear of free Blacks in Houston County may explain why William Jackson never gave his son Isaac his freedom formally on paper. As a black-belt region dependent upon enslaved labor, the number of free persons of color from 1840 through 1860 remained low in Houston County, ranging from only zero to eight free people of color. Since racially they were in the minority, especially in black-belt regions, whites in Houston County were constantly worried about slave rebellions. Free Blacks meant a loss of control, and a free person of color was therefore a threat.

Georgia officials made sure to account for Blacks living outside of the slave system, and for runaway slaves who were apprehended, the state required that there be a posting of their capture in the Milledgeville newspaper.[84] The Georgia legislature passed laws requiring living slave owners to petition the state assembly in order to emancipate their slaves, and as fears of free Blacks grew, the legislature revisited the issue and voted to require that all slave emancipations occur outside of Georgia, so that an emancipated person "could not return legally as a free person of color."[85]

By this time, much of William Jackson's family had relocated to Fort Valley. His mother and father and his youngest brother, Charles David Anderson, were there, and his older brother, John Saxon Anderson, who had been a blacksmith in Butts County, became a farmer and by 1860, owned $600 worth of land and a personal estate worth $2,000.[86] In the case of Isaac Anderson, William Jackson's blood ran through his son's veins, and his visage was reflected prominently in Isaac's high forehead and distinct nose. But although he was prominent in Fort Valley and his brother-in-law was a community leader, he was a businessman in Houston County and was dependent upon the favorable opinions of his neighbors. If he emancipated a valuable slave like Isaac, a carpenter in the prime of life, he may have been challenged to justify his actions by his white counterparts.[87] The lengthy process of emancipating Isaac may have drawn attention to the fact that the two men were not only master and slave, but father and son, and this was a reality that was not discuss publicly although most likely realized privately by many.

Moreover, Isaac's emancipation would have made him vulnerable since the shield of protection offered by his powerful father could easily disappear. A Black person, whether free or enslaved, was a valuable commodity, and it was not uncommon for them to be kidnapped and enslaved again. Georgia officials required that there be a posting of apprehended slaves in the Milledgeville newspaper, and local authorities could sell apprehended slaves as early as the first Tuesday of the month following the advertisement.[88]

The tension and unease experienced by slave children who lived in quasi freedom was tremendous, and enslaved children like Anderson would have experienced the constant reality that they could be sold at any time whether by displeasing a father or by his death. Moreover, having his white father and master's blood in his own veins was no protection necessarily, and this reality gave him a further reason to be wary of open and honest relationships with white individuals. Later in his life, Anderson would be known as a skilled businessman, but as a young man, he often portrayed himself to whites as being illiterate.[89]

Isaac Anderson would have been an easy target since slave labor was vitally needed for cotton production. If emancipated, his story may have mirrored that of Solomon Northrup, who was taken from his home in New York state, sold "down the river," and eventually rescued from a plantation in South Louisiana after twelve years of enslavement. Northrup's experience was dramatized in the critically acclaimed movie *Twelve Years a Slave*, released in 2013.

* * *

Original structure no longer standing. Current Mulberry Street Methodist Church. Courtesy of the author.

By 1850, William Jackson and his younger brother, Charles D. Anderson, had established themselves as "merchant princes" in Fort Valley.[90] Then the Civil War erupted. C. D. Anderson had served as one of the first county commissioners and briefly as a county judge of the Inferior Court in 1857. During the war, he built a distinguished military career serving in the campaigns of the Army of Northern Virginia, being captured, and nearly losing his life on several occasions. He earned the rank of brigadier general and was elected in absentia to the Georgia House of Representatives in 1863 and 1864 while serving in the war.[91]

William Jackson, who was forty-five, stayed in Fort Valley, and though he was eligible to serve, he raised money and support for the local war effort instead, earning the honorary title of Colonel Anderson. Although he had sustained an injury to one of his arms on his arrival to Macon in 1836, this was probably not his reason for failing to serve in the Confederate army.[92] Descendants of his son Isaac, in grasping glimpses of his unrecovered history, were told that his father and master did not believe in the war.[93]

As a local merchant and a part of the upper middle class in the burgeoning Bible Belt, William Jackson was wedged between planters and yeoman farmers who were growing increasingly zealous for Southern nationalism, but as a regional merchant and cotton commissioner, he had to cultivate a relationship with northern businessmen to maintain his livelihood. As a merchant in an area known for a strong Whig party, William Jackson was most likely a Whig in his politics, disdaining the demise of slavery but fearing

Picture of William Jackson Anderson and Rebecca Hollinshead Anderson. Courtesy of Carolyn B. Cunningham.

the rise of Southern nationalism and the impending civil war that would undermine the interdependent economy of the North and South. In the end, he openly supported the war, as did the rest of the Fort Valley community.[94]

As a wealthy merchant and businessman, he provided aid to the Confederate effort, and according to Wendell D. Croom, "A meeting had been held at the M. E. Church in Fort Valley, by the more prominent citizens of that place and vicinity, and after offering a prayer to Almighty God, invoking divine favor . . . gentlemen made liberal contributions to defray the expenses of the [Confederate] company." Listed among these contributors was "Col. W. J. Anderson," who contributed financially to the Butler Volunteers, a military unit of the Confederate army in which C. D. Anderson, his younger brother and business partner, was a captain.[95]

C. D. Anderson forever endeared himself to Fort Valley, and one history of Georgia records that at the end of the war, "A Federal force, unaware of the end of the struggle, was advancing on Fort Valley with hostile intent . . .

Rebecca Anderson portrait. Courtesy of Marilyn N. Windham.

General Anderson arrived just in the nick of time; went out, met the Federals with a flag of truce, explained the situation and accompanied them into town, where comfortable quarters were assigned the officers, and the community was fully protected."[96]

Before Union forces arrived in Fort Valley however, William Jackson and Isaac Anderson hid the cotton that was warehoused by Wm. J & Co. at that time, and because of his brother's warning, they were able to ship 150 bales of cotton saved from the wreckage of the war and fully repay "New York creditors of their flourishing mercantile establishment in Fort Valley."[97] Isaac's part in saving his father's business' from the ravages of the war will likely never be fully recovered; however, Mr. C. G. Gray, who authored his father's obituary, encountered William Jackson after the war and wrote of him, "He gave me his hand and in his candid off-hand way said, 'I just called you back to help you. I have a little money left that I borrowed from my negro man Isaac, to go to New York with. I want to divide with you, for I know you had a hard time in prison."'[98] In his address and subsequent obituary, Gray only mentions by name William Jackson's father, mother, and his "negro man," Isaac.

After the Civil War, William Jackson is said to have "fully realized his acceptance with God."[99] According to his obituary, this happened while listening to the Reverend Lucius G. Evans, who compared the salvation of some to "a man climbing a steep hill carrying a heavy bag of sand on his shoulder with a small hole at the bottom through which that sand so gradually ran out before he knew his burden was gone."[100] for William Jackson Anderson, it was as if God had softly removed a burden of guilt from his soul. Unfortunately, history may never uncover how much of that guilt came from wealth made from burdens placed on the backs of slaves like Isaac Anderson.

> 1844 Methodist Episcopal Church South Established—
> 1861 Civil War Begins—1865 Civil War Ends

Chapter Three

ISAAC ANDERSON

ON JULY 4, 1868, WILLIAM JACKSON WAS SWORN INTO GEORGIA'S LEGIS-lature as a senator representing the state's Twenty-Third District. Guided by the belief that former slaves were unfit for political office, his party opposed the "effort to establish the supremacy of the Negro race in the South, and to place the destinies of these States in the hands of adventurers and irresponsible persons."[1] Members of the Georgia Democratic Party in both the state's House and Senate acted on that belief months later by removing every Black state legislator from offices won by them in the election of 1868.

Even before this, Isaac Anderson's career in politics appeared to be over. He had left his growing family to run for office in the Georgia House and had suffered defeat, but by this time in his life, he had shown himself to be a natural leader, and his determination to lead would mirror the determination that his father had demonstrated decades earlier in the frontiers of New Alabama and in the boom-and-bust cycles of Macon. The two men were not distant from one another, and according to Isaac's family, "William Jackson ... employed him as a clerk in his cotton business and ... upon his death, left Isaac a substantial sum of money." After Emancipation, Anderson regularly entrusted matters to William Jackson, and he, his wife, Edith, and their children lived on three acres of land owned by William Jackson.[2]

Isaac Anderson was born at the end of the "Age of Jackson," a period that encompassed both the rapid settlement of the West and the religious fervor of the Second Great Awakening, which began twenty years before Andrew Jackson's presidency. Methodist camp meetings and Baptist revivals created "spiritual stirrings" that gave rise to the establishment of a number of churches in the frontiers of western Georgia and beyond. Methodism was a reform-minded movement that began with small "class meetings" and grew dramatically during the Second Great Awakening to become the Methodist Episcopal Church. Methodist camp meetings continued throughout the 1840s and 50s and were held yearly in Fort Valley. In 1834, James Abington Everett became a "new man" at such a meeting.

The evangelical zeal of the Second Great Awakening fueled Methodist slave missions and support for the training of Black clergy and lay leaders. In 1790, Methodism's first American bishop, Francis Asbury, encouraged ministry among people of African descent, and by 1797, Blacks comprised 15 percent of the denomination's membership. By 1800, the number grew to 20 percent.[3] In 1811, William Capers of South Carolina sent eight Black preachers to work with slaves and even though it "was forbidden by civil and ecclesiastical law, the Methodists skirted legal restrictions against Black preachers by simply licensing them as exhorters."[4] Between 1787 and 1829, preachers worked to integrate Black men and women into Methodist churches, and in 1829, Charles Cotesworth Pickney, the future lieutenant governor of South Carolina, asked that ministers be sent among his slaves.[5] By the late 1840s, separate Black Methodist churches existed in Athens, Macon, Atlanta, Augusta, and Savannah, and by 1864, Blacks were serving as class leaders and licensed preachers in Methodist churches.[6]

Not long after his conversion, Everett petitioned the Georgia Conference of the Methodist Church to send missionaries to work among his own slaves in Fort Valley.[7] He and another local slaveholder pledged one hundred dollars in support of the new slave mission's work, and James Dunwoody was secured as minister over the slave mission on Everett's plantation. Isaac Anderson benefited from a long tradition of Methodism in Houston County, and his ability as a leader developed over years of work in Fort Valley's Methodist slave mission.[8]

After arriving in Fort Valley broke and penniless, William Jackson joined the Old Pond Methodist Church, which was constructed in 1840 on the same camp meeting site where Everett was converted. Old Pond was the church home of the town's prominent families, many of whom were plantation owners and substantial slaveholders, and several years later, its members built a new sanctuary in what would become the center of the town on land donated by Everett and Matthew Dorsey.[9] The congregation's former building was donated to the Methodist slave mission and became the first Black church in Fort Valley.[10]

The building given to the slave mission was modest, unpainted, and defined most by its rectangular shape and shuttered windows. Its benches, which served as pews, prominently seated Black worshippers in contrast to the simple galley area reserved for them in Fort Valley's new Methodist church building, where prominent seating was designated for white parishioners.[11] By the 1850s, the slave mission in Houston County swelled with the growing Black population in central Georgia, and the number of slave missions in the adjacent counties of Dooly and Macon also multiplied. In 1866, its congregation of former slaves moved and eventually renamed their new church Usher's Chapel.[12] Isaac Anderson's first ministerial post was most likely at the Old Pond Church, and in 1866, he was one of the founders and a trustee of Usher's Chapel.[13]

As the number of slaves who embraced Methodism grew, the attempts of some slave owners to provide religious instruction to them were tempered by suspicions from others that Black leaders were using their "profession of religion" as a "cloak to rascality."[14] The formation of the all-Black African Methodist Episcopal (AME) and AME Zion Churches encouraged these suspicions since Black leadership grew independently from white influence in these congregations.

Around 1817, Denmark Vesey, a self-educated preacher and recently freed slave, joined the northern AME Church in Charleston and became a leader preaching weekly at a gathering of men who met at his home. In his sermons, Vesey focused on certain passages of the Old Testament, concluding that Blacks were the Israelites, and God's judgment on white enslavers was imminent. He believed that he was intended to be used as an instrument of God's judgment in Charleston, and he planned a slave uprising for July 14, 1822, which was also Bastille Day. He and over a hundred co-conspirators were discovered, thereby validating the fears of many Southern whites.

Outraged by this threat, white leaders in Charleston burned the AME Church affiliated with Vesey, and Rev. Morris Brown, its pastor, fled the city and found refuge in Philadelphia with Richard Allen, a founder and the first bishop of the AME Church. Vesey was tortured, tried, and hanged on July 2, 1822, and thirty-five other co-conspirators experienced a similar fate in the months afterward. After the war, Brown's church, Mother Emanuel, was rebuilt and remains to this day.[15]

By 1831, virtually every Southern state had enacted laws requiring a white presence in the meetings of Black congregations.[16] Earlier in 1829, Southern Methodists reacted to fears of slave insurrection by proselytizing slaves and thereby maintaining two overarching evangelical goals: The conversion of souls and the promotion of "public quietness and safety" via the message of Christianity for "both masters and slaves."[17] William Capers, a founding member of the Methodist Episcopal Church (MEC) South believed that the "master is under obligation to have his servant taught the duties he owes God and man."[18] Known as " a lifelong apostle to the Negroes," Capers ignored the law and sent Black pastors out among slaves, believing that "the Christian gospel could make negroes better people [and] less susceptible to incendiary leadership."[19] White Methodists concentrating their efforts on proselytizing slaves, first in South Carolina, and then in Georgia, and by 1835, five slave missions existed, mostly in Savannah, with a total of 846 members.[20]

In 1840, Everett and fellow planter Colonel Campbell pledged $100 to secure a missionary to preach to their slaves; that year, the South Georgia Conference sent James Dunwoody, a fifty-year-old Methodist preacher, to minister to Black Methodist congregants and to slaves at four slave missions. By 1845, the Fort Valley slave mission had 228 members worshipping separately from white Methodists.[21] Plagued with poor health throughout his ministerial career, Rev. Dunwoody faced a tremendous challenge even for a healthy preacher. Finding basic housing and food for a night was frequently a trial for him, yet his work resulted in a number of mission conversions, which was "evidence of genuine work of grace" in his estimation.[22] For five years, he labored along central Georgia's trails and paths, and without the use of modern roads or air-conditioned automobiles, he would trek a distance of twenty miles from Fort Valley to Hog Crawl, thirteen miles from Fort Valley to Perry, and fifty miles from Fort Valley to a slave mission located near the Flint River.[23]

Rev. Dunwoody worked to adapt his religious instruction to what he saw as the slaves' low "capacity of understanding," and his focus on "simplicity and plainness" resulted from his belief in the innate ignorance of Blacks. His instruction in slave missions emphasized the teaching of basic vocabulary and other prereading skills. "I would sometimes utter a word which I knew they did not understand but would always explain its meaning," he recalled.[24] By 1846, Rev. Thomas Coleman, a white Methodist, had replaced him, and the gospel message was simplified into a catechism developed by Capers and published along with tenets of faith and specific topics including duty to those who injure us: "Ye have heard that it hath been said, An eye for an eye, and a tooth for a tooth; but I say unto you, That ye resist not evil, but whosoever shall smite thee on thy right cheek, turn to him the other also"; and "Love your enemies, bless them that curse you, do good to them that hate you, and pray for them which despitefully use you, and persecute you. *Matthew* v, 38-44."[25] Capers's catechism was widely used by Southern Methodists alongside the Apostle creed and was considered, "less sophisticated and detailed than Charles Colcock Jones catechism for Presbyterian slaves."[26]

Since the number of Black members often exceeded that of whites in Methodist churches, Black congregations developed in other locations and met separately. The slave mission in Fort Valley, being separate from the white Methodist Church, provided a place for a distinct Black church to develop even if its pastor, the Reverend Thomas Coleman, was white.[27] As the slave population grew in Houston County, Fort Valley struggled with supplying its slave mission's pulpits, and with the Vesey plot serving as a reminder of a potential outcome of Black religious leadership independent of white influence, an increasing number of slaves who were trained and supervised by white pastors served in leadership positions as exhorters, deacons, and ministers.[28]

In 1847, Rev. Charles Colcock Jones wrote, "In all societies, some men possessing greater knowledge, zeal, and popularity of manners and excellency of character, than others, will become leaders *in fact*, whether they are made leaders by any *official act* of societies in which they move or not . . . All attempts to suppress this class of influential men among their own colour, have signally failed, and must continue to fail."[29] Jones, a Presbyterian minister, was from Georgia's low country where the slave population outnumbered whites by nearly four times and the fear of a slave uprising was not an abstraction.

For Jones and others who thought like him, religious instruction by white leaders was needed to prohibit Blacks from undermining white Southern society, which was a possibility that he documented with projections and statistics that forecasted the Black population surpassing Southern whites numerically.[30] Hoping to persuade his white Southern brethren of the need for "coloured helpers or watchmen" who would serve under the tutelage of white ministers, he wrote, "It becomes us to inquire, if, in the history of the world, any people have ever been thoroughly Christianized, without their employment of *their own agency* to a large extent, in diffusing the gospel amongst themselves? I know of no such people."[31]

According to historian Donald Matthews, slaves involved in ministry were "lay preachers who, although unable to celebrate the sacraments, did preach and administer discipline among their people. Usually responsible to the quarterly conferences of local churches, they sometimes worked as colleagues of white circuit riders even when it was illegal to do so."[32] Some slave owners, especially in small rural pockets, made allowances for Black ministers, and white Methodist churches developed a Black exhorter class of licensed ministers, believing that Black leaders could be shaped by whites and taught subservience as a central part of the Christian message. Henry McNeal Turner, who would be vital in establishing AME churches in Georgia after the Civil War, was part of this new group of licensed ministers.

In May of 1859, William Jackson Anderson and W. H. Hollinshead attended a Fort Valley Circuit meeting held at Wesley Chapel and voted to establish another slave mission provided they could find a missionary. They also voted in support of Caesar Taylor being licensed as the first Black preacher in the Fort Valley Quarterly Conference.[33] The following year, the slave mission in Fort Valley experienced the most dramatic increase in Black membership since its beginning. In 1858, membership in the Fort Valley Methodist Church totaled 397, and membership in the slave mission totaled 270, but in the year of Taylor's licensure, Black membership in the Methodist Church dropped to 288, while the number in the slave mission grew to 552.[34]

In the southern part of Houston County just southeast of Fort Valley, the town of Perry experienced a similar growth in the Perry Methodist Church as its slave membership grew from 291 in 1858 to 494 in 1859. Because of the massive growth, Black members in the Perry congregation opted, like their counterparts in Fort Valley, to establish a separate "Colored mission," or a distinctly Black space to encourage church growth among slaves, and membership in both the Perry Methodist Church and Perry slave mission reached a combined total of 804 slaves by 1860.[35] Although Caesar Taylor was never referenced in the Southern Methodist Church's conference minutes as serving a pivotal role in the growth in the slave missions, once licensed, he was certainly part of the massive growth in slave membership in Houston County.

* * *

Exactly when Isaac Anderson began to aspire to the "Gospel ministry" remains unclear, but he likely was influenced by his father's work as a superintendent of Sunday School in Fort Valley's Methodist Church. By 1866, he and Caesar Taylor, Paul Barnett, and Jim Staley were publicly recognized as Methodist preachers after meeting with Rev. William Jasper Cotter, who pastored Fort Valley's Methodist Church in 1866 and who described their training as a "literary and theological institute." Their study began with spelling since, according to Cotter, only some of the men could read adequately, but Cotter's assessment of Anderson's lack of ability in spelling and reading was false, as was an 1870 US census report referencing Anderson as unable to read or write.[36] In fact, Anderson often maintained the persona of a man with limited education, primarily when he interacted with whites who might be threatened by any learning acquired by a former slave.[37]

Cotter taught the men the first-year's study for itinerant probationers and deacons, which included courses on the Bible. He also made use of *The Preacher's Textbook*, *Wesley's Sermons*, *The Hymn Book*, Clarke's *Preacher's Manual*, and *English Grammar*. As part of their training, the four men under his tutelage were given a Bible text to study in preparation for a sermon they would give at the next night's meeting. An important tool in their training was *The Doctrines and Discipline of the Methodist Episcopal Church, South*, a small volume that was their handbook for ministerial life and set forth the qualifications for men aspiring to ministry as well as several important duties of the Methodist minister: how to conduct pastoral visits; how to marry a couple; how to administer the Lord's Supper; how to build church congregations. The latter section was most likely vital to the newly emancipated ministers and certainly important to Anderson. The book became the basis of *The Doctrines and Disciplines of the Colored Methodist Episcopal Church* and the denomination's book of church government and discipline.[38]

The rigors of their course of study were complicated by the fact that all four worked during the day and had responsibilities to their families. On June 16, 1866, after meeting in the evening two to three times a week for a year, the four men received formal recognition of their ministerial positions before members of the all-white Fort Valley circuit during its quarterly meeting at Providence Southern Methodist Church. Former slaves, especially those in Southern Methodist circles, understood the importance of literacy and how it validated their leadership, and Anderson, like many other Black leaders, understood that Black clergy would never be fully recognized as being on par with their white counterparts if they were not educated.[39] Anderson himself had been shaped by his formative years in Fort Valley where his father advocated for the education of both men and women and had served for nearly twenty years as Sunday School superintendent tirelessly supporting the usefulness of Sabbath schools.[40]

* * *

After Emancipation, the number of Blacks in the Southern Methodist Church decreased dramatically from 207,766 in 1860 to 19,686 by 1869.[41] In Fort Valley, the number of Blacks attending Southern Methodist churches fluctuated throughout the years of the Civil War, and in 1861, 387 Blacks attended services. In 1862, that number rose to 532, but by the following year, Black membership dropped to 472. By November of 1865, membership had decreased to 323 and then to 203 by December of 1866.[42]

In 1865, northern-based AME and AME Zion churches began sending pastors and missionaries south in order to make inroads into Black communities. As a consequence, competition to maintain Black members in Southern Methodist churches became so tense that white Methodist Church leaders sent ministers to "all colored churches' to persuade former slaves not to abandon their congregations. In a number of cases in Georgia, the white ministers at those churches had already been voted out before representatives could arrive.[43]

Second only to the Baptists, AME Churches established the largest number of congregations among freedmen in the South, while Southern Methodist churches watched Black members leave in droves. Initially, they viewed AME churches as allies and even issued a short-lived resolution calling for fraternal relations with the AME, but by the summer of 1866, their brittle alliance had crumbled.[44] Henry McNeal Turner was an AME pastor who returned to the South to establish AME churches. Often described as a mulatto, Turner was born a free man on February 1, 1834, in Newberry, South Carolina, and when he grew older, he converted to Methodism while attending a revival meeting and soon after decided to become a minister. In 1853, he received his preaching license in the Southern Methodist Church and traveled throughout the southeast. The bulk of his time was spent in Georgia, where he led several church meetings in Athens, Macon, and Atlanta. In 1865, he was commissioned to work with the Freedmen's Bureau in Macon but resigned his post to work in full-time ministry in Georgia. Well familiar with the people and culture of the Deep South, Turner organized AME churches throughout the state.[45]

By the summer of 1866, earnest discussions among Southern Methodist leaders began to take shape regarding the establishment of an all-Black denomination. In December of 1866, the Methodist General Conference formally announced a plan to establish the CME Church as a daughter denomination, and the plan was approved that year.[46]

Rev. Cotter of Fort Valley's Methodist Church embraced the Southern Methodist's position after having witnessed Black congregants leave the local church. To him and other Southern Methodist pastors, the AME undermined their influence in Black communities and fostered an interest in politics among former slaves. "Bishop Turner and his Church were in no way friendly to the Methodist Episcopal Church, South" he concluded in concern over the exodus of Blacks from Southern Methodist congregations.[47]

Many former slaves in Southern Methodist churches had long-standing relationships with whites, and many had said to Cotter, "We love our old pastors as well as our white brethren."[48] Black Methodists in fact may have been playing on the sympathies and fears of white Methodist leaders as a way to elicit support for a separate all-Black institution, using the threat of the AME Church and their fear of losing influence over people who stressed their love and devotion for their "old pastor[s]" and "white brethren." Alternatively, Cotter's report may have expressed the actual perspective of Black Methodists who were growing in their realization that they could not remain among white Southern Methodists as conditions for them grew increasingly worse, particularly in the fall of 1867 through the winter of 1868.

In 1866, Anderson and other Black Methodist leaders in Georgia may have believed in the promise of interracial cooperation with white Southern Methodists and may have perceived the AME Church's presence and work in the South as a threat.[49] Many AME ministers in the North refused to relocate to the South, and AME leaders willingly ordained illiterate Black ministers. In June of that year, Rev. John C. Simmons, a white Methodist minister, had presided over a biracial revival where fifteen Black men made professions of faith. Simmons, however, was weary of the AME pastor and revival organizer, Rev. Fortune Robinson. He doubted the minister's ability to shepherd the new converts because Robinson was illiterate and therefore not qualified to serve as the men's pastor, in Simmons's judgment.[50]

Other factors contributed to the decline in Blacks from the Southern Methodist Church. Southern Methodist leaders were often silent in condemning the surge of violence, particularly from the Klan and similar organizations, that plagued Black communities. Moreover, a number of Southern Methodist leaders believed openly that every former slave "must continue to be, the laboring man of the South, because he is not fitted either by talents, education or enterprise, for anything higher."[51] Consequently, many called on former slaves to be silent on issues of politics unless they were criticizing the Republican Party.

In August 1867, Isaac Anderson and Anthony Cobb were Republican candidates for the Georgia Constitutional Convention. Rev. George C. Clarke, a Southern Methodist pastor and presiding elder in Fort Valley, outraged former slaves at a church meeting when he strongly criticized the "radical party" and all who supported it. After the meeting, a fight nearly occurred among the racially mixed gathering. For many whites in attendance, Clarke's ideas reinforced their perspective that Black leaders like "Big Ike" and "Cobb," his political ally, were not to be respected. For Blacks in the audience, however, Clarke's comments undermined men they respected. Anderson was not only a political leader, but a pastor and spiritual leader, and his involvement in the state's Constitutional Convention was seen as an attempt to address the challenges facing their community.

In December 1867, Isaac Anderson left the Southern Methodist Church, becoming an elder in the AME Church. In that year, the number of Black Southern Methodists in Perry and Fort Valley totaled 613, according to the minutes of the South Georgia Conference, and by December of 1868, Black membership had dropped to zero.[52] Anderson's defection from the Southern Methodists was significant for two reasons: He was aware of efforts by Southern Methodists to establish a Black denomination, and he had completed the ministerial training needed to serve as a leader in the new denomination.

William Jackson Anderson portrait. Courtesy of Marilyn N. Windham.

That there were 613 Black Methodists in Houston County speaks to Anderson's influence and the belief of some freed people that they could have a measure of racial cooperation with white Southern Methodists. However, white Southern Methodists challenged this cooperation by their beliefs and positions, and leaders like Rev. Clarke openly espoused the belief that former slaves should not hold political office, which made membership in AME churches alluring since they were politically active.

The *Southern Advocate*, the Southern Methodist paper published in Macon, accused Anderson, Turner, and AME leaders of being representatives of the Republican Party in Washington and of "fomenting enmity against whites."[53] Yet, Anderson's defection to the AME and his involvement in politics were not simply bids for power, but attempts to combat persistent violence by white leaders towards freemen and the belief that former slaves were "not fitted either by talents, education or enterprise, for anything higher" than subservience.[54] Moreover, his defection to the AME Church possibly strained his relationship with his father and former master, William Jackson Anderson.

However, Anderson's defection from the Southern Methodist Church was short-lived. The promise that he had found in the AME Church was offset by what he may have seen as deficiencies, and following his loss in the state's election of 1868, he abandoned it. The AME General Conference in May of that year had been contentious as reports emerged that the Book of Concern, or the publishing arm of the AME Church, was several thousand dollars in debt. After traveling to Washington, DC with members of the Georgia delegation led by Henry McNeal Turner, Anderson was outraged over the extensive debt and mismanagement of the denomination, and before leaving, he made his disgust known, openly criticizing "ministers of the AME Church, whose sole object is to secure money to build up that iniquitous publishing house in Philadelphia that does not and never will benefit us or our children."[55] After Emancipation, Anderson had struggled to maintain a school for Black children in Fort Valley, which his children attended, and the thought of money being diverted from that effort to pay a debt in far off Philadelphia was unacceptable to him. Although the reason for Anderson's departure from the AME Church is not known, the message to Southern Methodists in Georgia was clear: Anderson was willing to join a powerful AME leader like Henry McNeal Turner, who was a threat to Southern Methodists.

By the summer of 1868, Anderson was laboring in ministry but was unable to make a living solely as a minister, especially since many of his congregants had little money to cover the needs of a pastor and his large family. Consequently, he worked, "tent making," on the Southwestern Railroad, which was the same line in which William Jackson was an investor. Anderson's ministerial duties on the Fort Valley circuit took him throughout central Georgia and to nearby communities like Vienna in Dooly County. As presiding elder, he would organize and minister at conferences, and as T. S. Lilly, a contributor to *The Christian Index*, writes, "When Rev. I. H. Anderson was Presiding Elder of this district, we had a grand time in our quarterly conference, he would always preach for us on Saturday." In recounting Anderson's spiritual influence Lilly remembers that "brethren would get up to express their feeling . . . the holy ghost would come down . . . [and] good old sisters [would] rise from their seat . . . and praise God in the highest."[56]

During this period, Anderson rekindled the political activity that had been muted by his loss in the election of 1868, and he may have been provoked to do so by the many reports of threats against families, destruction of property, whippings and assaults, and outright murders that he received while ministering to local congregations in central Georgia. Unfortunately for former slaves in Georgia, the fall of 1868 was marred with more violence and efforts by white leaders to exclude them from the political process.

In the months following his gubernatorial defeat, John B. Gordon traveled throughout the South addressing segregated crowds of whites and Blacks. In addressing white South Carolinians, Gordon decried Republican radicals "as enemies of the Constitution" and "enemies of the Union" who were advocating for "the peace of the bullet and the bayonet." He contrasted Republicans with the Democratic Party, which he described as the party of "law and order." Turning to address Blacks, Gordon ominously warned them not to listen to the counsel of "bad men," but only to good "southern gentlemen ... [less] the leaves on the trees now green would not be turned red by the autumn frost before they would be stained with the blood of the white man and the black."[57]

On September 16, 1868, General Gordon's revelation was fulfilled when violence exploded southwest of Houston County in the town of Camilla, Georgia, one hundred miles South of Fort Valley. The "Camilla Massacre" occurred as freemen prepared to join a Republican rally, and while they were three miles away from the town, they were informed by Sheriff Mumford S. Poore that no one was allowed in town with firearms. Leaders in the group of freemen gave their assurances that their intentions were peaceful, and though few men actually had weapons, Mumford gathered a posse of local whites and lie in wait for them. A shot was fired into the approaching crowd as townspeople joined the massacre, and while the approaching ralliers briefly returned fire, they quickly fled into the surrounding woods where many were wounded or killed trying to escape. Nine freemen were estimated to have died, and as many as thirty were wounded.

After the attack, agents of the Freedmen's Bureau including O. O. Howard and William Mills chronicled the events. Governor Bullock requested that the federal government send troops, but none were sent. The state senate launched an investigation, and in the final report adopted by the state legislature claimed that Poore and others were deemed to have responded appropriately.

William Jackson Anderson was one of the legislators who had approved the report. In the same month that the Camilla Massacre happened, both houses of the Georgia legislature voted to expel every Black politician who won office that year, arguing that they were unqualified because the state Constitution did not recognize the right of former slaves to serve in office. William Jackson joined white legislators in approving the action.

> 1865 Thirteenth Amendment Ratified—1865–1866 Ku Klux Klan Established—
> 1868 Fourteenth Amendment Ratified

Chapter Four

GEORGIA

AFTER HIS LOSS IN THE ELECTION OF 1868, ANDERSON FOCUSED ON MINistering to Methodist congregations in Houston County and establishing the Anderson primary and Sabbath schools in Fort Valley. While William Jackson began his tenure as a newly elected state senator during the summer and fall of 1868, Southwest and Central Georgia increasingly became a dangerous place for Anderson and for thousands of freedpeople like him.[1]

In December of 1865, months after the Civil War ended, white leaders in Georgia moved quickly to end Reconstruction by passing the Thirteenth Amendment as required by Congress for Confederate States to rejoin the Union. White Georgians wanted the removal of Union troops from the state and a return to the familiarity of white dominance, which had been the marrow of Southern society dating back to before Georgia was a colony.[2] The romanticized vision of the Antebellum South held by many whites necessitated the return of freedpeople to subservience and a system of quasi slavery. This vision would eventually develop into a misshapen nostalgia called the "Lost Cause," but in 1868, the fulfillment of this vision was temporarily undermined by interloping Federal forces like the Freedmen's Bureau.

Under the umbrella of the US Military, the Bureau of Refugees, Freedmen, and Abandoned Lands was a federal presence in Georgia that included troops and maintained a presence in Georgia that included medical facilities, schools, and field offices. Each field office had a civilian agent, or in some cases, a former soldier from outside of the region. The Georgia Bureau employed more than two hundred agents who were deputized to transition freed people into a free economy, and it oversaw roughly 59,000 square acres that included isolated cotton plantations, rice plantations, and barrier islands.

Working with a population in Georgia of roughly 545,000 Blacks and 639,000 whites, bureau agents frequently experienced hostilities over their presence.³ In February of 1866, bureau agent James D. Harris, who was stationed in Perry, wrote to his superiors, "I am quite at a lapse to know how I am to carry out instructions from the Bureau not having any one to assist summoning parties. The civil officers refuse to act. Could you furnish me with a soldier to act. There are a great many cases where the freedmen has not been paid for last years labor and I think they ought to be paid." ⁴ Freedpeople, however, understood that because Georgia was under military rule and had not rejoined the Union, the bureau had the final word and had the military and the force of the government behind it if needed. According to historian Paul Cimbala, "[Freedpeople] understood the Bureau was an important ally in their quest for security and land ownership. Some complained about the insensitivity of individual agents and officers, but a significant number by their own actions reaffirmed their belief that the agency remained their Bureau."⁵

After completing the federal requirements for Reconstruction in 1866, the Georgia legislature instituted Black Codes in a concerted effort to deal with the state's growing labor shortage. In *Reconstruction, America's Unfinished Revolution: 1863–1877*, Eric Foner writes that "their centerpiece was the attempt to stabilize the black work force and limit its economic options apart from plantation labor. Henceforth, the state would enforce labor agreements and plantation discipline, punish those who refused to contract, and prevent whites from competing among themselves for black workers."⁶

With Black Codes instituted to give more control to local jurisdictions, officials could target freedpeople and apply laws randomly as they wished. Additionally, in 1866, Georgia legislators reduced felonies such as larceny to misdemeanor offenses, which allowed local counties and communities to use the law autonomously as they saw fit. By lessening the charges to misdemeanors, local officials could arrest people on vague charges such as burglary or vagrancy.⁷

Moreover, railroads were vital to Georgia's economy before the Civil War, and afterwards, they were essential to rebuilding the state. In 1860, Georgia had maintained a higher quality and length of track than had any other Southern state, and its railroad was tied to its agricultural output of corn, wheat, oats, rye and of course the state's most important crop cotton.⁸ The state's railroad transported goods throughout the South, and before the war, Georgia was the third largest cotton producer in the country.⁹ However, businesses like the Central Railroad Company of Georgia found recruiting labor quite difficult, as did many white landholders.

Black laborers considered wages earned at rail lines like the Southwestern Railroad to be inadequate, and many often worked just long enough to find better paying jobs elsewhere. In the spring of 1868, General Thomas Ruger, Georgia's military governor, leased 100 Black convicts for $2,500 a year to William A. Fort of the Georgia and Alabama Railroad in North Georgia. As the use of Black Codes increased, so did the number of Blacks incarcerated, and by the end of 1868, 109 Blacks were shipped to work on the Macon Brunswick line, and 134 more were sent to work in Selma, Rome, and Dalton.[10]

Among the first convicts from Houston County that were leased out to work on railroad construction were Richard Cain, Jack Fagan, and Taylor Glover, who were convicted of vague burglary charges by an all-white jury in Judge Carlton B. Cole's court. In 1851, when the Macon circuit was created to serve Dooly, Bibb, Crawford, Macon, Twiggs, and Houston Counties, Judge Cole was selected to serve as a judge, and after being reappointed to the circuit in 1868 by the governor, Cole made quick work of a number of cases.[11]

Born in Massachusetts, Judge Cole lived in Georgia much of his adult life, was a Whig, and had even considered running for governor of Georgia. As a stockholder in Central Railroad, Cole along with his son, who was also in the banking industry, knew the importance of rebuilding Georgia's railroad in order for the state's economy to rebound. Although no evidence exists showing that Judge Cole had any personal vendetta against Cain, Fagan, and Glover, he most likely was aware that the three would ultimately end up in the state penitentiary, which meant the men would probably be sent to work in railroad construction.

Black Codes and their usefulness in capturing the labor of former slaves became apparent to agents of the Freedmen's Bureau as men were wrongfully sentenced to years of labor in the state's penitentiary. In describing one case, Bureau Agent J. D. Harris reported that "contrary to the charge of [the presiding judge] I understand that Judge Cole was surprised at the verdict . . . [The accused] provided an alibi." Harris concluded in this case that the accused "together with many others . . . are innocent. Some of the prisoners broke jail, but [the accused] would not go. I ask then why they did not go with the others and they replied that they were innocent of the charges and believed they would be released eventually."[12]

By the summer of 1868, the actions of Judge Cole and local Houston officials had drawn the attention of Freedmen's Bureau agent Daniel Losey who was from New Jersey and was a visible extension of the federal government in Fort Valley and Perry. On June 16, 1868, four Black men and one white man were convicted of stealing cotton from the Southwestern Railroad Company, and according to Agent Losey, Judge Cole sentenced them to different terms of imprisonment: "All of the colored but one was released by paying costs and a light fine and hiring themselves out, the employer becoming responsible. This [white] man Corbett was sentenced to 6 months imprisonment or pay a fine of $250." Days later, Losey spotted Corbett walking about town as a free man, and when he questioned the sheriff about Corbett's release, he was told that the white man's release was due to the death of his daughter and that Judge Cole had allowed him to attend to the family and then return to jail. Days later, Losey reported that "no later than yesterday I saw him again on the streets walking as if he was at as much liberty as any other citizen."[13]

Throughout his tenure, Losey repeatedly received reports of Black workers who were not getting paid. In April 1868, he received a report from several freedmen in Houston County about Lewis M. Houser, who had been an inferior court judge, and earlier in 1860, had been a wealthy plantation owner in Houston County with nearly 1,400 acres of land and 41 slaves. By April 1869, Houser was bankrupt and still trying to hold onto his farm, and he falsely claimed that he employed only eight when he actually hired between fifty and one hundred freedmen and had sold all of the crops raised that were on his farm without paying any of the workers. Losey reported that Houser was trying to defraud the freedmen and that the best course of action was to present the case to Judge Erskine for further investigation.[14] Losey's report put him at odds with Houser, who had at one time been a wealthy man and a leader in the Cotton Planters Convention who represented the county. Moreover, Losey was supporting the complaint of a Black man over that of a white man, and by that summer, he was receiving death threats.

In another case, Losey brought a suit on behalf of Sam Gilbert, a freedman, against C. M. Lester for violation of contract. In August of that year, Gilbert had begun attending what were most likely Grant Club meetings in and around Houston County. Lester, who did not approve of Gilbert's attendance, changed the terms of the labor contract and began deducting five dollars from Gilbert's pay for every meeting he attended, and when the freedman refused to stop attending the meetings, he was fired. Losey, who was frustrated by Lester's refusal to recognize his authority in mediating the contract, wrote to his superior, Captain L. N. Hill, for direction: "Mr. Lester in regards to this matter says I have nothing to do with the case, now if we have no authority and men are going to settle such as they think proper, the colored man is in a very bad position."[15]

In 1868, Black Codes in Georgia worked to return freedpeople to subservience and a system of quasi slavery. Apprenticeship laws in the state effectively extended slavery and the trauma of family separation associated with it beyond the Civil War. In the Antebellum North, where apprenticeship laws first developed, the practice served as a 'safety net' of sorts for orphaned or wayward children, but by 1830, it became a way for children and youths to earn wages. Throughout the country, the practice was most often used in skilled professions like that of a baker, coachmaker, blacksmith, or dressmaker, but in the South, apprenticeship laws were applied to white women with illegitimate children or illegitimate children of free women of color.[16]

In March 1866, Georgia changed its apprenticeship laws to harness the labor of Black teens and preteens.[17] In *Slavery and Freedom on the Middle Ground: Maryland During the Nineteenth Century*, Barbara J Fields writes that "Apprenticeship served a complex social purpose for former slaveholders. One of its tasks—arguably the most important—was to provide a temporary landmark for people as yet unable to orient themselves in the new landscape of emancipation." She concludes that in essence, "Apprenticeship satisfied ... an impulse of revenge against former slaves for the fact of emancipation, of punishment for disloyalty."[18] As former slaveholders instituted policies that undermined Black parental control, children of freedpeople were compelled to labor, whether in the fields or in the plantation house, without compensation.

The fear of children being "sold away" from their parents, or wives from their husbands, was a constant companion to slave life, and these fears made family and kinship ties even more important to Black men and women following the passage of the Thirteenth Amendment, which ended slavery. Unsurprisingly, after the Civil War and through the early twentieth century, many formerly enslaved people who had been separated from loved ones placed advertisements in newspapers and requested that their ads be read in churches. In one notable case, sixty-seven-year-old Nancy Russell of Perry had been brought to Houston County from Virginia as a slave, and she sought help from the Freedmen's Bureau to be reunited with her children. With her former owners unwilling or unable to support her, Russell asked Losey for money to pay for transportation back to Washington County, Virginia, where her children were in "tolerable good circumstances and perfectly satisfied to provide and take care of their mother and [were] anxious for her to come."[19]

Georgia's apprenticeship laws were effectively directed at and applied to the children of former slaves, and the practice gave broad powers to the County Court or local ordinary to "bound out" these children, in many cases, to former slaveholders. Apprenticeship laws applied to "all minors, whose parents [were] dead, or whose parents reside[d] out of the county, the profits of whose estate [were] insufficient for their support and maintenance; also all minors whose parents, from age, to infirmity or poverty [were] unable to support them."[20]

By allowing the ordinary or County Court to determine the ability of parents to care for their children, apprenticeship laws ignored the sovereignty of parents to determine the care of their children as did slavery. Furthermore, apprenticeship laws ignored the necessity of the labor needed by families in the rural South were Black children labored with their families raising crops, tending to livestock, selling produce, caring for siblings, and helping to maintain the household.[21]

Only a local ordinary or a judge of the County Court could dissolve an apprenticeship, and since Georgia's law in 1866 prohibited freedmen from testifying against whites, Black youth and their families had no viable legal recourse to dissolve an apprenticeship other than by appealing to officials. One such official would have been none other than Inferior Court Judge Lewis M. Houser of Houston County whom Agent Losey had investigated for trying to defraud freedmen in April of 1868.[22]

Most apprenticeships in the county, however, were decided by county ordinary William T. Swift, who was known throughout the region for his hostility toward former slaves.[23] Eleven-year-old Cereal Zass had been "bound out" by Ordinary Swift to work as a house servant in April of 1866, but unlike other children, her apprenticeship was facilitated by three leading men of Houston County. William F. Postell was one of several Houston County justices of the peace and was described by agent Losey as "a man prejudiced particularly against freedmen" and "not well enough acquainted with the law."[24] Reverend W. J. Cotter was the pastor of the Fort Valley Methodist Episcopal Church and was to serve that year as Zass's master. William Jackson Anderson, who was serving as the Sunday School superintendent at Cotter's church, was the last facilitator of Zass's apprenticeship, and he paid a bond of one thousand dollars for the apprenticeship arrangement.[25]

The apprentice record describes Zass as an "aptless girl" bonded to serve Reverend Cotter and "his successors in office." Like other Black children who were "bound out," she was to be trained in the "business of house servant," which tacitly was an extension of slavery, which had ended only one year earlier. The apprenticing of children like Zass was ideal for those looking for laborers since they were less likely to challenge the authority of a white adult and former master, and they had limited avenues and resources for escape due to their age. William Jackson's unique role in facilitating Zass's apprenticeship with a one thousand dollar bond possibly pointed to her labor being a unique gift to Reverend Cotter, who at the same time was providing extensive ministerial training to his son and former slave, Isaac Anderson.[26]

The Freedmen's Bureau was the only recourse for freedpeople trying to escape the apprentice system, which in some cases, allowed for the abuse of children by "masters." Bing Faircloth of Dooly County was given the right to "moderately" whip the children apprenticed to him, and this transference of authority was allowed under apprenticeship laws that stated that masters could use "the same degree of force to compel . . . obedience as a father may use with his minor child."[27] Jeremiah Robinson of Houston County was determined to recover his children from mistreatment under the apprenticeship system by two white men in Dooly County but was unfortunately arrested in the process. In two other cases, Amanda Foy and Charlotte Walker from nearby Taylor County were powerless to fight local officials and the mistreatment of their apprenticed children by white masters and consequently requested help from Bureau agents.[28]

An apprenticeship arrangement could legally be dissolved in the case of "cruelty in the master . . . [or] by reason of the masters depraved conduct."[29] In one case detailed in a letter dated September 30, 1867, agent Losey reported the "inhumane treatment . . . of a 'col'd boy named Warren Johnson." According to his report, "White citizens . . . saw Mr. Josiah Vincent and his Son strip and beat the [14-year-old] boy Warren Johnson."[30] Since Georgia law prohibited Blacks from testifying against whites, the "white citizens" who saw the abuse were the only valid witnesses to Vincent's actions, and Losey recommended that he be fined and Johnson's "apprenticeship" be canceled.[31] Losey's actions put him at odds with the white power structure of Houston County.

Children "bound out" under the apprenticeship laws ranged from five to twenty-one years of age, and young women usually served until they were eighteen, while young men served until they were twenty-one. Between 1866 and 1870, roughly eighty-four of the eighty-six children subjected to the apprenticeship system in Houston County by Ordinary Swift were free persons of color, and of that number, only three were apprenticed to a relative. In most cases, Swift listed the childrens' parents as deceased.

On October 8, 1866 Washington Hughes was "bound out" to J. R. Haddock by Swift, and three months later, Agent Losey reported that Hughes, who claimed to be eighteen, was "dissatisfied" and seemed "determined not to stay with him, [had] been absent two or three times from his premises without [Haddock's] consent and [had stayed] a week or more at each time." Losey informed Hughes that he was "properly bound to Mr. Haddock and must go back and serve his time out," but Hughes refused to return.[32] Southern landholders understood the value of a seventeen-year-old male like Hughes, who before Emancipation would be valued between $1,000 and $1,400 because of his potential as a laborer, yet under apprenticeship laws, he was only guaranteed food, clothing, shelter, and training in domestic service or farming. Children were supposedly "taught to read the English language," but this rarely occurred. By 1870, Hughes remained a farm laborer working alongside his wife, Sophronia with their six-month-old son, Augustus.[33]

The majority of boys "bound out" in Houston County ranged in age from twelve to seventeen years, and younger children comprised only a small portion of the forty or more males under the system in the county.[34] Young men were normally listed by local white officials as younger than their actual age so that they could be "bound out" before the age of twenty-one years. Willie and Henry Taylor, who were fourteen and sixteen years of age respectively, were "bound out" by Swift, who listed their mother as dead and sent them to work for John S. Taylor as farm servants in December 1866. Born in South Carolina, the Taylor brothers most likely had been John Taylor's former slaves, and by 1870, the two were living with their sister, Laura, and working as farm laborers, but not for Taylor.

On December 26, 1867, Fanny Everett, who was fourteen and recently married, visited the office of Agent Losey to request the return of her four siblings. She and her family had lived on a plantation in Fort Valley owned by James Abington Everett, the former benefactor of William Jackson Anderson, but following the death of her mother, her two brothers and two sisters were apprenticed on the recommendation of Myles Greene, a leading figure in Houston County. Greene was the executor of Everett's estate, and Fanny and her family had most likely been Everett's slaves. Moreover, Greene was known as a cruel master, and as one report goes, "Old Myers Green[e] would make his Niggers steal and he would say, 'If you get caught, I'll kill you.' One or two of them let themselves get caught, and he would whip them."[35]

As Losey reported, "I have the honor to state that Fanny Everett a freedman barring a very good character for industry & etc. (and also her husband) by this present employer have made application to me to have their Brothers and Sisters returned to them . . . Fanny should have them by right."[36] Unfortunately, her petition was denied, and Reverend George Clarke, who was the former pastor of the Fort Valley Slave Mission, refused to return Fanny's sister Mary, who was nine years old. Clarke's petition to keep Mary had previously been guaranteed by the former bureau agent, most likely J. D. Havis, who had agreed to maintain her service as an apprentice as long at the bureau existed. Moreover, Reverend Clarke most likely needed Mary's service for his wife, Martha, who was due to give birth to their first daughter.

By 1870, the Freedmen's Bureau was just a memory, and Mary remained the Clarke's domestic servant and the only person unable to read and write in their household, which was a reality that often befell children subjected to the apprenticeship system. For Mary and thousands of other children of freedpeople, the apprenticeship system meant enduring separation from family, uncompensated labor until the age of twenty-one, and little or no hope of attending an educational institution like the nearby Anderson School.[37]

Following his election loss in 1868, Anderson focused on ministry to Black Methodists and the establishment of the Anderson School as ways to fight the many injustices like the apprenticeship laws that plagued freedpeople in his community. As a father with several children of his own and a pastor with a special interest for the welfare of Black children, the separation of families in his community must have been difficult to watch, and the zeal that he had shown for his theological training quickly translated into zeal for the education of Black children.

Under his leadership, the Anderson School in Fort Valley was established and funded by freedpeople. The school also exemplified the resoluteness of freedpeople in Fort Valley to have an institution all their own. Well aware of the limits of interracial cooperation, Black leaders acquired a church building that had served as the Blind Academy during the war and a funeral home afterwards.[38] The building was quickly adapted to serve both religious and educational purposes and was paid for in installments with freedpeople often soliciting help from former masters when "payments fell due." Adapting the building to worship lessened the fears of local whites, and Caesar Taylor, Paul Barnett, Jim Stanley, and Isaac Anderson's continued connection to their former masters and their ministerial tutelage under Rev. Joseph Cotter also lessened the concerns of local white leaders even if a school for former slaves was being established in Fort Valley.[39]

In September of 1868, Anderson solicited financial support from the Freedmen's Bureau for repairs to the building. Agent Losey met with Anderson, describing him as a "colored" carpenter and "a leading man among his people" and reporting that "an upper portion of the Colored Church [was] used for school purpose by the freedmen in the vicinity of Fort Valley but was ... quite out of repair." After inspecting the building with Anderson, Losey forwarded an estimate of repairs to his superiors with a notation that freedpeople in Fort Valley promised to "put the lower portion in good repair at their own expense which they intend doing before cool weather sets in." As he concluded, "I am satisfied that the amount of said repairs and cost is as low as it can be done and the freed people will have a comfortable school house."[40]

Exactly when the Anderson School began classes is not clear, but by January of 1868, the school was up and running with Adeline Wallace, a twenty-five-year-old Black woman, serving as its primary teacher. The school was supported entirely by freedpeople and served an average of ninety-five students during the month of August. Ten of the students were older than sixteen, and most could spell and read "easy lessons."[41] The school also housed a Sabbath school, which provided additional space for educating former slaves and emphasizing literacy, civil engagement, and religious instruction. The Anderson School allowed former slaves to pursue two goals that were important to them: literacy and Bible knowledge. The place of worship established in the Anderson School would later become Usher's Chapel, and the primary school would form the beginnings of Fort Valley State University.[42]

Schools provided a space for work that often extended to advocating "civic and economic equality." Black teachers strengthened this environment and illustrated the changing status of freedpeople.[43] Adeline Wallace served in this role at the Anderson School in Fort Valley, and in nearby Perry, George Ormond, who was a Union league organizer and vocal Republican, served as a teacher. Churches and schools, two powerful institutions among freedpeople, would incubate a dramatic political upset by Republicans in Houston County in December of 1870.

* * *

In September of 1865, Brevet major general Davis Tillson was named assistant commissioner for the Freedmen's Bureau in Georgia. Tillson considered the bureau to be an extension of the federal government and a protection for freedpeople, helping them to transition from slavery into a free market economy. Tillson, who was a New England native striving for a fair contract system in the South, was an intruder to white Georgians, and under his bureau's protection, he began to require landholders to pay male laborers twelve to fifteen dollars a month and female laborers eight to ten dollars a month[44] This rate was a far cry from the three to eight dollars a month typically offered by white landholders, and when they balked and refused to pay Black laborers the required wage, Tillson began funding efforts to relocate Black Georgians to other Southern states that were clamoring for laborers.[45] By sending freedpeople to Mississippi and Arkansas, he hoped to force Georgians to raise their wages for Black laborers.

After four months, the Freedmen's Bureau had aided at least four hundred Black laborers in leaving the state, and this number grew to 1,124 by January of 1866. That year, legislators in Georgia enacted Section 4428 of the Penal Code in order to stop the exodus of freedpeople from the state. The penal code stated that if any person knowingly employed the servant of another while he or she was already employed, or if any person knowingly enticed or persuaded any servant to leave his or her employer either by offering higher wages or in any way whatever during his or her term of service, that person would be guilty of a misdemeanor and fined up to two hundred dollars or be jailed for up to three months.[46]

In Houston County, landholders responded by opting for day laborers for whom contracts were not required, and workers could be paid whatever the landholder desired. In other parts of Georgia, landholders frightened Black workers into signing low-paying contracts by circulating false stories that laborers "sent by the Bureau to Mississippi and South Western Georgia . . . were sold into slavery, and that women were drowned."[47]

The stories were flatly denied by the bureau, but Tillson did have a plan to establish a freedmen's colony in southwest Georgia and had approached General Oliver Otis Howard, the head of the bureau, about the effort. The plan was to have the Massachusetts-based American Land Company acquire inexpensive tracts of land in southwestern Georgia and resell them to freedpeople at a reasonable cost. Tillson's free market perspective was most telling in a speech that he gave before the Freedmen's Convention: "You have the same right with all other men to accumulate, hold and enjoy property; the right to be as rich as you can make yourselves by your own energy, industry and economy . . . With the blessing of providence your, future is almost wholy in your hands. You are no longer chattels but men."[48]

In January 1865, before the Civil War ended, Union General William T. Sherman had issued Special Field Order 15, which was a military directive setting aside nearly 400,000 acres of prime land confiscated from whites fleeing his infamous march along the coast of South Carolina, Georgia, and Florida. Many freedpeople treasured the hope of owning land, but Sherman's plan was short lived, and by August, the allocated land was returned to wealthy white landholders, many of whom had directly asked then President Andrew Johnson for a pardon for their complicity in the war. In June 1866, the passage of the Southern Homestead Act, which granted access to public land in exchange for a ten-dollar registration fee and an agreement to improve the land for five years, rekindled the hopes of freedpeople in the possibility of land ownership.

Initially, the Southern Homestead Act barred access to the land from those who had "borne arms against the United States," and Tillson worked to provide to freedpeople information about and transportation to the 46 million acres of public land made available in Alabama, Arkansas, Florida, Louisiana, and Mississippi. His efforts further encouraged them to seek opportunity outside of Georgia, and while some agents encouraged Black laborers to remain in Georgia, reports quickly spread across the state about the bureau's relocation efforts. Among those leaving the state was a group of freedpeople who settled in Panola County, Mississippi. Isaac Anderson would one day find himself in Mississippi after leaving Georgia as had that group.[49]

Unfortunately for freedpeople in Georgia, Tillson's tenure at the bureau ended on January 14, 1867, due in large part to the constant criticisms of his policies, yet even after his departure, white landholders continued to be frustrated throughout the late fall and winter of 1868 by freedmen who refused to sign labor contracts.[50] Moreover, rumors began to spread that Isaac Anderson and other Black leaders who were serving that year in the Constitutional Convention would also pass measures providing land to freedpeople, and in response, many of them throughout southwest and central Georgia refused to sign contracts with white landholders.[51] A month later, bureau captain M. Frank Gallagher published an impassioned plea to Black Georgians: "No convention will, or can, exempt you from labor for the support of yourselves and families. People whom you cannot hold responsible tell you not to go to work; while the Agents of this Bureau, as officers of the United States Government, tell you that you should go to work at once, making the best contracts that you can, under the circumstances . . . Make contracts before the Agents of the Bureau; they will try to secure for you the best possible wages, and to ensure their payment when due. Now is the time you must make contracts if you make any for the present year. Now is the time when land must be plowed and prepares; and planters must know how much to cultivate. If you do not contract now it is more likely that when you are ready to contract you will not be wanted, and cannot get employment."[52]

Throughout his tenure in Fort Valley and Perry, Agent Daniel Losey was a visible extension of the federal government and the Freedmen's Bureau, and freedpeople continually sought its help. However, by September of 1868, tensions in the county concerning Reconstruction had reached a crescendo, and Black legislators across Georgia were expelled from office by white leaders. In Atlanta, tensions were high over the upcoming presidential elections, and dozens of freedpeople were killed on their way to a political rally.

Whites, emboldened by the racial tensions, made Losey a target of animosity, and the agent appealed to Brigadier General Silbey, who was the new head of the Georgia bureau: "I have been informed by several colored persons that they have overheard at different times that I must be got away from here [and] that if this is accomplished . . . the whites can do with the Nigger what they please." He concluded, "I cannot alone among so many violent men feel that my life is safe. Please instruct what course to pursue and in what manner the government will protect its representatives."[53]

By December of 1868, the Freedmen's Bureau effectively ended most of its operations in Georgia. In his last two reports, agent Losey wrote, "From present indications it seems to me that combinations are being made by the planters to reduce the price of labor to such an extent, that the interest of the freed people will be very materially affected to their injury... My impression is that the freed people are again having to have pretty hard times they are commencing already to show it to them that the Bureau is run out."[54]

Writers in the *Fort Valley Leader and Tribune* have described this period as a time of "terrible oppression of the Yankee Bureau, presided over by Captain Losey, of the USA."[55] Moreover, in *A History of Houston County*, Warren Grice writes, "Backed by the radicals at Washington, the policy sustained by Federal Troops in the South, 'egged on' too often by the officials of the Freedmen's' Bureau, and assisted in some instances by renegade whites, this mistaken policy of the conqueror made for Houston county in the late sixties and early seventies its darkest period."[56] Barring a handful of academic books, the dominant story of the Freedmen's Bureau accepted by most white Georgians and reinforced by many local histories for over a century is often devoid of Black voices and virulent with a romanticized vision of the Antebellum South and the need to return freedpeople to subservience.

In 1869, after the departure of Agent Losey and the Freedmen's Bureau from Georgia, Houston County's court docket exploded with Blacks being arrested and indicted for larceny, burglary, and a slew of other misdemeanor offenses. The all-white grand jury was composed of some of Houston County's most respected citizens, and the judge presiding over the cases, as he had for the last eighteen years, was the Honorable Carlton B. Cole. That year, the grand jury issued a bill of indictment against a "colored" woman, identified only as Lydia, for violating an 1866 law that prohibited individuals from leaving their current employer. According to court records, Lydia was indicted for encouraging someone "to leave the employment of said D. H. Houser, the said Lydia... knowing the said [person was] in the employment of said D. H. Houser and that her term of service had not expired."

Houser, a successful grist mill owner, was related to Lewis M. Houser, the former inferior court judge about whom agent Losey had received a report in 1868 concerning several Black laborers not being paid. Moreover, Houser was both the plaintiff in this case and a member of the grand jury that issued Lydia's indictment. Judge Cole found Lydia guilty and fined her five dollars, and in his judgment, a message sent to Black laborers: Their labor is not their own and the laws of Georgia will reinforce that truth.[57] The indictment and conviction of Lydia was also a reassertion of power by local white leaders.

That same year, Mack Watkins was arrested and indicted by the grand jury for "[carrying] about his person a certain pistol not in an open and fully exposed to view." Watkins, who was found guilty, was forced to pay five dollars, and if he were not able to do so, he would have joined the thousands of freedpeople across the South whose labor was purchased by local white landholders to work off their debt. Watkin's conviction served to warn men in Houston County like George Ormond and Isaac Anderson that carrying a weapon could result in their arrest and that the interpretation of how "visible" a weapon was would be determined solely by white residents serving on the jury.[58]

In August 1869, Judge Cole adjudicated the cases of John "Newton" Glover, Richard Cain, Jack Fagan, Taylor Fagan, and Wesley Glover, who were indicted on vague burglary charges. All of the men were between the ages of seventeen and thirty, and all were sentenced to hard labor at the State Penitentiary in Milledgeville.[59] That previous year, Georgia began contracting convict labor with 205 inmates housed in Milledgeville. Of the inmates there, 177 were Black, and only 28 were white, and as the use of Black codes increased, so did the number of Blacks incarcerated.[60] By 1870, 597 out of 737 prisoners in the state penitentiary were Black, and the number would continue to grow to 1,582 out of 1,809 prisoners by 1880.[61]

Carlton B. Cole, who had served as a circuit judge for Dooly, Bibb, Crawford, Macon, Twiggs, and Houston Counties since 1851, would have been aware of where prisoners ultimately ended up as he sentenced them to work in the state penitentiary or "anywhere deemed acceptable by the state." This meant that incarcerated men would be sent to work in railroad construction, and as a stockholder in the Central Railroad, Cole knew the importance of rebuilding Georgia's railroad in order for the state's economy to rebound.[62]

William Jackson Anderson consistently supported the Macon and Brunswick Railroad, which was considered essential to Fort Valley's growth and to the economic recovery of the state. In addition, he was most likely aware of the Macon and Brunswick as well as the Southwestern Railroads' need for the labor of freedpeople. It is no wonder, therefore, that William Jackson also supported the policy of leasing out convicts to railroad companies following his election to the Georgia Senate in April of 1868. State officials like him were so concerned about rebuilding railroads in Georgia that in 1868, they promised ten thousand dollars a year for each ten-mile track of land laid by 1870 with full completion by 1873.

While traveling throughout Georgia ministering to Black Methodists, Isaac Anderson would have most likely learned of former slaves being ensnared by the state's Black Codes and returned to a system of quasi slavery. Before Emancipation, the Southwestern Railroad had owned nearly a dozen slaves who primarily worked to construct and maintain the track, and afterwards, roughly 200 prisoners were leased to the Macon and Brunswick

Railroad in order to complete its Macon-to-Augusta line. By the end of 1870, the number of convicts leased for railroad construction had increased to 385, and by 1875, more than 800 miles of new track were constructed with convict labor.[63] Moreover, the leasing of convicts to rebuild railroads was deadly, and from May to December of 1868, 16 of the 211 convicts leased to work died of exhaustion and disease.[64]

* * *

In 1869, the *Macon Union*, a local Republican paper, reported the arrest of F. Y. Fyall, who was one of the thirty-three Black legislators removed from office in September 1868. His charges, which changed like shifting sand, ranged from attaining office while not living long enough in Macon County to being ineligible for office for being one-eighth Black. The paper reported that while in Fort Valley, he had been "dragged off to jail," held there for over two months, and sent before Judge Carlton B. Cole's court. Henry Turner, who visited Fyall reported, "he has been in prison sixty-four days, because he would not promise to join the Democratic party . . . He told them he would remain in jail till he rotted before he would forsake his principles. I found the jails generally full of colored men, for all kinds of falsely charged offenses."[65]

Fyall was eventually released, and he subsequently called for the investigation of a group of local Blacks from nearby Randolph County who had been mistreated. Hoping for federal protection, Fyall, along with Joel Griffith, secretly requested that federal troops be sent to southwest Georgia. As Willard E. Wight conjectures in *The Negro in the Georgia Legislature: The Case of F.H. Fyall of Macon County*, "following his removal from office Fyall [was] 'made conductor on a freight train, from which he fell and was killed.'"[66]

The new Georgia Constitution, which was ratified the previous year, guaranteed Blacks the right to vote and participate in the political process, and in exercising that right, Isaac Anderson, Jack Ballard, Hugh Dean, Isaac L. Primus, George Ormond, and other Black leaders began to establish Grant Clubs throughout the state in anticipation of Ulysses S. Grant's run later in November as the Republican presidential candidate.[67] Local white leaders were determined to squelch what they described as the "radical" element, and a month after the spring 1868 election, the first documented escalation in racial violence occurred in Dooly County. John Woodward, a white resident of the county, was ecstatic over the election of Democrats who were all white: "If the State [had] done as well as Dooly County, Radicalism [would be] dead in Georgia."[68]

On May 23, 1868, a white mob gathered around Jack and Mary Ballard's home in Vienna, the county seat of Dooly. Jack Ballard most likely had been a slave and was a carpenter by trade. He was also known for his political activity and had been warned by local whites to stay away from politics, and that night in May, several men torched the Ballard home. Jack and Mary were away at a church meeting, and their two children, who had remained at home were trapped inside and burned alive. Days later, a paper in Macon callously referenced to the arson and murder stating that "no one felt sorry [for] him [Ballard]."[69]

Hoping to find some justice, the Ballards reported the arson and murder of their two children to the Freedman's Bureau, which was only months away from effectively ending most of its operations in Georgia. Agent Daniel Losey immediately faced opposition to his investigation, and he reported to his superiors that local whites had threatened him, saying that "he better leave that section or he would go up next."[70]

Ballard's oppression mirrored the experience of many Freedmen who were targeted for contradicting the stereotypes of most Southern whites concerning Black manhood. In their eyes, his participation in the political process and his work as a skilled carpenter made him equal to them and put him in direct competition with them, provoking them to emasculate Black men by undermining their role as the heads of households, among other things.[71] No evidence exists showing that anything was ever done to respond to the murder of the Ballard children, and the reality of such acts of violence was shared by Black men and women living near the Ballards, and especially by those who attended the political meeting with the Ballards on the night their children were burned alive. The trauma of events like these often had such an impact on freedpeople that adults who knew the perpetrators of such crimes kept silent for decades, fearing retribution.

August brought more violence in Georgia. In another report, agent Losey recounted that Dennis Lewis and seventy-five other Black men "were taking initiatory steps to organize a Grant and Colfax club in the county of Dooly ... [when] about four hundred white men and boys well-armed surrounded the place." James Cobb, Dooly's former sheriff, and William Graham, its current sheriff, were among the armed group, and they loudly declared that they "did not respect or recognize the laws which placed Governor Bullock in power that he was going by the laws enforced before Bullock was ever thought of."[72] The group demanded the surrender of Hugh Dean, the president of the local Grant Club, along with other club officers, and when the freedmen refused, the sheriff punched George Cobb, one of the organizers, in the mouth twice and drew his weapon on the other Black men. Earlier, Dean had requested that members of the club leave their weapons at home in order not to alarm local whites, and consequently, the armed mob was able to apprehend Dean and remove him to the courthouse in Vienna where Shep Rodgers, the local judge, immediately tried and convicted him. Judge Rodgers had vowed that if Ulysses Grant were elected, "his party would kill every negro in the southern states," and to emphasize his ability to carry out his threat, he made it known that local whites had powder kegs and were willing to start a war in Dooly if necessary.[73]

The Freedmen's Bureau was only months away from effectively leaving Georgia, and its failure to protect freedpeople led many to conceal weapons in their homes for protection and organize militias through the Grant Clubs. Historian Paul Cimbala records that "even before the end of the war up and down the coast in Sherman's Reservation, Black Georgians supervised by [Freedmen's Bureau] officials mustered militias to protect their freedom and common good." Formerly enslaved men openly drilled for warfare, and in some cases, they organized armed groups to investigate suspected Klan activity.[74] In one instance, George Ormond reported after receiving numerous death threats, "[I] soon called 12 or 15 armed men to my protection and kept them all night with me."[75]

As the violence escalated, Joel Griffin, who had become a member of the Executive Grant Club committee, wrote to Governor Bullock late in August. After visiting the Dooly county jail he reported that, "The jail there seems full of political prisoners, the Officers there are certainly perverting justice if all reports be correct for there is a semblance of martial law established . . . I am afraid [that] Outrages will commence soon in my County." Six days later, Griffin wrote the governor again in a private and confidential letter: "[The] Judge of the County Court in Dooly County . . . has no authority what ever to be issuing warrants and having them executed on Negroes by Sheriffs of the county and his underlings, and these Negroes being incarcerated in the prison of that county for weeks till they [face] utter starvation [and] renounce their political faith."[76]

Unlike Dooly, Houston County was successful in establishing Grant Clubs, and the Freedmen's Bureau reported that "whites in that county think that their chance of electing their Democratic ticket are small." However, Grant Club organizers like George Ormond soon became the targets of whites who were emboldened by the violence in nearby Dooly County. In a report to the bureau, Ormond wrote, "We have met peaceably at all our meetings . . . [A]gain we want nothing but Justice and again we don't intend to trouble the white people if they but let us alone and they very well know that we will not trouble them too."[77]

* * *

Following his loss in the election of 1868, Anderson had focused on ministering to Methodist congregations in Houston County and establishing the Anderson primary and Sabbath schools in Fort Valley, but escalating violence coupled with the departure of the Freedmen's Bureau made Southwest and Central Georgia a dangerous place for him and thousands of other freedpeople.[78] In 1869, life for Blacks in Georgia meant the constant threat of arrest and the enforcement of Black Codes and apprenticeship laws that worked to return freedpeople to subservience and a system of quasi slavery. In reflecting on Emancipation after his election to the state's Senate, Anderson would write in 1873 that "the reason [Blacks] were leaving was on account of the fact they could not get protection in Georgia."[79]

> 1868 Grant Elected President—1870 Fifteenth Amendment Ratified—
> 1870 CME Church Established

Chapter Five

1870

ON JANUARY 13, 1869, AS BISHOP CHARLES T. QUINTARD, A FORMER CONfederate chaplain, offered an opening invocation, William Jackson Anderson sat among his political peers, ready to proceed with the business of the Georgia Senate. To white Southern leaders like him, the state seemed to slowly be making its way forward, but the meddling of the federal government remained a constant hindrance. The Freedmen's Bureau was making its departure from Houston County and the state, and if federal oversight would totally disappear, Georgia would be ready to set its own terms in defining the New South.

Earlier in 1868, the state had met federally mandated conditions of Reconstruction for a second time, but Congress was increasingly concerned about the defiant tone of its leaders. During his inaugural year, William Jackson and many state senators resisted congressional efforts to implement Reconstruction in Georgia by opposing the passage of the Fourteenth Amendment, and even though it was ratified against their wishes, the state failed to protect the rights of former slaves as mandated in the amendment and also expelled Black leaders from its legislature.

Henry M. Turner, Tunis Campbell Sr., and a delegation of Black leaders from Georgia visited Republican leaders in Washington to make a case for increased federal intervention. Congress, dominated by progressive Republicans, had a reason to act on their behalf. Despite a sizeable Black electorate, Georgia was one of only two Deep South states that Ulysses Grant had failed to carry during his presidential run in November of that year.

Throughout 1868, the House Committee on Reconstruction held hearings to investigate complaints leveled against the state, and several individuals, including Turner and Rufus Bullock, Georgia's Republican governor, gave testimony highlighting the unfair dismissal of Black state legislators and the mistreatment of former slaves in 260 cases documented between January and November of that year. The congressional testimony was later published in 1869 as *The Condition of the Affairs in Georgia*, and Nelson Tift who represented Albany in southwest Georgia and was later recognized as that city's founder, countered accusations during the hearings. Tift, who was a Democrat, was born in Connecticut and sworn into the US House of Representatives on July 25, 1868, following Georgia's readmittance to the Union. He had moved to the state in the 1830s and established himself as a merchant, newspaperman, and land speculator, and although he had opposed secession, he built warships for the Confederate navy and provided supplies for Confederate soldiers during the war and had acquired a pardon in 1865. Tift was a vocal critic of the numerous reports that Georgia was ignoring the rights of freedmen and women, but he saved his harshest criticism for Governor Bullock.[1]

Joel Griffin, who had earlier petitioned congressional leaders in Washington concerning the mistreatment of former slaves in Houston County, and George Ormand, the Perry school teacher and Union league leader, also appeared at the hearings. Concerning Houston County, Ormand testified that "Mr. E. M. Hulsey, justice of the peace, and one of the managers, did refuse votes . . . [and] hundreds were refused their votes."[2] Griffin was one of several Houston County notaries who had questioned the actions of William F. Postell and Brad Brown, two precinct managers in Fort Valley, and had submitted a signed affidavit on behalf of Black residents. According to Griffin, the two men had repeatedly questioned the qualifications of Black voters "while hundreds of citizens were waiting to vote, [which] closed polls for better than an hour, thereby absorbing the time allotted [to vote]." Underneath his affidavit were the names of 169 Black Fort Valley residents who made their "marks," or signatures, acknowledging that they were denied access to the polls.[3]

Hoping to offset the accusations, Tift had Houston County officials challenge the validity of the freedmen's accusations. William T. Swift, a County Ordinary, issued a written response stating that no organized effort to disenfranchise Black voters existed, election officials had fulfilled their duties, and the treatment of Blacks by whites was "kind and conciliatory."[4] Tift also tried to stem growing support for the removal of former Confederate leaders from Georgia's legislature by arguing that their fitness for office had been settled during the state's previous tenure of Reconstruction from 1867 through 1868 under military general Meade. In a scathing rebuke, he addressed accusations made by Governor Bullock, writing, "I must confess with sorrow and humiliation . . . [and] defend the people and State of Georgia against the slanders and machinations of her governor. Whatever may have been the motives which dictated his course, instead of acting as a guardian and defender of her rights, her honor and her interest, as duty and manhood required, he has been foremost among her defamers, and the chief enemy of her peace and prosperity."[5]

In December 1868, following the hearings, Samuel Clarke Pomeroy, the Republican Senator from Kansas, sponsored a bill to reinstate federal oversight and again place Georgia under Reconstruction. Tunis G. Campbell Sr., one of the three Black senators who had been expelled, was also one of the most vocal Republican leaders lobbying in Washington for the reinstatement of federal oversight in Georgia.[6] By the summer of 1869, William Jackson's hopes and the aspirations of many other Democratic leaders dissipated as two out of three members of the Georgia Supreme Court ruled that Black legislators were wrongfully expelled and had a right to hold office.[7] Months later, on December 22, Congress reinstated military rule in Georgia a third and final time sending Union troops to enforce federal oversight in the state.

* * *

In January 1869, as Congress considered whether or not to reinstate federal oversight in Georgia and William Jackson began his second year in the state's senate, the consideration of the 15th Amendment was among the measures on Georgia's legislative agenda. The proposed amendment would guarantee "the right of citizens of the United States to vote shall not be denied or abridged by the United States or by any state on account of race, color, or previous condition of servitude." The measure that had already passed in both houses of Congress would have to be ratified by two-thirds of the states in the union before it could become an amendment to the Constitution.

In the spring of that year, William Jackson and fifteen other state senators voted against the amendment, and it failed, but Governor Rufus Bullock and the new military commander, Alfred H. Terry, were aware of the political necessity for Republicans to pass the amendment. Leaders in Georgia understood that federal control would remain until the amendment was passed. By expelling leaders who had Confederate ties in the Georgia Assembly and had also opposed the Fourteenth Amendment, Congress hoped to return Georgia to a path of Reconstruction that was satisfactory in its eyes.

Earlier, Tunis G. Campbell Sr., had protested state legislators whom he believed were sympathetic to the Confederacy, and with the protection of a reinstalled military governance, Campbell, Aaron Alpeoria, and George Wallace had been officially reseated as the state senate was called to order on January 13, 1870. Yet, even before the session began, Campbell sought the removal of several legislators who had aided Confederate efforts or held Confederate office and had not received a presidential pardon for these actions.[8] Animosity toward his actions were palpable among supporters of the senators in question, and as Campbell himself recalled, "It now became common talk that the old Negro Senator of the Second was destroying Georgia, and the Negroes would be unruly unless he was put out of the way."[9] In months to come, Campbell and other Black legislators in Georgia would understand the lengths to which many white Georgians were willing to go to protect their state.

Minutes before the opening session that January, Campbell was told that none of his senate colleagues would sign a resolution to remove the senators and that "there [were] eight men stationed in front of the side gallery, above the Republican members, [ready] to shoot down any member who should attempt to read a protest." Campbell recalled a packed gallery and a sea of white faces, and ten minutes before the call to order, he clarified his intent to protest the seating of Confederate sympathizers. He later remembered that immediately "all the Senators then moved away from my seat."[10]

As the clerk read the names of elected senators and the district they represented, he began his protest by citing Senator John J. Collier from the Fourteenth District. When Campbell began to read the resolution, he recalled that "Democratic members arose almost in a body to object, and would not obey any calls to order. With the permission from the president . . . I continued to read, raising my voice above their clamor."[11] The roll call continued without protest until the call for the seating of W. J. Anderson, the senator from the Twenty-Third District. At William Jackson's seating, Campbell rejoined his protests, and C. A. Wooten, who represented the Ninth District, spoke out in opposition to him but was ruled out of order. Names continued to be read and ended with M. A. Candler from the Forty-Fourth District and W. T. Winn from the Thirty-Fifth District, both of whom had served the state before or during the war. Campbell opposed their seating, and arguments again erupted among the senators. Eventually, Senator Candler "demanded the authority for filing printed protests against the eligibility of Senators," and at this, applause broke out in the gallery.[12] Campbell recalls that Governor Bullock, who was concerned with rising tensions in the chamber, "sent for me and told me not to read anymore as the house had to adjourn without doing anything."[13]

Bullock, General Terry, and Republican leaders in Georgia needed the Fifteenth Amendment, and to ensure its passage, they still needed to expel some Confederate sympathizers from office. Consequently, they moved to expel several legislators from the House and Senate, including William Jackson.[14] In March 1863, as the Civil War raged, the Georgia Assembly had passed a bill to "relieve William J. Anderson ... and other persons, from the pains and penalties of the laws of this State against the issuing and circulating of change bills, upon certain conditions, and for other purposes." Such actions provided the needed justification to oust William Jackson from office, and at the request of Bullock and Terry, State Attorney General H. P. Farrow charged William Jackson with being a notary public for the Confederacy and aiding and abetting the rebellion.[15]

For his part, William Jackson "admitted that he acted as a notary public, though never qualified as such, and admitted aiding and abetting the rebellion,"[16] and although he was removed from office only months before the end of his term, his tenure had been a great success personally and by the standards of his party. His position as president of the Fort Valley and Loan, his efforts to incorporate the Cotton States Insurance company where he served as a local agent, and his support of the convict lease system had allowed his business interests to flourish. Railroads that traveled through Fort Valley were either built or restored from the damages of war, and his status among Southern leaders had risen sharply. Moreover, because of his refusal to pass the Fourteenth and Fifteenth Amendments and his ousting of Black leaders from the Georgia Senate, he had become a symbol of Southern resistance. "Colonel" Anderson's tenure expanded his wealth and influence and ultimately made him one of the wealthiest and most influential men in Houston County. William A. Matthews, a Fort Valley doctor and member of Fort Valley Methodist, completed the remainder of his term.[17]

* * *

Once reseated in the Georgia House and Senate, Black legislators busied themselves pushing through measures of importance to the Black community. James Porter, who represented Chatham County, worked on civil rights and education, while Henry McNeal Turner, representing Bibb County, pushed for improvements in public education. Turner, along with James M. Sims representing Chatham County with Porter and George Wallace representing Baldwin County, served on the committee investigating conditions at the state penitentiary and also proposed legislation to promote lawful elections.[18]

Isaac Anderson had lost his run for the state legislature, and by 1870, he had seen the ouster of Black leaders, the seating of Confederate sympathizers in Georgia's legislature, and the violent curtailing of voting rights for former slaves like himself. Two of these injustices had been righted, and on August 6 of that year, he joined Joel R. Griffin and Samuel A. Cobb to contest the seats of Houston County representatives C. C. Duncan, H. R. Felder, and J. W. Matthews based on "the charges of fraud, bribery, and intimidation in the elections held in [Houston] county for Governor, members of Congress, members of the General Assembly and county officers in 1868."[19] Griffin had contested the three representatives immediately after their election in 1868, and Anderson and Cobb's decision to join him in renewing the protests of these seats spoke to their growing frustration with the conditions of freed people in Houston County and their hopes for the support of newly reseated Black members.

Anderson, Griffin, and Cobb appealed to the Georgia House Committee on Privileges and Elections, claiming that they should be seated as representatives since they had received the next highest number of votes.[20] In the end, the House dismissed the petition on the grounds that the "General Assembly had no power and could not go back of the acts of General George G. Meade . . . by whose order the honorable members from Houston county are now holding seats upon this floor."[21] With the door shut to reclaim these legislative seats, Anderson and Griffin made plans to run again and bring about a massive political upset in the election of 1870, but this time they would do so by maximizing their respective areas of influence: the press and the pew.

Earlier in 1868, Governor Bullock had provided funding for Republican newspapers throughout the state hoping to counter newspapers that staunchly supported the Democratic Party. As a Republican, Bullock, made these papers the official media outlet of Georgia and guaranteed financial support from the State despite opposition from many white Democratic-leaning Georgians. With the growing number of freedpeople who could read, the Republican papers provided a counterbalance to the portrayal of former slaves and their leaders. Instead of *The Houston Home Journal*, which was stridently antagonistic toward Black leaders even in its first weeks off the press in 1870, Republicans in Houston County opted to read Griffin's *Southwest Georgian*, an official paper supported by Republican leaders and funded by the state. Reportedly, Griffin was mistreated for his support of the Republican Party, and Captain J. W. Lowe, a writer for the *Southwest Georgian* and a local merchant, had his storehouse "vigorously assaulted by KKK while . . . absent on business."[22]

Anderson set about the work of claiming the state senate seat that had been vacated by his father and former master, William Jackson, and he also set his mind on gathering political support from voters in Black churches. Often referred to as the "invisible institution" before the Civil War, the Black Church was vital to formerly enslaved people and provided a cohesive and liberating space to them following Emancipation. From 1860 through 1875, the number of Blacks who were Methodists grew from 31,000 to 75,000 in Georgia alone, yet freedpeople wanted their own, separate spaces to worship, and during slavery, either the slave mission or the "Brush arbor," a place of secrecy for enslaved worshippers, allowed them to worship in physical and spiritual proximity with people like themselves.[23]

* * *

In *Under the Sentence of Death: Lynching in the South*, W. Fitzhugh Brundage examines how members of the Black community gathered their own "collective history" of the violence and repression perpetrated on them by whites.[24] Many of these perpetrators were prominent churchmen, and in Fort Valley's Methodist Church, Myles Greene was one such man. To whites, Greene was the wealthy grandson of a prominent local Methodist preacher. More importantly, he was the brother-in-law of Fort Valley founding father James Abington Everett and the executor of his estate. Greene was also a trustee at the church, and he and William Jackson sat in prominent seats near each other in the church's sanctuary.

The memory of Greene was different in the Black community. He was known for his unusual cruelty, and as H. B. Holloway of Fort Valley recounted, "Old Myer Green[e] would take a Nigger and tie his feet to one side of the railroad track and tie his hands to the other side, and whip him till his blood ran. Then he would take him down to the smoke house and rub him down with lard and red pepper. 'rub plenty in,' he would say, 'Don't let him spoil.' Then I have seen them take up a ten-rail fence and set it down on a Nigger's neck and whip him. If he would rare and twist and try to jump up, he would break his neck."[25]

The collective memories of such men and events spurred Blacks to leave white churches behind. All too often, their white leaders were complicit in such atrocities as the murder of Jack and Mary Ballard's children, the threats against Hugh Dean during his run for office in Dooly County, the arrest and mysterious disappearance of F. Y. Fyall after his election in Macon County, and the separation of blood kin like Fanny and Mary Everett. Freedpeople stood collectively in witness to these injustices, and consequently, their establishment of a separate and distinct Black Church was the most visible form of collective protest in the years after Emancipation.

After Emancipation, Black churches increasingly functioned as places of witness and testimony to the separation of parents from children, the reality of work with little or no pay, and the constant fear of being caught on the road alone. Black churches gave spaces for parishioners to testify to acts of violence and sing of an afterlife free from pain and sorrow. As one Black

Methodist minister reflected joyously in a hymn, "O rapturous scenes that wait the day, When Thou shall call me home, When I shall here no longer stay, No longer weep and moan."[26]

In *The Negro Church in America*, E. Franklin Frazier describes the Black Church as "a refuge in a hostile white world." The pastor was central to the vitality and cohesion of the Black Church, and following Emancipation, former slaves overwhelming choose Black pastors to lead them, and they did so by 'speaking with their feet' and leaving churches and denominations lead by white leaders. For former slaves in Fort Valley, the Church was a refuge from both the presence and the message of white leaders like Rev. George C. Clarke who had been the pastor of Fort Valley's Slave Mission.[27] Emancipation meant that they could openly and freely oppose their former pastor who had violently denounced the "radical [Republican] party, and everybody who sympathizes with, or endorsed it."[28]

To former slaves, white clergy served either as perpetrator or bystander with bystanders reinforcing the power of perpetrators by not challenging their actions. As Edward L. Wheeler writes in *Uplifting the Race: The Black Minister in the New South 1865–1902*, "As the leader of the church, the black preacher held an exulted position which gave him visibility and influence... To inspire the community, the ministerial leader had to know its suffering."[29] The Black pastor therefore validated pain and sorrow that could not be fully understood by a white pastor, and in doing so, served his flock as a defacto therapist and advocate engaging in political activity that furthered the well-being of his congregation and community.

Clearly, there were differences among Black worshippers in liturgy, leadership, music, and doctrine, but Black churches were places of safety, remembrance, and mourning for former slaves. Noted psychiatrist Judith Herman provides a valuable understanding of the essential place of Black churches to people who were dealing with the memory of enslavement and the reality of freedom. In her landmark book, *Trauma and Recovery*, she writes, "The ordinary response to atrocities is to banish them from consciousness. Certain violations of the social compact are too terrible to utter aloud: this is the meaning of the word unspeakable. Atrocities, however, refuse to be buried."[30]

To pastors like Isaac Anderson and their congregants, Black churches were safe havens of transformation, and as Herman concludes, such safe havens were essential to "transform the meaning of... personal tragedy by making it the basis for social action."[31] In her work, Herman delineates three distinct stages of recovery from trauma: safety, remembrance and mourning, and reconnection to everyday life. In the first stage, trauma survivors work toward the restoration of control and power in a place of safety, typically with the assistance of a therapist. For former slaves, Black churches provided places of safety, and Black pastors provided therapy through preaching and a validation of their trauma. In Herman's second stage, survivors remember the story of their trauma, and this remembrance and mourning often results in an increased difficulty in the survivors' use of words and a switching by them to nonverbal means of communication such as drawing or painting.[32] In safe spaces of the church, former slaves expressed both joy and grief through moaning, swaying, singing, or modes of spiritual expression that are intrinsic to worship in Black churches.

In Herman's last phase, survivors reconnect to everyday life through the creation of a new future. As she explains, "survivors recognize a political or religious dimension in their misfortune and discover they can transform the meaning of their personal tragedy by making it the basis for social action."[33] S. B. Wallace's sermon, given to the Israel CME Church in Washington DC, provides a glimpse into how the church and its pastor fostered a place of refuge for the formerly enslaved. In his sermon, which was published in 1894 and entitled, *The New System of Slavery in the South*, Wallace opened with Exodus 3:19: "And I am sure the King of Egypt will not let you go—not by a mighty hand." He then recounted the horrors of slavery by comparing the experience of former slaves with that of the Israelites and in doing so, he drew upon a common understanding of suffering that all hearers would understand well.

Wallace then went on to draw a connection with slavery and the present reality of the convict lease system practiced in the south. As he proclaimed, "the Southern white people are slowly but surely restoring slavery in that section which is far worse in its subjective and objective effects than that which cursed the country for nearly three centuries." The last portion of the sermon called for his hearers to "recognize the fact that providence never deserts one in the hour of distress" and to find healing in knowing that "our aims shall be higher and our progress shall be marked by definite results."[34] Wallace's message to his Black congregation was clear: Freedpeople were not forgotten since God was on their side, and they should act with this hope. As such, Black churches were essential as places to take action by acquiring an education, gaining and sharing financial burdens, understanding civil rights, and participating in the political process. Herman's analysis provides insight into why the healing provided within the context of Black churches was vital as former slaves established schools throughout Georgia. It also gives insight into why the Georgia Equal Rights and Educational Association (GERA), which was formed in 1866 to provide a political voice to Freedmen, was so closely tied to the Black churches.[35]

* * *

For Anderson, a political victory in 1870 would serve as a beacon to a new future for the many former slaves who he hoped would ensure his election. Consequently, the establishment of Black churches in Georgia was as vital to his personal wellbeing as it was to his political success. The need for Black churches surged in importance as continual repression dominated every aspect of life for freedpeople in Georgia. The *New Orleans Christian Advocate*, a white Southern Methodist publication, admonished that "No true friend of the Negro can desire to see him put in authority over white men." A couple of months later, the paper added, "Let Negroes and Chinamen and Indians suffer the superior race of white men to whom Providence had given this country, to control it. A good government for the white man will be good enough for the Mongolian, the African or the aboriginal American."[36]

Many Black Methodist leaders knew that there was no place for them among Southern Methodists, which was a reality that Richard Vanderhorst and William Miles had grasped when they joined the AME and AME Zion churches after attending Southern Methodist churches as slaves. Deeply rooted in their Southern Methodism was their identity as Southern white men, and that identity ordered their impulses to maintain power over Black brethren and their unwillingness to share power with Black Methodist leaders.

Black Methodist leaders like Isaac Lane, Elias Cottrell, and Anderson understood something that Lucius Holsey would himself learn decades later: white Southern Methodist leaders were virtually incapable of seeing their Black brothers and sisters in Christ as equals. The hope of racial reconciliation led Holsey to believe that Black and white Methodists could coexist in the same denomination with white leaders providing guidance to, and not control over, Black leaders and churches. The realities of Reconstruction in the South led Anderson to understand that Black and white Methodists could only coexist through the creation of a distinct and separate denominational sphere where Black Methodists controlled their churches. The latter model would dominate evangelicalism well into the twenty-first century.

* * *

On December 16, 1870, in the midst of a Georgia's campaign season, Anderson and lay clergy from the Annual Methodist Conferences in Tennessee, Arkansas, Alabama, Kentucky, Mississippi, South Carolina, and Georgia gathered in Jackson, Tennessee, for the founding meeting of the CME Church. Robert Paine, a white Southern Methodist Church bishop, presided over the Conference, and as the chair of the Committee on Church Organization, Anderson delivered its report. In it, he explained that "the time has come in our history when we believe it will be for the glory of God and the best interest of the Church we represent, that we have a distinct and independent organization." Continuing with the report, he read, "Whereas the Methodist Episcopal Church in America was the name first given to the Methodist Church by its Founder Mr. John Wesley; and Whereas we are a part of the same Church never having seceded or separated from the Church . . . and now as we belong to the Colored race we simply prefix our color to the name as we are in fact part of the original Church and as old as any in America."

The message of the committee's report was clear: the CME Church was not attaching itself to a Southern identity, but was instead to be a church for "colored" Methodists distinct and separate, but in the line of John Wesley. Hoping to soften any offense to the Southern Methodist Church, Anderson and the Organizing Committee added a second resolution stating, "We shall ever hold in grateful remembrance what the M.E. Church, South has done for us, that we shall ever cherish the kindest feeling towards the Bishops and General Conference."[37]

After the conference had unanimously adopted the committee's report, two major issues came to the floor: The first was a requirement that all clergymen be educated, and the second concerned political speech and property.[38] The newly created denomination followed the Southern Methodist's book of church order, but for the CME Church, an amendment was offered to the book's eleventh chapter stating, "Let all our churches be plain and decent, and with free seats, as far as practicable . . . And they shall, on no account be used for political assemblages or purposes."[39]

Without hesitation, Anderson opposed the amendment arguing that "it was a poor reflection on their own races, as though they did not know how to treat such applications when made."[40] Unfortunately, he gained only one supporter the next day when a second vote was taken on the amendment. White Southern Methodist leaders were still in attendance at the CME Church's founding meeting, and they likely influenced the lack of public support from Black CME leaders for Anderson. Although he did have the potential leverage of his father, who was wealthy and influential in Methodist circles, and his own influence as a religious leader in central Georgia who could challenge the AME Church, many CME leaders felt it necessary to portray themselves as nonpolitical in order to play to the paternalistic perspectives of Southern Methodists, especially those who read the *Christian Advocate* which, as the periodical of the Southern Methodist Church, covered the new denomination's founding in detail.[41]

Fitzhugh Brundage explains in *Under the Sentence of Death: Lynching in the South*, that by using the language of deference, "Blacks publicly performed in ways that conveyed submission even while they sustained an ongoing dialogue of protest. Outside the intimidating gaze of whites, blacks gathered and voiced the words of anger, revenge, and self-assertion that they normally had to choke back when in the presence of whites. In black social spaces ... a rich culture of opposition flourished."[42] Brundage's analysis gives insight into why Anderson was able to maintain his political activity and never be ousted by CME leaders who were certainly aware of his campaign for state office only four days from the denominations founding meeting.[43]

The conditions that existed in Georgia, however, highlighted the need for Black ministers to serve in public office, and Anderson understood the potential political power of Black churches. Moreover, many Black legislators in Georgia were also ministers: Henry McNeal Turner was an AME minister and also ran for re-election to his Macon House seat in 1870, and Tunis Campbell served AME Zion congregations as a minister and a Georgia constituency as a state senator.[44]

Anderson's support for political engagement in the CME Church set him at odds with Lucius H. Holsey, who would become the leader of the CME Church in Georgia and, for many, the face of the newly formed denomination. Holsey believed that "as ministers of the Gospel, we make no stump speeches and fight no battles of politicians."[45] The similarities between Anderson and Holsey were striking: Both were sons of enslaved women and their white masters, both were conceived in the frontiers of Georgia, and both were known for their distinctly white features.

Holsey was born in the Georgia frontier near Columbus in 1842. He recalled that his father, James Holsey, "Like many others of his day and time ... mingled, to some extent, with those females of the African race that were his slaves—his personal property."[46] At five years of age, his father died, and he became the property of his white cousin, T. L. Wynn. In 1857, on his deathbed, Wynn asked him to select his next master, and Holsey selected Richard Malcolm Johnston, a close friend of his cousin. He moved with Johnston to Athens, Georgia, and secretly learned to read.

Several years later, when the Civil War began, Johnston returned to his home in Hancock County, and Holsey met and married Harriet Turner, a house slave owned by George Foster Pierce, a Southern Methodist minister. The relationship between Holsey and Pierce was amicable, and Holsey's wedding ceremony was held in Pierce's home. Moreover, Pierce mentored Holsey for ministry and also secured land for him when he became pastor of Ebenezer Methodist Church. In 1868, Pierce was on the credentials board when Holsey was issued his license to minister, and in 1869, he ordained Holsey as an elder.[47]

While the Southern Methodist Church formed, influenced, and ordained both Holsey and Anderson, similarities between the two concerning the identity and direction of the CME Church ended there in 1870. Holsey's desire for interracial cooperation was key to his goals of racial uplift for former slaves, and he was adamant in his perspective of whites as tutors and Blacks as students. Much later, in 1882, he would address the General Conference of the Southern Methodist Church and proclaim, "To you we sustain a three-fold relation: 1. As your servants. 2. As citizens with you. 3. As your Church-children ... It seems natural that we should follow you, and make ourselves duplicates of you as far as we are able ... We ask your sympathy, aid and cooperation in redeeming your friends and former slaves from the long night of darkness and degradation. Who will come to the rescue? Who will hear the cries of the children of Ham?"[48] In 1919, in discussing the problem of race, he would also write, "I have always been impressed and so understood from boyhood, that no matter what might take place in the rise and fall of American civilization; and no matter what social or political changes or upheavals might appear, the white man of the South would be on the top."[49] Ironically, Holsey's hope of interracial cooperation with white Southern Methodists would all but vanish later in his life.

Concurrent to the first general conference of the newly established CME Church in 1870, the South Georgia Conference of the Southern Methodist Church was convened at the Fort Valley Methodist Church. Bishop George Pierce, Holsey's mentor and the former master of his wife, presided over the gathering. Among the conference's highlights was its Sunday School Anniversary which drew a large crowd and certainly warmed the heart of William Jackson who was the Sunday School superintendent at the church. Yet, the sermons, clergy examinations, and mission fundraising at the conference were mere distractions for Houston County residents who were preoccupied with the upcoming election where "Big Ike" Anderson was again running for office. Joel Griffin, the self-described "lone white Republican in the County," George Ormond, a Loyal League leader and freedmen's school teacher, and A. Simmons, a sixty-five-year-old Virginia-born carpenter, also ran for state legislative offices along with him.[50] In reporting the proceedings of the conference, the *Houston Home Journal* wrote, "Our little town is quiet and peaceable; business very good, and politics has assumed a veil of tranquility which must be the dreaded lull just before the election storm."[51]

On December 20, as the Southern Methodist's South Georgia Conference ended in Fort Valley, the first of four days of voting in the state's legislative elections began. Records from the CME's founding meeting do not show who proposed the prohibition on its leaders participating in political activity, but the prohibition most likely served as a warning to Anderson in his bid for office in the state's Senate. Anderson would have been aware of Pierce's position on Black Methodist leaders participating in political activity since he had served as the bishop's secretary at the Southern Methodist's Georgia Colored Annual Conference a year earlier.[52] Pierce was known for his avid support of the Confederacy and his close ties to prominent politicians who were Southern Methodists and who vehemently opposed Black political leadership. Yet his campaign went forward regardless of Pierce's lack of approval. Anderson's primary concern was the mistreatment of his congregants who, as his constituency, could find justice in his political victory.

Methodists claimed the vast majority of Black political officeholders during Reconstruction with fifty-three from the AME Church, seven from the AME Zion Church, and thirty-six from the Southern Methodist Church. Baptists followed with fifty-six Black officeholders.[53] A major reason that the CME Church had gained the support of the Southern Methodist Church was because of white Methodist leaders' fear of the AME Church and its leaders whom they considered to be too political. Unlike other Southern states, Georgia was increasingly becoming a stronghold of both the AME and CME Churches even though the latter was much smaller than the former. In most of the South, the AME outpaced the CME Church, especially in urban areas where Blacks increasingly migrated for greater economic opportunity.[54] Henry McNeal Turner also held great influence in the vibrant AME Churches of Macon and Savannah. Following the war's end, the massive scramble among Methodists to establish a presence in the South encouraged Turner to ordain illiterate Black men as preachers less the AME Church lose territory to other Methodists.[55]

Both denominations vied for control in the state, and Pierce understood the influence that Anderson had developed in Black churches in central Georgia. Earlier in 1867, Anderson had left the Southern Methodist Church and become an elder in the AME Church, but his defection was short-lived. The promise that he had found in the AME Church was offset by its glaring deficiencies, and following his loss in the election of 1868, he had abandoned it. If he were to again join the AME Church, his defection this time would mean a loss to white Southern Methodist influence in many Black churches and a gain for AME churches as well as increased political influence for AME leaders in rural parts of central Georgia.

As a presiding elder in the newly forming CME Church, Anderson built upon the relationships he had developed with Black congregants in both the Fort Valley Southern Methodist Church and the slave mission. As they organized their appointed districts, presiding elders had a number of duties: directing elders, deacons, local preachers, exhorters, and candidates for ministry; changing, receiving, or suspending preachers; calling church members to quarterly meetings; adjudicating questions of law which arose in quarterly conferences; and ensuring that the *Book of Church Discipline* was being enforced.[56]

Using the "garb of a presiding elder," a technique learned from Henry McNeal Turner, Anderson established the Fort Valley District.[57] Here he supervised the communities of Butler in Taylor County, Montezuma in Crawford County, Hawkinsville in Pulaski County, and Perry and Hayneville in Houston County. These communities became essential parts of his political base, and the Fort Valley District became the largest and most well-staffed conference in the CME Church with roughly twelve circuits and an equal number of circuit pastors.[58]

Anderson's effectiveness as a spiritual leader made him influential in the lives of freedpeople like Jesse and Eliza Minnis Hunter and Bob and Charlotte McCas Felder for whom he performed marriages following emancipation.[59] His work provided the necessary cover to plan his political return, which was further motivated by reports of injustice and oppression that he received from both lay people and ministers as he traveled throughout central Georgia. Anderson saw the struggle of day-to-day living as a spiritual issue. and he also understood the politics of leadership outside the confines of the church. His involvement with Grant Clubs and work as a registrar in Houston County were extensions of his spiritual leadership.

Georgia was distinctive within Methodist history in that all five branches of Methodism vied for influence among former slaves who felt empowered by aggressive Black leadership and consequently were drawn to the all-Black AME and AME, Zion, Churches.[60] The AME Church, with its history of protest, high profile leaders, and roots steeped in Methodism's earliest beginnings, was a draw for Anderson and thousands of other freedpeople who rallied behind its message of promise and possibility. Richard Allen, James Forten, and Absalom Jones demonstrated both a spirit of protest and a well-established tradition of Methodism, and following Emancipation, Richard Cain of South Carolina and Henry McNeal Turner of Georgia furthered this tradition.[61]

Anderson's effectiveness as a spiritual leader, however, made him a threat to the AME Church's attempts at significant inroads into Fort Valley and Perry. By 1870, his efforts to establish CME Churches in Central Georgia were so fierce that Henry McNeal Turner described the reception of the AME in Perry as one of "deadly opposition of A.M.E. ism." It was not until 1890 that St. Peter's AME Church was established in Fort Valley, but by then, 22,840 men and women in Central Georgia and in rural communities belonged to CME churches, and the denomination also claimed 20,107 members concentrated in north Mississippi, Tennessee, and Alabama.[62]

The founding of the CME Church put Black Methodist at odds with one another and slowed the vigorous work of the AME Church, even leading some AME ministers like Richard Vanderhorst to leave the denomination and become one of the first CME Bishops.[63] William H. Miles belonged to the AME Zion Church before being ordained as another of the first CME bishops.[64]

Trinity Methodist Church in Augusta was known as "one of the finest colored churches in the South," and Bishop J. J. Clinton worked tirelessly to include the church in the Georgia Conference of the AME Zion Church, but by 1869, Trinity became a CME Church. Bishop Clinton and his fellow leaders were so disappointed at losing Trinity that twenty-five years later, AME, Zion, Bishop J. W. Hood wrote, "Our hopes for Georgia were lost. Augusta was one of the three important points in Georgia at the time. The Methodist Episcopal Church held Atlanta, the African Methodist Episcopal held Savannah, but if we could have held Augusta we should have been in a good fix as any of them; but we failed to hold Augusta and lost Georgia."[65] The AME Zion Church never gained the presence in Georgia that it attained in Alabama, North Carolina, and South Carolina.[66]

* * *

Having developed political support from voters in CME Churches, Anderson successfully claimed the seat left by William Jackson, his father and former master, in the election of 1870 and became the first Black state senator from Houston County.[67] Griffin, A. Simmons, and George Ormond were also victorious in winning seats in the Georgia House.[68] In neighboring Crawford County, several Black men also ran for office, which was a major feat in that Blacks in Crawford had never done so previously. Their run may have been infused by the political organizing of Anderson as he ministered in the adjacent county.[69]

The tactic of developing political support by accessing the press and the pew in Houston County had proven successful for these Republican leaders. However, the election of 1870 brought a dramatic Democratic victory throughout the rest of the state. Henry McNeal Turner, the AME Church leader who had regained his Macon House seat after being forced from office following the election of 1868, lost his bid for re-election in 1870. As Drago concludes in *A Splendid Failure: Black Politicians and Reconstruction in Georgia*, "less than a year after [ousted Black legislators] were reseated, conservatives, relying heavily on the terrorism of the Klan, won an overwhelming electoral victory, virtually nullifying the black vote."[70]

In Georgia, violence during the election often took the form of candidate intimidation. In the fall of 1871, nearly a year after the election, Henry McNeal Turner appeared before a congressional committee investigating conditions in the South and testified, "Well, I will state that I cannot say that I have ever seen any Ku-Klux, that is, as a band roaming about at night. I have, however, had my life threatened, and I am satisfied that on two or three occasions, I may say in a dozen instances if I had not secreted myself in houses at times, in the woods at other times, in a hollow log at another time, I would have been assassinated by a band of night-prowlers, or rovers."[71]

For Turner, the violence directed at him and others was systematic: "[During the election after delivering a political speech] I saw two men standing by the side of the road; they fired off four guns, firing them into the bushes . . . I arrived at the river, and there I met seven or eight white men with guns and horses . . . [T]here are organized bands of night assassins, murderous villains, who have banded themselves together to roam about and kill republicans, kill any man who has got the mane of radical attached to him, especially if he is a leader." In his testimony, he also described voting tampering in Macon that replicated that of Houston County two years earlier in the election of 1868: "The white people turned out in great numbers . . . They were pulling, snatching tickets and doing a great many things of that sort . . . I know I was advised personally to go away, or otherwise I would be killed before the night."[72]

Previous to his testimony before Congress, Turner had brought evidence of voter fraud to local authorities in Macon. Judge Carlton Cole of the Macon Circuit dismissed Turner's claims of voter irregularities and seated the Democratic candidates.[73] Cole, who was a Democrat, disliked Turner so much that in June 1869, he had traveled to Washington, DC to protest Turner being named as Macon's postmaster. He blamed the AME leader for much of the political uproar in Macon following the Civil War.[74]

* * *

Following the December 1870 election, the *Houston Home Journal* applauded its outcome and proclaimed that Democrats had "smitten radicalism with such a mighty stroke; that hideous monster now lies writhing at their feet—a maimed and helpless mess."[75] However, very little celebration followed local elections in Houston County as Republicans swept the state and county elections. Shocked and outraged, white residents blamed results on everything from young men being distracted in drinking clubs to voters being too lazy to go to the polls. For weeks, the *Houston Home Journal* wrestled and editorialized concerning the outcome of the election.[76]

Days after the election, on the morning of January 4, the newly formed CME Church held its first state conference in Augusta. Meeting at Trinity Methodist Church, Bishop Pierce served as the chair and opened the meeting with a reading of the fourth chapter of First Corinthians. Pierce was most likely disturbed by Anderson's election, but he possibly understood the influence that Anderson held as a religious leader and knew that Anderson could easily return to the AME Church and expand Henry McNeal Turner's influence from urban centers such as Macon into smaller towns and communities such as Fort Valley. Pierce may not have been alone in his frustration over Anderson's election: Lucius Holsey, his protégé and advocate for barring political talk among CME clergy, understood the tremendous cost if Anderson left the newly formed denomination.

On the last day of the conference, Anderson was appointed missionary agent for the conference and a Sunday School agent responsible for collecting funds for missionary causes.[77] Anderson's power was significant not only in the number of churches that he influenced, but also in the financial support that the Fort Valley District pledged to the newly elected bishops.[78] Along with R. J. Brown and Lucius Holsey, Anderson was also appointed to "memorialize to the Georgia legislature to incorporate the Georgia Colored Conference, one of the conferences of the CME Church in America."[79]

Before adjourning, the conference adopted a resolution transferring property to the presiding elders in each station.[80] As the conference ended, Anderson was left with the responsibility of maintaining the organization of the newly created Georgia Conference, working as a Sunday School agent and establishing CME congregations throughout the state. He had maintained his position as a presiding elder overseeing districts that had been important to his political victory.

The election of 1870 transformed Anderson's congregants into a potent political constituency. Unfortunately, the election also resulted in the ouster of Henry McNeal Turner, the AME Church's greatest champion and reformer, and Tunis Campbell Sr., the AME Zion Church's strongest voice in Georgia. In 1872, Campbell would again lose his state senate seat in a contested election, and later he would be sentenced to one year of hard labor on the dubious accusation that he had improperly arrested a white man as a justice of the peace. In 1876, Campbell would be leased to a convict labor camp at sixty-three years of age. "Heavily ironed [and] dressed in prison clothes," he would join 119 other convicts on a chain gang.[81] By the end of 1872, Anderson would become the lone Black Methodist leader in the Georgia legislature and his strategic position among Southern Methodist would be greatly diminished. Campbell's fate would be one that Anderson himself would barely escape.

> 1870 Hiram Revels of Mississippi First African American Elected to US Senate—1870–71 Enforcement Acts—1872 Grant Re-elected

Chapter Six

EXODUS

THE 1870 ELECTION OF ISAAC ANDERSON AND AN ENTIRE SLATE OF REpublican candidates shocked white residents of Houston County, who, just two years earlier had proudly proclaimed themselves to be the "Banner County" for the election of an all-white slate of Democratic candidates. The election results were particularly painful for whites in the majority Black county because throughout much of Georgia, Democrats were able to outmaneuver Republicans, win a Democratic majority in the legislature, and reclaim Georgia, a strong proponent of secession.[1] The *Houston Home Journal* justified Anderson and his fellow Republicans' victories by explaining, "When honest men were asleep or attending to their lawful businesses, [Republicans] were meeting with poor ignorant negros in their league rooms, or other dark and secret places for months before the election. . . . [and] the Radical leaders secured their own election over the candidates of our choice—all estimable worthy men . . . to put the black race over the whites."[2]

Local frustration over the election was such that nearly sixty years later, Warren Grice would call the 1860s-70s Houston County's "darkest period." In *A History of Houston County*, he writes, "Conservative white people met in mass meeting and formally requested the Hon. A. O. Bacon of Bibb County then in the legislature, to represent Houston in any and all matters that affected her interest; for they felt that they had no one to represent them among the three elected from Houston. But the resourceful whites, though largely outnumbered by the blacks, finally put a stop to this orgy of ignorance, insolence and corruption." By 1872, disgruntled whites would find a solution in the methods utilized by the Ku Klux Klan and similar organizations.[3]

The beginning of Isaac Anderson's tenure as a state senator coincided with a political earthquake that hit the Republican Party in Georgia as Democrats took control of the legislature. Accusations of corruption and malfeasance had plagued Republican governor Rufus Bullock, and since Republicans held a slim majority in the legislature, he had been able to stave off challenges to his administration, but all that changed when Democrats took control after the elections of 1870. Hoping to avoid impeachment by the newly elected Democratic majority in both houses of the legislature, Bullock quietly resigned and left the state days before his resignation was made public on October 30.

Benjamin Conley, the Republican president of the Senate, was quickly sworn in as governor just days before the legislature convened in Atlanta. Though Conley refused to give up the governorship, Democrats overturned all of his vetoes and elected a Democratic president of the Senate to replace him. James M. Smith, a former Confederate soldier and Democratic House speaker, was elected without opposition and sworn in as governor a year later on January 12, 1872, resulting in Democratic control of the House, Senate, and governor's office.[4]

Ten days after the election, Florida native George Ormond, who had won a seat in the state's House of Representatives, found himself detained in the Perry prison and charged with a misdemeanor offense of election tampering. Shocked by Ormond's win and unwilling to wait for the next election, local officials charged the former Freedmen's School teacher and Grant league leader with instructing Jake Anderson, a Black man from Dooly County, to vote for him at the Perry Court House even though Anderson did not live in Houston County. Ormond proclaimed his innocence, claiming that he did not know Anderson and that he was handing out tickets on the second day of voting when Anderson came to him and received one. Ormond testified that after Anderson voted, "he came back to me looking very scared [and] asked me what difference it made living in one county and voting in another . . . I told him there was a great deal of difference—that he ought not to have voted living in another county . . . [and] about that time he was arrested."[5]

The entire case, which was argued before Judge Carlton Cole in Superior Court, proved to be a farce. Anderson was the main witness for the prosecution and admitted that he couldn't read or write and didn't "know whether he voted for legislation or county officers."[6] Moreover, Sheriff John R. Cook, the arresting officer, testified, "I did not arrest Jake—I arrested Ormond [and] a warrant for his arrest was put in my hands."[7] Sheriff Cook's statement before the court was baffling and demonstrated the questionable tactics used to convict Ormond. The person who gave the warrant to Cook was not identified, and Jake Anderson was never charged.

Redding Pace, a local doctor, and W. L. Grice, a Houston County Democratic Party leader and former colonel in the Confederate army, also testified against Ormond at his preliminary hearing, claiming that Ormond knowingly gave Jake Anderson a ballot even though he lived outside the county.[8] By May of 1871, Ormond's arrest had drawn attention throughout Georgia just as Congress passed legislation allowing greater federal oversight in the state's trials and elections. Five months after his arrest, Ormond was found not guilty.[9]

The political storm that marked Isaac Anderson's first term in office was strengthened not only by state politics, but also by congressional hearings in Atlanta investigating the surge of Ku Klux Klan activity first manifested during his first run for state office in 1868. The hearings were part of an effort to deal with rampant violence and intimidation tied to Klan-like activity occurring throughout the South, and they would later be described in two volumes of congressional testimony known as *The Condition of Affairs in the Late Insurrectionary State in Georgia*.[10]

Local white leaders had long maintained control over freedpeople in their communities through slave patrols, which checked Black power by restricting free movement and stoking fear. As H. B. Holloway of Fort Valley recounted, "The pateroles [sic] were for Niggers just like police and sheriff were for white folks. They were just poor white folks."[11] After Emancipation, the legacy of slave patrols was visible in agricultural clubs, which intimidated those opposed to the "traditional agricultural system," planter militias, and the Ku Klux Klan, which was often comprised of Confederate veterans and powerful local leaders.[12] In *Slave Patrols: Law and Violence in Virginia and the Carolinas*, Sally E. Hadden explains, "The Klan also allowed militant whites to assert psychological dominance over freedmen who seemed such an ominous threat, just as patrols had done in the prewar period . . . Freedom for slaves elevated the status of African Americans, but in the minds of southern whites that freedom implicitly lowered the status of all whites in society."[13]

Warren Grice describes the Klan in noble terms in *A History of Houston County*: "The ingenuity of the white man created the Ku Klux Klan. These knights of the Klan mounted on horses and arrayed in linen sheets, and pillow cases, carried torches and rode at night . . . The white clad riders paraded the roads at night at about the time the darkeys would be going home from their political meetings. The Ku Klux published blood curdling "General Orders" in the newspaper." They placed, "Their notices [which] were posted along the public roads, the skull and bones always appearing. The Klan frightened the negroes into good behavior and without violence had a large part in overcoming the influence of the carpet baggers among the negroes, in restoring Houston County and its affairs to the control of the whites, and in making it again a good place in which to live."[14] For most white Southerners, the realities of the postwar South demanded action, and many deferred to the actions of a culture long built on the idea of self-help and the willingness to use violence as necessary.[15]

The *Rome Courier* described the congressional hearings as an "inquisitous body" and arguing that "the Spanish Inquisition was not more disgraceful and dangerous."[16] The hearings, which were not nearly as aggressive as those that had occurred in South Carolina, began in July 1871 in Washington, DC and by October had moved to Atlanta where Governor Bullock, who was weary of growing public animosity towards federal intervention in Georgia, hoped that state and local leaders under Republican leadership would undermine Klan efforts and avoid additional federal oversight. During the hearings, the congressional subcommittee heard the testimony of General John B. Gordon, who spoke of the "noble" tenets of the Klan. Henry McNeal Turner, however, testified about threats to his life by groups and individuals in and outside of the Klan and about voting tampering that cost him his re-election bid to the state legislature earlier in December of 1870.

Outdone by what he viewed as unwarranted federal intervention into Georgia, state senator James R. Brown challenged the legitimacy of the hearings, claiming that they "greatly [defame] the people of the state," and offered a resolution in the Georgia state senate that stated, "Certain politicians North and South, who esteem the success of the party to which they belong and the accomplishment of their political purposes ... And whereas this Senate is satisfied that no such political organization [as the Klan] exist in this state. ... And whereas this Senate is satisfied that the people of this state never were at any time in the history of this country more peaceable, quiet and law abiding than they now are."[17]

In response, Anderson and nine others, including the four Black senators—George Wallace, James Deveaux, Thomas Crayton, and Tunis Campbell Sr.—voted against the resolution. The five men were all too aware of the Klan activity that wracked the state and made them direct targets. Anderson's vote was important as a first-term senator, signaling his willingness to challenge the idea that Georgia was fairly treating its citizens of color.[18]

Early in October, federal arrests were made primarily in the northern part of the state, where Deputy Marshal James Skiles led soldiers in arresting roughly a dozen Klansmen.[19] The growing number of arrest further inflamed the animosity of most white Georgians and reminded them of the Republican-led Congress which had placed their state under Reconstruction three times, defied President Johnson, supported the Freedmen's Bureau, and denied the seating of Georgia's representatives to Congress until they complied with the passage of the 13th, 14th, and 15th Amendments.

Former State Senator Amos T. Akerman also led efforts to challenge the Klan and was appointed by President Grant to head the Justice Department in June of 1870. Akerman, a devout Presbyterian and the lone Southerner in President Grant's cabinet, vehemently opposed the Klan and supported measures to aggressively go after the secret organization. He was well acquainted with violence of the Klan as he his family had been threatened by individuals tied to the organization. George W. Ashburn, a fellow Republican who had served with him in the Georgia Constitutional Convention of 1867, had been murdered in the middle of the night just days before the 1868 elections, and though all indications were that his murderers were Klansmen, no one was ever brought to justice despite several arrests. Moreover, Akerman "did not think it adequate to hope that [the Klan] would desist once they had achieved the intimidation of the former slave."[20]

The passage of the Enforcement Acts by Congress in 1870 and 1871 aided Akerman, and these pieces of legislation were direct responses to the massive Klan violence that targeted Blacks, white Republicans, and former union soldiers. The acts strengthened the recently constitutionalized Fifteenth Amendment and among other things, made it a felony for two or more people to disguise themselves with the intent to deprive a person of citizenship. This provision was designed to curtail Klan activity, but in *White Terror: The Ku Klux Klan Conspiracy and Southern Reconstruction*, Allen Trelease concludes, "The new law's effect upon the Klan in 1870 was wholly negligible. Voter intimidation took place on a large enough scale to reverse the will of the majority [in Georgia]."[21]

The Ku Klux Klan Act, which was passed in February 1871, focused on strengthening the Fourteenth Amendment and for the first time made acts of violence a federal offense. The most controversial part of the act allowed for Klansmen to be purged from federal juries and granted President Grant the power to call out the military to suppress law breakers and suspend the writ of habitus corpus. Penalties for violating the Act ranged from $500 to $5,000 and/or imprisonment.[22]

Akerman supported the measures, believing that the only way to deal with the Klan was with the threat of government action and the dispatching of federal troops.[23] His efforts were fruitful, and by 1871, federal grand juries throughout the South had returned 3,000 indictments with roughly 600 convictions.[24] Unfortunately, the hope of similarly aggressive tactics reaching Georgia were dashed as Akerman was relieved of his duties by President Grant on December 2, 1871.[25]

* * *

In 1871, with the legislative session quickly drawing to a close in Georgia, Black Republicans scrambled to make legislative changes where they could, which was difficult in a Democratically controlled legislature. Legislators, hoping to build up state revenues, began a debate in the Georgia Assembly on how many convicts to lease at one time to individual businesses in order to ensure maximum profit and meet growing demand. State Senator John A. Jervis proposed a charge of no less than fifty dollars per convict per year, which was a substantial increase from the twenty-five-dollar minimum passed in the House of Representatives.[26] Tunis Campbell Sr., however, led an effort to challenge rather than improve upon the convict lease system by offering a resolution to reconsider the passage of a penitentiary bill to "provide for farming out the convicts of this State." According to the *Atlanta Daily Sun* (December 7, 1871), Campbell, who represented the Black legislators and a handful of white Republicans who were sympathetic to those entrapped by the convict lease system, argued that Senator Jervis's proposal did not "accomplish the object of the Penitentiary which is the reformation of convict."

Unfortunately, lacking any support from the majority of Senators, Black legislators and their handful of Republican allies watched their resolution lose.[27] Their concern over the convict lease system stemmed from an 1870 investigation of the treatment of prisoners led by legislators from the entire state assembly including Henry M. Turner from the House and George Wallace from the Senate. Both men viewed the system as unfairly pressing a large number of Black Georgians into a new system of quasi slavery, and the reality of this concern was confirmed by the fact that following Emancipation, the racial dynamics within the prison system flipped as white convicts became a significant minority and Blacks became the majority, constituting 84 percent of all prisoners in the Georgia State Penitentiary.[28]

* * *

In June of 1872, Isaac Anderson traveled to the National Union Republican Convention in Philadelphia as a delegate representing Georgia's Third District, which included Fort Valley. Excitement was in the air as one of the largest contingents of Black officeholders attended the convention and as Ulysses S. Grant was nominated for a second term along with Henry Wilson, the vice-presidential candidate. Anderson was one of forty-nine Black delegates at the convention, and J. R. Lynch, a member of the impressive Mississippi delegation comprised of several leading Black Republicans from across the nation, rallied support for Black Republicans in Mississippi and throughout the South, declaring the Democratic Party to be dead due to Grant's Presidency and the growing federal oversight strengthened by the

Enforcement Acts passed in the 1870 and 1871. According to Lynch, Grant was an undertaker of sorts of the Democratic Party who would, "dig a grave for this corpse so deep and so wide and bury it so that it will ever more be resuscitated." Lynch also encouraged his fellow Black delegates by recognizing that "without the black man the cotton States cannot be developed."[29]

L. J. "Little John" Scurlock, Anderson's co-laborer in ministry, also attended the convention as part of the Mississippi delegation representing Water Valley in Yalobusha County. Scurlock had attended the CME Church's founding conference in 1870 and was elected Publishing agent and assistant to the editor. Although Anderson had been the lone voice for political involvement at the founding of the CME Church, he was not the only CME leader with political ambitions. Emboldened by Anderson's election, Scurlock resigned his position as assistant to the editor less than two years after his appointment and ran for public office in Mississippi.[30]

Also in attendance was William H. Grey, a delegate and formidable Black leader from Helena, Arkansas, who served as commissioner of immigration and states lands. Addressing the convention, Grey boasted of the Republican Party's national efforts to stop the Klan and reminded Black delegates of their need to stand together and vote for the party. The enthusiasm in the convention hall was palpable as cheers interrupted his speech and he seconded President Grant's nomination.[31]

Following the convention, Anderson continued to minister to CME congregations in Georgia as he awaited the new legislative session in July, and as a presiding elder, he worked to ensure that his circuit grew in membership, in subscribers to the *Christian Index*, and in contributions to fund the salaries of the bishops. But in July 1872, the fledgling denomination lost its founding bishop with the death Richard Vanderhorst, who was fifty-seven, and with Vanderhorst's passing, the denomination's General Conference would need to meet the following year to select a new leader. Anderson's elevation to Bishop was certainly on the mind of some of his supporters.[32]

* * *

As a new legislative session began in Georgia that July, Black Republicans faced new challenges as Tunis Campbell Sr., Thomas Crayton, and George Wallace were all up for re-election. During the last legislative session, all five Black Republicans opposed legislation to reinstate the collection of poll taxes, but their efforts were defeated. The collection of poll taxes was supported by the Democratic majority and directly undercut the ability of freedpeople to vote, and hoping to avoid the inevitable, Black legislators moved quickly to pass resolutions and legislation before fall 1872 elections.[33]

As a Republican minority in the Democratically controlled state senate, Anderson and his fellow Black senators focused on issues that most impacted their communities such as reforms to the legal system, franchise, and labor. Seemingly, the only way to pass any legislation of consequence was to propose legislation directed at their home counties so that white Democratic legislators wouldn't consider it a threat to their respective communities. Moreover, since the convict lease system could not be directly dismantled, Anderson took another approach at fighting injustice in Georgia's legal system. He challenged the legality of all white juries.

The issue had arisen in 1866 when Congress passed the Civil Rights Bill and later, the Fourteenth Amendment, which ultimately allowed Blacks to serve on juries.[34] Data conclusively demonstrated that between 1866 and 1879, Blacks were three times more likely to be convicted than whites for the same crimes.[35] The 1868 Constitution in Georgia did not explicitly give Blacks the right to serve on juries but instead emphasized the need for "upright" and "intelligent persons" to serve as jurors, and these phrases were often interpreted by local white officials as a pretext to exclude Blacks. Moreover, Houston County ordinary W. T. Swift ensured that local Blacks would never receive jury duty.[36]

The idea of Blacks serving on juries for many white Southerners was analogous to equality between the races, and with their exclusion from juries, freedpeople had a much higher conviction rate than did whites who were charged with the same crimes. The reality of the faulty jury system coincided with the rise in Black arrests and the growth of the convict lease system, and this was a leading motivator for Black legislators to reform the jury system.[37]

On July 25 of that year, Anderson introduced a bill proposing mixed-race juries for the trials of Blacks, but by mid-August, he withdrew his bill most likely because of potentially violent realities that faced him.[38] As an active Black legislator, his life was at risk, his wife, Edith, was hours away with their growing family, including his sons, Henry and Isaac, who were on the verge of manhood. Moreover, any suggestion of mixed juries for the trials of whites was noticeably absent from his bill. Unlike Anderson, Tunis Campbell Sr. pushed for the seating of Blacks on any jury in Georgia, and to many, this meant that Blacks could judge the guilt or innocence of whites. His continual promotion of civil rights legislation led to constant legal battles that plagued him for the rest of his political career.

Unable to change the jury laws, Anderson and the cohort of Black senators worked to stop the passage of sunset laws, or codes that undermined Black labor and free enterprise.[39] These laws were a common tactic used in many southern legislatures in the 1870s to hamstring Black farmers from selling their crops in the evening hours, which was especially important for sharecroppers or tenant farmers who grew crops independently and needed to sell them during the more convenient evening hours. Whites argued that the sunset laws were necessary to curtail theft by laborers. In 1869, state legislators had passed laws restricting the sale of crops after dark in two counties in southwest Georgia. But now legislators wanted to expand the law throughout the state.[40] Efforts to stop the passage of sunset laws failed as twenty-four senators voted in favor of them. Hoping to protect Black residents in their respective counties, Campbell moved to strike out McIntosh and Liberty Counties, Deveaux moved to strike out Jones County, and Anderson moved to strike out Houston County. All three senators failed in their attempt.[41]

Hoping to discourage Black voters from participating in the upcoming state elections, the Democratically controlled legislature moved them from November to October. By moving the state elections up a month before the presidential election, Blacks would not only face poll taxes, but also violence and intimidation due to a lack of federal oversight. The *New York Times* ascribed two rationales for moving the election up a month: "First, it was known that the negroes would be very likely to have lost their tax receipt of the previous year, and could only obtain duplicate of it from Democratic officials; and second the election was taken out of the operation of the law for the enforcement of the Fourteenth Amendment, and the Ku klux were left free from all fear of punishment for terrorism, except under State laws—ie., entirely free. The way having been thus paved, the scheme of disfranchisement was boldly carried out."[42]

Potential Klan activity was not the only threat to the state elections in October 1872. As historian Edmund Drago writes, "By 1872 the conservatives had reassembled most of their prewar military companies."[43] Now rather than using secret organizations like the Klan, recognized and honored state militias legally marched and, like the Klan, "defended" Georgians from "insolent and dolent" freedpeople.[44] Prosecutions of Georgians for violations to the Enforcement Laws fueled their resolve to reorganize state militias, and with their reorganization, the Klan became less important as a representation of white dominance and a reminder of the slave patrols that existed in the Antebellum period.[45] With the support of Democratic governor James M. Smith who was elected in 1872, state sponsored militias were established under the guise of promoting peace and civility and as an extension of Georgia's government, they received guns and munitions as state sanctioned organizations.[46]

In Houston County, the Southern Rights Guard based in Perry was officially recognized as a militia in 1859, but state militias were suspended throughout the South as part of the Military Reconstruction Act of 1867.[47] Two years later, many states were allowed by Congress to reinstate their militias under the guise of controlling Klan activity, but Georgia was not permitted due to the failure of state and local leaders to protect voting rights.[48] With the Democratic Party in control of the state, there was little need for pretense in reinstating local militias.

May 3, 1872, or Memorial Day, marked the official return of the States Rights Guard. In Fort Valley, former Confederate soldiers gathered to remember their service in a war that had ended only seven years earlier, and Georgians gathered at the Female Seminary to watch the Governor's Guard and the procession surrounding it move forward accompanied by deep and solemn drums with William Jackson's brother, General C. D. Anderson, serving as one of its marshals. J. W. Matthews led the Governor's Guard, and two schoolgirls carried "wreaths and bouquets" as veterans followed the procession to the town's cemetery. A similar scene played out in Perry, and when the Governor's Guard and veterans from the county reached the Perry courthouse, the Southern Rights Guard was re-established.[49]

Nicholas Johnson writes in *Negroes and the Gun: The Black Tradition of Arms* that the rise in the number of state-sanctioned militias like the States Rights Guard resulted in the "distinction between . . . official militias and terrorist organizations like the KKK [becoming] thin."[50] Moreover, petitions for militias formed by freedmen were largely ignored, and by 1874, only three "colored companies" existed in Augusta, Columbus, and Savannah.[51]

* * *

In spite of insurmountable challenges, Anderson experienced moments of happiness in 1872 such as the birth of his daughter, Ida Roberta, who like her father, was born in March.[52] In a home brimming with children, Ida would be the last of his children with Edith, his first wife, and the family's joy at the new arrival would soon be tempered by deadly realities outside of their home.[53]

The October elections of 1872 in Georgia were marked by reports of "negroes [being] driven away from the polls at every precinct where the Republican vote was supposed to be in the majority, and every specie of fraud and violence was resorted." In *White Terror: The Ku Klux Klan Conspiracy and Southern Reconstruction*, Allen Trelease concludes that the method of violence and intimidation later known as the "Mississippi Plan" and adopted by other southern states was first adopted in Georgia.[54] In Macon, freedpeople were "driven away from the polls by pistol shots and brickbats, [and] two of their number [were] murdered outright and others [were] severely wounded."[55] With only four polling stations and an electorate of roughly eight thousand, Savannah witnessed "polls . . . surrounded by armed Democrats, and the roads patrolled by Democratic 'Sabre Clubs' to overawed the negroes." Intimidation and violence virtually covered every part of the state.[56]

By the end of the 1872 term, poll tax collections had resumed, and the occasions for voters to register were scheduled for only three months during prime planting time, when many Black farmers were busy working their crops. George Wallace lost in a landslide to his white Democratic opponent, and many votes for Tunis Campbell Sr. were questionably thrown out. By the end of the election, he and Thomas Crayton had also lost their reelection bids to the state senate, and other election irregularities caused Campbell to struggle for two years to regain his seat.[57] The election also meant that the Houston County coalition of Griffin, Ormond, Simmons, and Anderson was broken. Ormond was defeated in his bid for re-election, Griffin did not compete, and Simmons's political fate remains unknown as one of the many "silences" in the retelling of this period. Four years earlier, twenty-eight Blacks had served in Georgia's assembly, and after the election of 1872, a handful remained with only Anderson and Deveaux in the state senate.

In Houston County, the Democrats newly elected to the House were George M. T. Feagin, William A. Mathews and C. H. Richardson. Feagin had been a slaveholder in the county and would later serve as a judge, and Richardson was a member of the Democratic Executive Committee in Houston County and the future mayor of Byron, a town he would help to incorporate in 1874.[58] Matthews served on the Board of Directors for the Planters Bank of which William Jackson Anderson was the director, and he was also a member with William Jackson at the Fort Valley Methodist Church. Originally, Matthews completed William Jackson's term in office when he was removed from office in January of 1870.

Anderson was not up for reelection until 1874, and he was the only Republican left in the senate from Houston County and the twenty third district. He, along with James Deveaux, were the only Black members of the Georgia Senate, and both men most likely understood that their time in office was limited.

On November 22, 1872, the *Houston Home Journal* celebrated George Ormond's election defeat by reporting, "The supper given by the freeds, last Friday night at the Courthouse was for the purpose of raising funds to pay the expenses of the Hon George Ormond, p.c., to Arkansas, to look out a place to colonize the discontented portion of his race in Houston County. George left this place, we are informed, Sunday to fulfill his mission. There is no doubt that a little emigration tried by such negroes as Ormond and few others will greatly benefit the county, but the industrious producers of his own or a little darker color, are needed here and will find it profitable to remain."[59]

Between 1870 and 1880, nearly 36,000 Blacks moved to Arkansas, and the majority were from Georgia. The number of freedpeople leaving central Georgia was so large that reporting of their exodus was carried as a national story by the New York Times on January 27, 1873. By the summer of that year, between 3,000 and 6,000 Blacks were estimated to have left central Georgia.[60] The following year, Georgia governor James Smith addressed the Colored Convention and lamented, "Two thousand colored people left Houston County on account of an election that went against them."[61]

Yet, the election in 1872 was not the only motivator for the exodus of freedpeople from Georgia. January of 1873 marked the beginning of a full-fledged economic crisis that was only rivaled by the Great Depression of 1929. The crisis quickly made its way across the country and was rooted in a downturn in the railroad boom that had swept the nation. Georgia was hit particularly hard since the state had invested significant resources to rebuild its railroads. Moreover, from 1872 through 1877, the price of cotton fell at least 50 percent and railroad construction came to a standstill driving many farmers into debt.[62] These conditions hit Houston County especially hard since it was a leading cotton producer and a center of railroad construction in the state. Groups like the Georgia Grange significantly influenced how much laborers, who were overwhelmingly Black, were paid, and these organizations worked to reduce wages from $100 to $60 a year, which further encouraged Blacks to seek economic opportunity in states further west like Texas, Louisiana, and Arkansas.[63]

The Georgia Senate's 1873 legislative session commenced on January 8, but just four days into the session, Isaac Anderson was given a leave of absence "on account of sickness in his family."[64] Several days later, a news story published in the January 16 edition of the *Savannah Republican* appeared and was mistitled the "Removal of Georgia Negroes to Alabama." The story verified a growing "exodus of negro laborers" from Georgia, and according to the paper, "Whole families of negro men, women, and children, chiefly . . . from Houston and adjoining counties were going west . . . several thousand had passed over that road, bent for the same destination, within the past three weeks, and that the volume . . . [is] increasing rather than diminishing."

According to the report, landholders in Arkansas held sway with certain Black leaders who were serving as immigration agents in Arkansas and enticing Black laborers by "the delights of buffalo hunts and living on game." The story ended with the dire warning, "If this thing goes on . . . the question of labor will soon be a serious one in Georgia."[65] The following month, the

Atlanta Weekly Sun reported that two attempts were made to stem the tide of Black laborers leaving the state by derailing the "Southwestern train off the track, between Fort Valley and Macon by placing iron bars and stringers across the road. The engine threw the obstacles off and proceeded without injury."[66]

After Emancipation, the Freedmen's Bureau had assisted freedpeople in leaving Georgia for better opportunities elsewhere. Brevet Major General Davis Tillson considered the bureau to help freedpeople to transition from slavery into a free market economy, and under his bureau's protection, he began to require landholders to pay male laborers twelve to fifteen dollars a month and female laborers eight to ten dollars per month which was a far cry from the three to eight dollars a month typically offered by white landholders.[67] When they refused to pay Black laborers the required wage, Tillson began funding efforts to relocate Black Georgians to other southern states like Mississippi and Arkansas that were clamoring for laborers.[68] After four months, the Freedmen's Bureau had aided at least 400 Black laborers in leaving the state, and this number grew to 1,124 by January of 1866. That year, legislators in Georgia enacted Section 4428 of the Penal Code which stated that if any person knowingly employed the servant of another while he or she was already employed, or if any person knowingly enticed or persuaded any servant to leave his or her employer either by offering higher wages or in any way whatever during his or her term of service, that person would be guilty of a misdemeanor and fined up to two hundred dollars or be jailed for up to three months.[69]

Tillson's free market perspective was most telling in a speech that he gave before the Freedmen's Convention: "You have the same right with all other men to accumulate, hold and enjoy property; the right to be as rich as you can make yourselves by your own energy, industry and economy ... With the blessing of providence your, future is almost wholy in your hands. You are no longer chattels but men."[70]

Efforts to lead freedpeople out of repressive communities were typically tied to emigration societies frequently hosted by schools and churches. According to historian Story Matkin-Rawn, "these groups pooled their savings and elected agents, often ministers or school teachers, to serve as advance scouts and arrange transportation."[71] With numerous reports of a freedpeople leaving Houston and surrounding counties, Anderson, who was both a CME minister and a Georgia politician, was accused of being an emigration agent.

In 1872, George Ormond had made plans to lead a contingency of freedpeople from Houston County to Arkansas, and Anderson most likely used his knowledge as a CME missionary agent and his connections with the Southwestern Railroad to help freedpeople leave the state as well.[72] J. H. Blount, who was the first African American to run for governor in Arkansas, left Georgia when he was thirteen with his mother and stepfather in 1873. In writing about Blount in *The National Cyclopedia of the Colored Race*, Clement Richardson recalled that "during the great exodus from Georgia, which took place in 1873, Rev. I. H. Anderson took many immigrants to Arkansas as tenants."[73]

Anderson traveled throughout the state as a CME missionary agent establishing churches and working with a number of CME congregations to build the fledgling denomination. His ministerial work gave him ample opportunity to meet with Blacks who were weary of the never-ending oppression by white leaders in Georgia. Moreover, he most likely met William Grey, who was head of the Arkansas Immigration Agency and had been part of the Arkansas delegation at the Republican Convention that previous summer in Philadelphia. Leaders like Grey emphasized the promise of higher wages, land ownership, and freedom from the strident racial oppression experienced in Georgia.

Anderson reminded white Georgians publicly of the inequalities and injustices spurring the Black exodus from the state. He also reminded Black Georgians publicly that the "white race needs our labor and . . . we need employment from them."[74] While representing himself in this manner, he began to lay the foundations for his own eventual departure from the state. By 1873, Ormond himself had made an exodus from Georgia to Arkansas with other freedpeople, and consequently there was little that Houston County leaders could do to attack him legally as they had when they arrested and tried him for voting tampering two years earlier, but there was something they could do to Anderson.

During that year's legislative session, a bill specifically tailored for the county was sponsored by the three newly elected state representatives from the Twenty-Third District: "Be it enacted by the General Assembly of the State of Georgia, that from and after the passage of this Act, the Ordinary of Houston County . . . is hereby authorized to hire out persons convicted of misdemeanors or other offenses not punishable by imprisonment in the penitentiary, to persons having charge of public contracts, or to employ them under the direction of any overseer, in cutting or and repairing public roads, building and repairing public bridges, and upon any other public works coming under his jurisdiction."[75] The bill coincided perfectly with Section 4428 of the Penal Code, which specified that any person who knowingly entices or persuades any servant to leave his or her employer either by offering higher wages or in any way whatever during his or her term of service will be guilty of a misdemeanor.[76]

The plan was to charge Anderson with the misdemeanor offense of encouraging Black laborers to leave the state for Arkansas and employment elsewhere, and the proposed bill would promptly allow him to be placed on a chain gang in Houston County. Moreover, the bill would purposefully circumvented Superior Court Judge Carlton Cole who might have been reluctant to prosecute Anderson for personal and professional reasons. In 1871, a Houston county case involving Cole's court and several Black laborers had made its way to the Georgia Supreme Court, which ruled that evidence allowed by Cole was in error as was the judgment for the plaintiffs, and although the case did not end his position, Cole would have been less likely to move forward on a similar case if the evidence was not strong and the person being tried was a high-profile leader like Anderson.[77] From a personal standpoint, Cole, with his frequent visits to Houston County, his connections to the Whig party, and his investments in the state's railroads, was most likely aware of Anderson's relationship to the influential William Jackson.

For the Twenty-Third District's three newly elected state representatives, the best option in prosecuting Anderson was to use the newly elected Houston County ordinary, Andrew S. Giles, who had served in the reinstituted Southern Rights Guard militia in 1874.[78] For Anderson, the threat of prosecution would be a huge scandal and would wreak havoc on his family. For a number of white Southern Methodist leaders, his political involvement was becoming unpalatable with Democrats firmly in place in Georgia's legislature and Henry M. Turner and Tunis Campbell Sr. virtually defeated politically.

A day before the bill went before the senate for its final reading, Anderson published a letter in the *Houston Home Journal* stating, "To all it may concern, Information having reached me that colored immigration agents in the habit of visiting the counties of Houston, Crawford, and Taylor and persuading colored immigrants to leave the above mentioned counties, using my name and influence to practice their nefarious business of pretending to carry emigrants to the State of Arkansas, when their real destinations, in many and most instances, are the States of Tennessee or Mississippi, this is to warn all who use my name in said connection that I will prosecute any and all parties to the fullest extent of the law who are now practicing said business in my name on the unsuspecting of my people." Keenly aware that the new law was directed at him, he denied any suggestion that he was involved in the duplicitous practice of telling migrants that they were headed to one place and then leading them to another, but he did not explicitly deny the charge that he was leading freedpeople out of Georgia.[79] Yet, even with his attempt to address the allegations of white leaders against him, he most likely understood that the end of his political and ministerial activity in Georgia was inevitable.

* * *

As Georgia's legislative session ended in 1873, Anderson's focus shifted from the senate to the church as the CME General Conference began in Augusta that March. Outside of CME circles, he was the delegate with the highest profile and the lone state legislator at the conference. A number of issues were on the docket, most notably, who would replace Bishop Vanderhorst, who had died a year earlier, and among the leaders being circulated was Lucius Holsey. Bishop Robert Pierce, his Southern Methodist mentor, would be in attendance at the Conference, along with many other white Methodist leaders, and their presence increased Holsey's chances of being elected to the post.[80]

A major issue at the conference was the CME Church's involvement in politics. Earlier in 1864, the Southern Methodist Church's publishing house in Nashville had been damaged when the military governor took control of the facility, and Methodist leaders sought damages from the federal government to restore the building. The Southern Methodists sent Dr. Richard Abbey to the conference to solicit support from CME leaders for this request believing that support from the Black denomination would put them in a favorable light with the federal government. The request, however, was "re-committed for further study," which most likely meant that the CME committee did not want to vote on the measure.[81]

For a number of CME delegates, a resolution to honor the Southern Methodists' request was a political matter and, as such, had been prohibited earlier at the denomination's founding in 1870, most likely at the request of Southern Methodist leaders who were now hypocritically involving CME leaders in "political matters." Moreover, the request most likely upset many Black leaders whose civil and political rights were increasingly being eroded throughout the deep South, and though Dr. Abbey suggested that the lack of support of the Southern Methodists' request was due to "outside influences," the reality was that a number of CME leaders opposed the measure.

The request's most outspoken critic was Anderson, who was facing extreme pressure from both the Georgia Senate and the CME Church because of his political activity.[82] For his part, Holsey encouraged CME delegates to pass the resolution out of "gratitude" to the Southern Methodists and also to "prove their individuality," but many Black leaders responded with outrage. During the conference, Anderson resolved never to agree with such a request.

He reminded the other leaders that there had been a "general hue and cry to cast politics out from the Church" and that he had been "threatened with expulsion from his own Church for asserting his civil and legal rights." [83]

* * *

Holsey's support for the measure was most likely due to his paternalistic relationship with Bishop Pierce and his perspective of racial reconciliation, which compelled him to maintain this type of relationship. Known for his support for education, Pierce worked tirelessly raising funding for Emory College, and among his more prominent donors were Benjamin Hill and Robert Toombs, two of Georgia's most powerful politicians. Benjamin Hill was known as an "earnest" Methodist, but Black Georgians knew him for his view of freedpeople. Earlier in 1868, Hill had mocked Anderson and other Black delegates to Georgia's Constitutional Convention in the *Georgia Weekly Telegraph* by "rephrasing" their preamble to the new Constitution: "*We the niggers of Georgia in order to destroy all permanent government, establish robbery, insure democratic disgrace and discord, and secure the curies of anarchy and despotism to all races and their prosperity.*"[84]

Hill's rhetoric had earned him his reputation as a voice for the rights of white Southerners. Toombs, who was no different, had served as secretary of state in the Confederacy under Jefferson Davis, and despite refusing to seek a pardon to regain his citizenship rights, he had resumed his law practice and become heavily involved in Georgia's politics as a Democrat. Pierce sought contributions from both men, and in 1873, each gave $500 to support Emory College at the same time that Holsey was openly discouraging political speech in the CME Church and Anderson, along with the remaining handful of Black legislators, was being targeted by Democratic leaders who were of the same mind as Hill and Toombs.[85]

Holsey's discouraging of political speech threatened Anderson's position as both a presiding elder and a state senator, and while he may not have been aware of the support given to Pierce by Hill and Toombs, he was aware of the strong ties between the three white men. Moreover, while he may not have realized that he was allied with men who were working to end the involvement of freedpeople in Georgia's politics, Lucius Holsey was elected to the position of bishop at the CME Church's General Conference in 1873. In a symbolic motion, Anderson called for Bishop George Pierce to preach the ordination sermon for the new bishops.[86]

In December 1873, Anderson sold his Fort Valley property to Andrew Hollinshead, a local Black farm laborer and attended the January meeting of the Georgia legislature which would mark his final tenure as a state senator.

During the legislative session, he was named to the Penitentiary Committee alongside of James Deveaux. The committee was involved in the investigation of convict abuses, but its viability was being increasingly questioned by white state legislators who saw the benefit of the lucrative convict lease system. Moreover, he and Deveaux were the lone supporters of the Civil Rights Bill that was introduced in 1870 by Senator Charles Sumner and was languishing in Congress with little political will behind it. As newspapers and political leaders decried the legislation as a tool of radicals and the Republican Party, Anderson and Deveaux published a letter announcing their support for the bill, which was placed in the senate minutes.[87] Anderson's forthrightness was most likely a sign of his intuition that his work in Georgia had come to an end. Days after the end of the legislative session in 1874, he left Georgia.

The *Macon Telegraph and Messenger* reported that "ex-senator Ike Anderson, of the man and brother persuasion, has emigrated to Arkansas in search of another office."[88] That fall, James Deveaux lost his seat, and former Confederate captain William Rutherford was elected to Anderson's former seat for the Twenty-Third District. The bill introduced in February 1873 by state representatives Feagin, Mathews, and Richardson foreshadowed Henry McNeal Turner's prediction that legal means would be used to remove Black leaders from office. In responding to earlier efforts to remove Tunis Campbell Sr. from office before the 1872 elections, he had written, "They mean to get him out of the Senate and defeat his re-election—they mean to put the colored race lower than they were in slavery—they mean to defy the laws of the land and crush republicanism from the state." As Turner concluded, "Colored men of Georgia, we must either leave the State or the United States Government must provide a speedier remedy."[89]

> 1872 Freedmen's Bureau Ends—1872 Grant Re-elected—
> 1874 Blanche K. Bruce of Mississippi Elected US Senator

Chapter Seven

PROMISED LAND

ISAAC ANDERSON'S EXODUS FROM HOUSTON COUNTY WAS INDESCRIBABLY hard, but he had no alternative. After years of tilling spiritual ground and harvesting political opportunities in Georgia, many people wanted him gone, and days before the opening session of the Georgia legislature on January 14, 1874, the CME minister and state Senator sold his three acres of land in Fort Valley and prepared an Exodus from the state. He knew that his future in Georgia was bleak as lawmakers passed a code allowing authorities in Houston County "to hire out persons convicted of a misdemeanor or other offenses not punishable by imprisonment in the penitentiary."[1] Because he could be charged under Section 4428 of the state Penal Code with the misdemeanor of persuading people to leave their employment in Georgia for higher wages elsewhere, Anderson joined his wife, their six children, and 36,000 other Black men and women in finding refuge in the "promised land" of Arkansas and Mississippi.[2]

Throughout 1873, white leaders continually worried about the growing exodus of Black laborers from Georgia, and in dealing with the crisis, the state legislature passed a law that year requiring all contracts between employers and workers to be written. By requiring a written contract, employers stopped laborers from leaving the state to secure other contracts since a signed contract had to be in place before they were allowed to leave the state.[3]

White leaders also promoted fear in freedpeople by exaggerating the difficulties encountered outside of Georgia. In December, 1874, Governor James Smith stated at the Colored Convention in Atlanta, "If it is to your interest to leave, in God's name go! But it is a fearful risk." Seizing upon the economic challenges in places outside of his state, he exclaimed, "In 1866 I recollect there was an exodus of negroes to Mississippi from Georgia. Many of my old servants went. Scores of those who went, now sleep under the sod along the banks of the river. They were unacquainted with the climate or its people."[4]

As the emigration surge continued into 1874, other southern states impacted by migration adopted stories of hardship outside of their borders. The *Daily Phoenix*, a regional paper from Columbia, South Carolina, re-published an article from the *Houston Home Journal* titled "An Arkansas Emigrant Returned." The column described conditions of emigrant laborers forced to live in swamps and drink lagoon water, and in this account, an unnamed "Houston County Negro" who had been a former hand of George Slappey returned to Georgia and left several friends behind in Arkansas who were too sick to return home with him.[5]

Later that year, the *Houston Home Journal* and the *Columbus Inquirer*, ran a column entitled "Bad Luck" in which Matthew Keen, a Black farm laborer who had left Houston County for Arkansas, claimed, "emigrant agents told lies to get negroes to go to Arkansas, and take them about and hire them to the highest bidder like they used to do the 'niggers' in slavery times. There is much suffering yet in the overflowed district." Keen's letter, which was published throughout central and southwest Georgia as direct evidence of the fate of Georgia emigrants, ended with a brief mention of George Ormond who was employed along with his wife, Eliza, by Dr. George Bodie Peters, a planter in Lee County, Arkansas.[6] Immediately below the letter, editorial comments by the Houston County paper added, "This is bad on an ex-member of the Georgia Legislature and prominent politician, Work won't agree with him."[7]

By October, news of it reached Ormond, Peters, and Matthew Keen himself, and frustrated by the 'fake news', all three men wrote letters in the *Memphis Daily Appeal* challenging the column's authenticity. Writing flatly. Keen responded, "I wrote no such letter, for I am in the State of Arkansas, living with Dr. Peters, and doing well, also every one that came from Georgia." Ormond also responded, writing "Yes, myself and wife are working for Dr. Peters, and we feel proud to work for such a man as he is. As a general thing we both have been quite healthy this year. In this State it is an honorable thing to work for one's living, and we gladly exchange Arkansas for Georgia on that account."

Peters ended the three-fold response by describing Ormond as "strictly honest and trustworthy" and "a well-behaved man, strictly temperate, and respectable to both the white and colored race." Peters' reputation as a gentleman and his desire to attract Black laborers may explain why he wrote the lengthiest response, explaining "I always instructed my agents never to offer inducements to any one not already determined to leave the State, and especially to those living with their former owners. I depreciate the loss of labor to any community . . . but when the colored race, en masse, have determined to leave the State they feel, they have the right to do so, and being lost to Georgia, the editor should not blame us for furnishing homes and employment to the poverty-stricken emigrant."[8]

White leaders throughout Georgia promoted fear of life outside the state especially in Arkansas by highlight the difficulties which were often exaggerated. The realities were that Arkansas did have a number of challenges in the early to mid-1870s. In his travelogue, *The Cotton States in the Spring and Summer of 1875*, Charles Nordhoff who was a British visitor to the states described Arkansas in 1875 as full of economic challenges that stemmed from two economic problems: First, state and local governments were saddled with an estimated $20 million dollars' worth of debt from investment in the states limited railway system. Secondly, that Arkansas's leaders allowed different types of scripts to be issued by the state as well as individual counties, townships, and schools which he argued further undermined Arkansas's economy. [9]

* * *

In a speech given at the Colored Convention in Atlanta in 1874, W. A. Pledger, a proponent of Black migration asked bluntly, "Shall we stay in hell on earth or find a home elsewhere?"[10] At the convention in Atlanta, Black Georgians gathered to debate the merits of leaving Georgia, and as the promise of Reconstruction waned, many Black leaders were persuaded that the only refuge for freedpeople would be found in a land they considered to be free of white control. Henry McNeal Turner stated in a letter read at the convention, "Ultimately the final exodus of the race will be to Africa. The prejudice against the colored man is on the increase north and south."[11] For others, the call was not to leave the United States but to find refuge in other areas of the country, and as early as the mid-nineteenth century, Black leaders like Martin Delany called for safe spaces through the creation of an all-Black state. Delany had not been formerly enslaved, but had been born as a free person.[12]

Lucius Holsey would follow Turner's call for Blacks to leave areas dominated by whites, but like Delany, Holsey preferred to remain in America. During the first decades of his ministry, he called for interracial cooperation, but nearly twenty years later, he would advocate for racial separation. Weary of racial violence and economic oppression, Holsey would conclude that "there is a vast legalized scheme throughout the South to set the iron heel more permanently and desperately upon the head of the Black man as a race, and as individual characters."[13]

As highlighted in Nell Painter's *Exodusters*, many Blacks, weary of the South, moved westward taking advantage of the opportunity to settle recently seized Native American land and create all-Black communities in places like Nicademus, Kansas, and Boley, Oklahoma.[14] Likewise, freedpeople who stayed in the South founded communities like Mound Bayou, Mississippi, Eatonville, Florida, and Cameron Place, Alabama. For others, opportunity and safety were found in Arkansas and the Mississippi Delta in pocket communities initially established through the efforts of the Freedmen's Bureau, the Southern Homestead Act, railroad companies, and white landholders looking to attract Black laborers.

The Delta region of Mississippi and Arkansas was a frontier with dense forests, swamps, gray and Black timber wolves, alligators, and venomous snakes.[15] Following the Civil War, landholders, hoping to turn the rich alluvial soil into viable farmland, worked tirelessly to recruit laborers, and the Freedmen's Bureau aided them by relocating a number of Blacks to these areas. According to historian Story Matkin-Rawn, freedpeople who moved to Arkansas settled in the Arkansas Delta and in areas south of the Arkansas River near Pine Bluff, and because of the developing demographics of these areas, Arkansas drew many formerly enslaved Georgians as did the Mississippi Delta.[16]

In his travelogue, Nordhoff described an environment with little emphasis on regional and political affiliations, and he quoted an unnamed Confederate General who downplayed sectional differences and proclaimed, "We are all Union men." Nordhoff also noted that a year after its enactment and with fifty-three federal commissioners providing enforcement, no cases were filed under the Enforcement Acts of 1870-1871. Moreover, a civil rights bill that mirrored the Congressional bill being debated in 1875 was passed in Arkansas a year earlier and in it, hotels, bars, and most public accommodations were prohibited from discriminating on account of race. Any officer of the peace who did not enforce the law was subject to prosecution, and as Nordhoff observed, the results of the law were dramatic: "I noticed that some drinking-saloons had two bars, one for each color; but I also saw in several cases Black and white men drinking together." Regarding state elections, he observed, "whatever happens, the negro is safe, for his vote—which can only be got by kind treatment—will be sought by the leaders of both parties, and he who wrongs a black mean loses votes."[17]

For Black Georgians steeped in years of political elections that were ripe with violence, threats, and in some cases death, the possibility that political leaders from both parties might value their votes was a phenomenon, and this possibility coupled with higher wages and legislation protecting their civil rights drew many to Arkansas in the early 1870s. Frederick Douglass praised the state for being "thoroughly reconstructed" and demonstrating obedience to the laws enforced, the people protected in their persons and property, and their civil and political rights permanently secured without regard to race or color."[18]

William Grey, who was the Immigration Commissioner of Arkansas, gave freedpeople a concrete example that the state's civil rights laws were more than anecdotal references. Grey, who was born free in Washington, DC, lived in Virginia and Missouri before settling in Helena Arkansas and serving at the Arkansas Constitutional Convention in 1868. He was elected twice to the state's legislature and was an active Republican leader serving as vice-president of the Union league in Arkansas. In Houston County, George Ormond had also been a leader in the Union League, and Isaac Anderson had attended the Republican convention with Grey in 1872 where the latter had seconded Grant's nomination to the presidency. Grey led a state agency that was responsible for settling Black laborers, and though his tenure in office was short, his success was justified as 36,000 new Black residents arrived by the end of the decade. The majority were from Georgia.[19]

Although there is no evidence that Anderson returned to politics after leaving Georgia for Arkansas, Ormond became a delegate to the Phillips County convention to nominate officers. Unfortunately, in 1872, Democratic leaders who were worried about the tide of Black laborers coming to the state called their exodus a conspiracy by Republicans to take over Arkansas. By 1875, white leaders who had initially tolerated Black migration and Blacks in office began to undermine Black leadership in the state.[20]

* * *

In *The Slave Community: Plantation Life in the Antebellum South*, John Blassingame writes that slaves, distrustful of whites, "generally developed a strong sense of loyalty to all blacks." This sense of loyalty was particularly strong with slaves who lived on the same plantation since a measure of solidarity often developed among them.[21] After Emancipation, this sense of loyalty continued to develop among freedpeople even as their communities changed geographically.

After leaving Georgia, Anderson retreated to a community in Arkansas where more than 60 percent of the population was Black, and he was most likely drawn to Arkansas not only because of the large surge of freedpeople migrating there from Georgia, but also because of previous ministerial connections that he had made. Three years earlier, he had been selected to establish churches throughout Georgia, and by 1873, he was serving as vice-president of the CME's Missions Board. In Hempstead County in what was the second largest pocket of Black settlement in Arkansas, Reverend Richard Samuels served as founding pastor of St. Paul CME Church of Washington. Like Anderson, Samuels had attended the denomination's founding meeting in 1870, and like Anderson, he was both a CME minister and a state legislator in the Arkansas General Assembly.[22]

Where Anderson lived upon his arrival in the state is shrouded in silence, but he and his family most likely settled quietly in Hempstead County. Although a large number of freedpeople from Georgia settled in the Delta counties of St. Francis and Phillips, the largest number of CME churches and members were located in Hempstead County, and by settling there, Anderson and his family would find a modicum of protection among fellow CME members.[23] The reality was that he could not let anyone know where he was, which may explain why the record of his life is so sparse. Anderson most likely lived with the constant reality that he could be arrested and taken back to Georgia if discovered, and unlike George Ormond, he and his wife, Edith, cared for 7 children.

No family stories have survived that uncover the life of Edith Anderson, but details about her exist in historical records. She, like her husband, is listed as a "mulatto" who was born in Georgia, and she was most likely among the 239 mulatto women listed as slaves in Houston county since only sixteen free Black mulatto women are recorded as living there, and because slave schedules only listed slaves by their owner and their age, color, and gender, there is no clear evidence to indicate who owned Edith. William Jackson did not own a female "mulatto" slave that was the same age as Edith in 1860, nor did his brother, Charles, so she most likely belonged to another slaveowner.

Anderson's skill as a blacksmith and carpenter, which was frequently given to slave owner's sons, may have enabled him to hire himself out and subsequently buy his and his wife's freedom, which was a practice among slaves with a favored trade. Anderson may have also bought the freedom of his two oldest children, Henry and Isaac, who were born in 1858 and 1859, respectively, and were owned by the same master who owned Edith.

Over the years, Edith Anderson, who was the mother of seven children, shouldered a huge burden as she faced the constant threat of violence directed at her husband and family. She, like countless freedpeople in her community, remembered the murder of the Ballard children, and with her sons coming of age, she knew the risk of false accusations that they faced because of their father. Moreover, with Anderson traveling frequently, she also understood that she or any of her children could be targeted to punish her husband for his actions, which may explain why George Smith and Harriet Anderson are listed as "farm laborers" who lived with the family.[24]

Edith Anderson's fear would have only increased in 1873 as the legislation that threatened to put her husband on the local chain gang was passed, and this fear would have impacted her mental and physical wellbeing. The deleterious effects of racial oppression have been well documented, most recently in a study published in Lancet in 2018, where researchers noted the correlation between police killings of unarmed people of color and "increased fear of victimization and greater mortality expectations" among Black Americans not directly impacted by these events.[25]

Although historical records do not indicate that the Anderson family experienced violence from vigilantes or local officials, hostility was palpable, and Edith Anderson understood what could happen to Blacks who challenged the status quo. The exact cause of her death in 1874 is unknown, but threats to her husband and family assuredly did not improve her life and health. In the end, the responsibility of raising his children in a new land was Anderson's alone, and he gained a measure of safety living quietly in a new place where 75 percent of the population were freedpeople like him.

Anderson's need to flee from his home and community in Fort Valley and the loss of his wife may explain why nearly four years of silence enshroud his already sparse historical record for this time period. The experience of Black politicians and their families during Reconstruction also explains why many disappeared from public life and historical records. It also explains why those stories that were shared by Black politicians were typically told decades later when they were outside of the South.

Unfortunately, the promise of respite in Arkansas changed soon after Anderson arrived as Democrats gained control of the state's government in 1875, Black political power began to wane, and economic conditions worsened. Of the forty thousand Black settlers who arrived that decade, nineteen thousand left Arkansas, relocating to the West, and in some cases, immigrating to Liberia.[26] In January 1877, Anderson transferred his ministerial call to the North Mississippi Conference of the CME Church where he became the presiding elder.[27] By the late 1870s, North Mississippi was a fertile ground to establish new CME congregations as freedpeople settled land stretching from the heart of the Mississippi Delta into the hill country in the northeastern part of the state. The growth in population led CME leaders to split their denomination's Tennessee Conference and create the North Mississippi Conference.

Anderson settled in Panola County in the vibrant community of Sardis and rented land from George Ballentine, an investor in the Helena, Sardis, Pontotoc, Birmingham Railroad Company, incorporated by 1882. Like many tenant farmers, he worked Ballentine's land while slowly improving his own and hoping to eventually become self-sufficient. In October 1878, he purchased land south of Holly Springs in the community of Chulahoma, which straddled Sardis and Holly Springs. Chulahoma was located roughly sixteen miles southwest of Holly Springs near the Tate County line and former Chickasaw land, and it had been heavily destroyed during the Civil War but had rebounded briefly in the 1870s just as Anderson arrived.[28]

Labor agents highlighted the region as one of the best places for Black men and women to relocate, and north Mississippi soon was known as a place that welcomed African Americans regardless of whether they were freedpeople or free-born. Following the end of the Civil War, whites had encouraged Black laborers to work and clear the land, but with the Depression of 1873 and the drop in cotton prices, the Delta suffered with the rest of the nation. African Americans faced diminishing economic opportunity and growing animosity from whites who were devastated by poor economic conditions, and many left the region for better opportunities in Oklahoma and Kansas.[29]

However, those who stayed in Mississippi found the state's massive forests of oak and hickory to be lucrative, and settlers cleared the land, hoping to utilize the rich alluvial soil for cotton. Settlement in the region continued to grow, and in *Forgotten Time: The Yazoo-Mississippi Delta after the Civil War*, John C Willis writes, "African-American farmers of humble means frequently purchased Delta land in the decades during and after reconstruction. By the mid-1880s the economic rise of these backcountry farmers—and their accompanying political strength—had transformed the Delta's interior into a promised land for poor but hopeful farmers and an implicit challenge to riverside planters."[30]

Panola County, located in the center of the state, was considered the inland part of the Mississippi Delta and was known for its majority-Black population. In 1860, 8,557 of the county's 13,794 residents were slaves, and by 1870, its total population was 20,754 with a Black majority of 12,585 and white minority of 8,169. Adjacent to Panola were Tate and Marshall Counties, and by 1880, Black residents in Panola had grown to 28,352, while the total Black population for the tri-county region was 46,795 compared to a white population of 29,607. This demographic drew both freed and free-born African Americans seeking opportunity and security.[31]

By the time of Anderson's arrival, Sardis, which was at the center of Panola County, had a Black population that was more than double that of whites. The town had been the location of a Freedmen's Bureau, and by 1868, it had a chapter of the Union League, which was led by Urbain Ozane, a white leader. The league's efforts were strengthened by the occasional presence of federal troops, and even after the league waned in Mississippi, individual branches in Panola County held significant power and helped former slaves deal with white planters and transition to freedom. Moreover, by 1869, African Americans were serving on juries that typically chose six Black and six white individuals, and this eventually led to mixed-race juries becoming the norm in the county.[32]

Josiah T. Settle is an example of the African American leadership that flourished in North Mississippi during this period. Settle arrived in Sardis to establish a law practice two years before Anderson. He previously had attended Oberlin College in Ohio, and in 1872, he transferred to Howard University in Washington, DC where he was part of its first graduating class and also one of the first graduates of its law school. Before moving to Sardis in 1875, he served as a clerk for the Freedmen's Bureau in Washington and as a trustee for the capital's school district. After an unsuccessful run for district attorney in Sardis, he served as a delegate to the Republican National Convention in 1876 and 1880 and won a seat in the Mississippi legislature in 1883 as an independent.[33]

Moreover, four Black Republicans served on Panola County's Board of Supervisors from 1871 through 1877, and by 1875, the county's Democratic Party had split from a more progressive Democratic wing within it that was arguing for a Black franchise as part of the party's platform. This was done to garner support from African Americans, and it resulted in the election of two Black Democrats in the county: Felix Eldridge as circuit clerk, and M. G. LittleJohn as chancery clerk.[34]

Along with Sardis, the towns of Old Panola and Como were communities in Panola County where Blacks outnumbered whites nearly five to one. In Como, the local Black Union League was led by J. H. Piles, who was born a free man in Springfield, Ohio. Piles also attended Oberlin College and studied law in Ohio before moving to Mississippi, where he served on Panola County's Republican Executive Committee, and later, in the Mississippi House of Representatives. In 1875, he served as the assistant secretary of state.[35]

The CME Church made its first efforts to establish schools in Sardis and in Louisville, Kentucky. The educational initiatives were first conceived by the denomination's first bishop, Henry Miles, who believed that Sardis would serve as an ideal location for a CME school. In 1869, four schools existed in Panola County, two of which were managed by freedpeople with support from the Freedmen's Bureau. By 1874, Bishop Miles had purchased land in Sardis hoping to establish a high school and believing that a school for children and adults would allow African Americans to acquire the education needed to attend the normal, or teachers' school in nearby Holly Springs.[36]

Anderson fervently supported the education of former slaves, and as the presiding CME elder in North Mississippi, he labored alongside of Miles. With skills as an organizer, expertise in business, and experience operating the Anderson School in Fort Valley, he was an ideal choice to work in the area. Moreover, Anderson had worked with Black and white leaders and locals to establish the Anderson School nearly a decade earlier.

Unfortunately, things grew dire as Miles pleaded for funding to complete the schools in both Sardis and Louisville, and by 1878, the bishop ended his efforts, disheartened and disappointed by the thousands of dollars in the loss of the property and investment.[37] Anderson, however, remained undaunted and ever mindful of the educational needs of freedpeople, and under his leadership as presiding elder, the North Mississippi Conference would soon become one of the largest in the region, outpacing other Black Methodist denominations in the area. He also lent his support to Elias Cottrell, a dynamic and increasingly popular Holly Spring resident who would eventually become a CME bishop and establish Mississippi Industrial College in 1906.[38]

Along with the dissolution of Bishop Miles's efforts in Sardis, Anderson faced another challenge: the yellow fever outbreak of 1878, which ravaged Holly Springs in nearby Marshall County. Roughly forty-five miles northeast of Sardis, Holly Springs was an extension of the Black powerbase found in Panola County, but with broader political reach. Secretary of State James Hill lived in Marshall County, and from 1873 to 1880, he was one of eight Black Mississippi representatives and senators from north Mississippi.[39]

Like Sardis, Holly Springs was home to a Freedmen's Bureau and Loyal League, both of which were led by Nelson G. Gill.[40] Holly Springs was also another safe haven for African Americans and was most famously known as the hometown of civil rights activist Ida B. Wells. During Reconstruction, Union generals stationed nearly two hundred soldiers in the county, including a number of Black troops, which further heightened a sense of security for Black residents.[41]

Holly Springs also provided another key magnet for African Americans: education. Rust College was a direct outworking of the Asbury Methodist Episcopal Church, which was known as the "mother of Rust College" and was established in Holly Springs in 1866. Both institutions were funded by the Northern Methodist Episcopal Church, and Rust, which was initially known as Shaw College, gave northern Methodists an opportunity to provide an education to African Americans, and in doing so, differentiate itself from

Southern Methodists. By 1878, Rust had established the first law school in the South for African Americans in response to Blacks being barred from the University of Mississippi's law school.[42]

Holly Springs was also the home of the State Normal School, which was one of only two public colleges in the state training African Americans teachers.[43] The Normal School, with its teacher training and preparatory track, was an indispensable pipeline for Black education and boasted of training "more graduates than any two colored schools in the State ... The faculty of the Normal are all colored. They are all Mississippians. The colored people of the State are proud of the Normal and Alcorn because our colored have a chance to demonstrate the colored man's abilities as an educator."[44] By 1890, 162 students were enrolled in the school's normal and preparatory programs, and by 1900, enrollment had increased to an average of 250 students.[45]

When the yellow fever outbreak first struck the mid-South in the summer of 1878, people from around the region flocked to Holly Springs believing that the Hills surrounding the community gave protection from bad air which was believed to cause the disease, and by September, many whites with means fled Holly Springs as the disease continued to spread. By the end of the outbreak roughly 51,737 people throughout the region were infected, and 12,164 were dead. In Mississippi, there were 12,703 cases and 3,277 fatalities, and as the number of sick grew, rumors spread about Blacks purposely spreading the illness as well as claims that Blacks had an innate resistance to the fever. The latter claim was tragically proven false as James and Elizabeth Wells, the parents of Ida B. Wells, and her brother, were among those taken by the fever.[46]

From 1860 to 1880, Marshall County's Black population grew from 17,447 to 18,338, while whites decreased from 11,376 to 10,992, and in October of 1878 in the middle of the yellow fever outbreak, Anderson purchased land in Chulahoma on the outskirts of Holly Springs from a white landowner for thirty dollars. The circumstances around the purchase are not known, but it is likely that Anderson was able to buy the land so cheaply because the money was used to either escape or forget horrible memories of the fever.[47]

Roughly a year later, on December 23, 1879, Anderson, who was forty-four, married Louisa Allen Byrd, who was twenty-one and from Sardis. According to the Anderson family history, Louisa was born in Sardis in 1860, and like Anderson, she was owned by her father and master who formally educated her mother as well as Louisa and her two brothers.[48] Although census records in the 1880s place Anderson's family in Holly Springs, they actually lived partly in Sardis where Anderson and Isaac Jr. worked the land. His other children from his marriage to Edith also lived near him: Henry worked as a farmer and was married, and Victoria was married to a man who was a farmer and a schoolteacher.[49]

Roughly a year after Anderson's marriage, Louisa gave birth to Celestine Lucy, who sadly died five days later. The next year, Rebecca Louisa was born, followed by James Christian, John Ernest, Ernestine Minerva, and Benjamin Franklin. Eventually, Anderson moved his new family to the land he had purchased in Chulahoma near Holly Springs in order to access the town's schools for his children, and he continued to minister to Black Methodists from Holly Springs to the Mississippi Delta.

* * *

By 1882, Paine Institute in Augusta, Georgia, and Jackson High School in Jackson, Tennessee, were both established. Lucius Holsey had led efforts to establish Paine, which was named after a prominent white Southern Methodist leader who had provided substantial funding for the school. He also served on Paine's board of trustees, which consisted of three members from the CME Church and three Southern Methodists.

Bishop Isaac Lane had been instrumental in establishing Jackson High School, which was directed by a board composed heavily of CME pastors, including Isaac Anderson. By 1885, the school became known as Lane Institute, and during the first twenty years of operation, it fluctuated between white and Black leadership until it became a college in 1896 and James Bray became its first Black president in 1902. Paine Institute would not have a Black president until 1971.

Advertisements for both schools appeared in the *Christian Index*, and Paine emphasized its focus on industrial education and the school being operated under the sponsorship of the Southern Methodist and the CME Churches. In contrast, advertisements for Lane, which usually were placed under Paine's advertisements, emphasized that the school was for young men and women and that it offered a Christian Education and instruction in music and in ancient and modern languages. Strikingly, Lane noted that it was founded and sponsored by the "C.M.E. Church" in bold capital letters.[50]

For Anderson, Jackson High was the ideal school to support due to the fact that it was primarily under CME leadership. Moreover, he most likely considered Holsey's involvement with Paine, his differing perspective on racial reconciliation, and his efforts to gain support from white Georgians who disapproved of Blacks being involved in politics.[51] In addition, the school's proximity to his family most likely encouraged his decision to support the school by serving on its Board of Trustees as a representative from the denomination's North Mississippi Conference.

In North Mississippi, financial challenges overshadowed much of Anderson's work, and the fact that the CME Church was based in the rural South only made these challenges more difficult. Problems plagued the denomination, including a lack of housing for ministers, difficulties with members' paying subscriptions for the denominational newspaper, and funding to support four CME bishops, yet by June of 1889, Anderson and other CME leaders instituted their plan to plant a congregation in Holly Springs.[52] Writing in the *Christian Index*, he asked for locals to give their presence and money for the new church: "We want to build a respectable church . . . Nothing will hoist the banner of the CME Church at this place but a new church. Come together let us have it."[53] A couple of months later, construction began on a new church building that would eventually become Anderson Chapel.[54]

Around the same time, construction began on a CME Church in Sardis. The work was overseen by J. P Hightower, a local blacksmith, Silas P. Patton, a local carpenter, Walton, R. D. Leake, a local school teacher, and B. M. Moore, a local farmer. Once completed, the congregation of the Sardis CME Church began to meet in a 30 x 56 building constructed from Mississippi pine lumber with frescoed walls and a sky-blue ceiling that was twenty-two feet high. Before its completion, the construction of the church's edifice had brought the congregation together in raising $1,600 in six months, and the building grew to be a labor of love built with the congregation's own resources by their own hands. The Sardis CME Church would be renamed Miles Chapel a few years later.[55]

One of Anderson's goals in North Mississippi was to establish churches along the railroad since these communities guaranteed the growth of the denomination. His work brought him to communities like Hollywood, which had been established along the LNO&T and Illinois Central Railroads.[56] By 1890, the region boasted a sizeable CME presence with the North Mississippi Conference recording a membership of 12,661 eclipsing the Mississippi Conference and the rest of the state's reported membership of 7,446.[57] Yet, Mississippi was changing, and Anderson began to sense the danger for African Americans behind these changes just as he had previously in Georgia and Arkansas.

* * *

Sardis and Holly Springs provide a case study in the rural South that mirrors the Black urban community discussed in John Blasingame's work, *Before the Ghetto: The Making of the Black Community in Savannah, Georgia, 1865–1880*. Blasingame argues that urbanization, unlike rural communities, "created the preconditions for the emergence of an intelligent leadership class, a sense of unity and the will and economic means to fight against white oppression." He further concludes that urbanization gave African Americans "a large arena to develop a variety of social, intellectual and creative talents to build the community infrastructure denied to them as slaves and as quasifree men." Sardis and Holly Springs demonstrate that the community infrastructure delineated by Blasingame could develop in semirural communities as well.[58]

Both freed and free-born African Americans migrated to Sardis and Holly Springs, and their migration and settlement in Panola County fostered the unity needed to spur economic growth and positive leadership in North Mississippi. This environment also allowed for the development of the Black nationalism that Steven Hahn emphasizes in his book, *Nation Under Our Feet*, and in this environment, competition developed between the Northern Methodist and the CME Church. White Northern Methodists were often paternalistic in their leadership of African Americans, but they did provide funding and resources for the education of former slaves. On the other hand, Black CME leaders often maintained ties with white Southern Methodists for whom the education and political activity of freedpeople was not a priority, but the educational efforts and the very formation of the CME Church demonstrated the desire of CME leaders like Anderson for greater Black autonomy.[59]

The Northern Methodist Episcopal Church established Asbury Chapel in 1866 and maintained a multiracial congregation there, even encouraging CME pastors to preach from its pulpit.[60] According to historian William Montgomery, the Northern Methodist's "missionary program was bountifully endowed and effectively planned, focusing on the spiritual needs of the freedmen but not to the exclusion of education and attainment of civil and political rights."[61] The missionary program of the Northern Methodists did result in significant support from freedpeople even though African Americans understood that they were not considered fully equal to their northern white Methodist brethren, who excluded Blacks from the office of bishop. This was keenly realized by many in North Mississippi where Blacks talked openly of African American autonomy in leadership, and the power dynamic caused by the ratio of Blacks to whites as well as the number of CME members was such that Northern Methodist leaders understood their need for positive relations with CME leaders in order to maintain influence among African Americans. Conversely, CME leaders needed friendly relations with Northern Methodists since many Blacks in the area attended Northern Methodist schools such as Rust. The internal politics at play in Holly Springs explains why Elias Cottrell, after becoming a CME Bishop in 1892, established Mississippi Industrial College as a rival to Rust in 1906.

Isaac H. Anderson picture. Courtesy of Carolyn B. Cunningham.

Communities such as Sardis and Holly Springs where African Americans held a majority powered the legitimacy of Blacks to obtain economic and political power, to the dismay of many Southern whites. For freed and freed born people alike, Sardis and Holly Springs promoted opportunities to rebuff white dominance and to separate themselves within the confines of safe spaces where African Americans could "capitalize on race pride."[62] With worship, fellowship, and Annual Conference meetings, African Americans in the CME Church could support one another and testify to each other about how each one had persevered through hardships. The CME Sabbath schools that ministers like Anderson established in the heart of the Mississippi Delta not only instructed CME parishioners on the Bible, but tacitly called African Americans as a people to embrace the potentiality of civil engagement much like the slave missions had done out of a fear of the slave master and a competing desire to be free.[63] Moreover, as white leaders began to question the validity of Black education throughout Mississippi in the late 1880s and early 1890s, Black churches and Sabbath schools proved to be valuable foundations.

Communities such as Sardis, Holly Springs, and Como allowed Blacks to develop as leaders both within their communities and in their interactions with whites. Even whites with paternalistic views of Blacks understood that some compromise was needed with a strong Black power structure in place, and such was the case with E. H. Crump, a Holly Springs native and future mayor of Memphis. As a white leader, Crump grew up within a vibrant Black community that prepared him to interact productively with the powerful Black community in Memphis during his tenure as that city's political boss.[64]

* * *

For many, the story of African Americans in Mississippi is marked by the *Plessy v. Ferguson* decision in 1896, which validated segregation, and the Supreme Court's *William v. Mississippi* decision two years later which gave federal sanction to poll taxes and literacy tests.[65] Both of these decisions solidified repression and seared a negative image of the state into the American consciousness, but this was not the Mississippi that Isaac Anderson knew on his arrival in the late 1870s.[66] Yet, with growing segregation codified by the state's passage of Jim Crow legislation in 1888 and the ratification of its new Constitution in the fall of 1890, he began to sense an all too familiar turmoil in Mississippi that mirrored his earlier experiences in Georgia and Arkansas. In March of 1889, he sold a large portion of his land in Chulahoma and rented land from the Ballentine family in Sardis.[67] He and his family would reside on the Ballentine land for at least three more years before leaving Mississippi and migrating to Jackson, Tennessee, roughly eighty-five miles northeast of Sardis.[68]

> 1875 Civil Rights Act passed—
> 1892 Ida B. Wells Launches Antilynching Campaign—1905 NAACP Founded

Chapter Eight

THE COLORED METHODIST EPISCOPAL CHURCH

IN 1894, LUCIUS HOLSEY WAS STILL NOT ABLE TO TRAVEL TO NEW MEXICO and recover from tuberculosis as dictated by his doctor, and he was physically tired, emotionally spent, and mentally weary. CME leaders faced constant accusations of being "democrats," "bootlicks," and "white folks niggers," and Holsey faced the majority of these insults.[1] His role as a fraternal delegate to the Southern Methodist Church, his advocation for Black ministers to stay out of politics in Georgia, and his writings and speeches validating slavery and the inferiority of freedpeople all intensified the accusations against him. According to someone who witnessed his struggles while establishing Paine College and the CME Church, he was "so overcome by a hemorrhages that blood in great quantities would flow from his nose and frequently left him white and helpless."[2]

Moreover, Holsey had become disillusioned with the prospect of working productively with white Southern Methodists by 1894. When it became clear that the education and political activity of freedpeople was not a priority even among men whom he had counted as friends, he wrote in the *Christian Index*, "I see no hope of the M.E. Church South, of doing anything much to help us. The prejudice against any movement to help us on the part of the Church, is too great for us to expect anything."[3]

* * *

Like many in search of a new beginning, Isaac Anderson was filled with hope when he and his family joined thousands of freedpeople converging in North Mississippi. A few years later, on December 23, 1879, twenty-year-old Louisa

"Lula" Byrd Allen became his second wife. Lula Anderson represented the new Black woman in an era when African Americans sought respectability as a tool to combat the rampant racial stereotypes, and in her case, stereotypes of women who were identified as mulatto. In the eyes of many white men, her mixed racial heritage cast her as a "jezebel," or someone who was sexually accessible since her birth was the result of interracial sex.[4] Lula Anderson had been formally educated by her white father, and her relationship with her family was complicated. When questioned by her granddaughter years later about why she was distant from members of her family, she answered, "They know where I am if they want to see me."[5]

Although she was born just before the Civil War, Lula Anderson was influenced by the growing economic, political, and educational opportunities available to African Americans after Emancipation. In North Mississippi, Black women like her had a chance to get an education by attending Rust College or the State Normal School which were near her hometown of Sardis, forty miles east of Holly Springs. The importance of education was a hallmark of the Anderson home, and Ida and Edella, his youngest daughters from his first marriage, attended Lane Institute in Jackson, Tennessee, which originally opened as Jackson High School in 1882. The couple's oldest son, James Christian, also pursued further education and eventually became a CME pastor like his father. Anderson's second eldest son, John Ernest, earned a master's degree in mathematics from Harvard, and in 1913, his middle daughter, Ernestine, became the first woman to graduate from Lane after the school was established as a college in 1896.[6]

Lula Anderson was a contrast to most wives of early CME leaders. The wives of many CME founders like Miles, Holsey, and Lane were born enslaved, had married before Emancipation, and had borne many of their children while still in bondage, and this may explain why many of them were not openly and actively involved in the work of early CME bishops. This contrast may also explain the growing tension between leaders and women in the CME Church as it moved past its initial years and younger women pushed for a greater voice in the denomination. In 1878, Evangelist Alice Courtney addressed the CME General Conference, and by 1886, a Women's Missionary Society was formally organized within the denomination.[7] Efforts to establish a Women's Missionary Society, however, have been credited to Lucius Holsey, who is reported to have organized its first chapter in Fort Valley in 1894.[8]

Roughly a year after the couple married, the Andersons had their first child, Celestine Lucy who died five days later. Five more siblings quickly followed with Rebecca Louisa born in 1882, James Christian in 1883, John

Ernest in 1885, Earnestine Ginevra in 1888, and Benjamin Franklin in 1889. Months after giving birth to her last child, Lula Anderson established the North Mississippi branch of the Women's Missionary Society, where she served as president, and this coincided with the establishing of social and fraternal organizations by African American women like the National Association of Colored Women (NACW), which was organized in 1896.

Anderson's support for his wife's efforts speaks to his success in escaping his upbringing as a slave and an environment where Black women were forced to be strong but were excluded from educational opportunities and public spaces, unlike wealthier white women who were typically afforded access to even a modest education. Anderson was similar to his father, William Jackson, who had actively supported the education of women and in 1852, had served as a founding board member of the Fort Valley Female Seminary.[9]

* * *

While Anderson was starting anew in Mississippi, William Jackson Anderson's life in Georgia was drawing to a close. His investments in the Southwestern Railroad made him a very wealthy man, and he furthered his investments by tapping into the growing need for fertilizer in Georgia, becoming one of the main purveyors of bat guano and locally made fertilizer in Houston County. In the 1870's, Georgians were spending tremendous amounts of money on fertilizer in an attempt to outproduce neighboring states, and this competition sparked what would be known as the guano craze.[10]

On March 4, 1872, William Jackson's world was firmly shaken when in the early hours of the morning, robbers made off with $15,000 in currency and $2,000 in gold pieces from the Planters' Bank of Fort Valley. Using gunpowder to explode the safe lock, robbers went undetected as neighbors dismissed the noise.[11] In a time when banks were uninsured federally, the robbery of Fort Valley's main bank was a huge blow to William Jackson. The Depression of 1873 followed these events and brought with it a number of railroad bankruptcies, which further undermined the solvency of the Planters's Bank and William Jackson's interests as a Cotton States Insurance agent. By late September things had grown from bad to worse with the death of Rebecca, his wife of twenty-four years.

By 1890, at the age of eighty-five, the man who was once a "merchant prince" of Fort Valley was now a farmer in the community he had helped to build. Similarly, his son and former slave farmed on rented land, and he also worked on improved land that he owned in Holly Springs while also serving as a minister.[12] This was a common practice for freedpeople who had little cash to buy land outright, but Anderson's fortunes would change with William Jackson's death in March of 1890.

According to Anderson's descendants, "upon his death, [William Jackson] left Isaac a substantial sum of money."[13] William Jackson's will does not mention Isaac Anderson, and unbeknownst to his family, he may have maintained a connection with his son and former slave through an intermediary who also delivered a monetary gift to him at his father's death. A more likely explanation is that Anderson briefly returned to Fort Valley upon learning of his father's impending death and saw him one last time. Any record of their relationship before William Jackson's death has been lost to silence, but reports in the *Christian Index* clarify that Anderson kept in contact with CME leaders in Houston County and had traveled back to the area, visiting Americus in Sumter County, less than fifty miles away from Fort Valley.

His return home was most likely influenced by the fact that roughly sixteen years had passed since Anderson's escape from Georgia, and the threat of his arrest had subsided. With Democrats firmly in control of state and local politics, he was no longer a threat, and the need to honor William Jackson, a prominent figure among white leaders in Houston County, most likely softened any hard feelings of local Democratic leaders. Preventing the two from meeting could only harm the memory of the "honorary colonel" who, in the words of his obituary, was "quick to resent an insult either to himself, family or friends . . . ready upon the first sign of penitence to forgive . . . [and] quick to forget when he forgave."[14] William Jackson's published eulogy given by his friend C.G. Gray mentions only three people: His mother, Anna, his father, Robert, and his man, Isaac.

* * *

The story of African Americans in Mississippi is a negative one in which Black men and women were stripped of their voting rights and survived within rigid lines of segregation. These lines were strengthened by two Supreme Court outcomes: The 1896 *Plessy v. Ferguson* decision, which validated segregation, and the 1898 *William v. Mississippi* decision, which sanctioned poll taxes, literacy tests, and grandfather clauses.[15] These decisions solidified repression and seared a negative image of Mississippi into the American consciousness, but this was not the Mississippi that Anderson knew when he arrived in the late 1870s. During this period, he experienced a state where African Americans still had significant power in municipal communities well into the 1880s.[16] In the Mississippi Delta and in overlapping borders of the Mississippi Hill country, Blacks still maintained significant control and served in leadership positions ranging from school superintendents to state senators. In *Black Mississippians in the Age of Jim Crow*, Neil R. McMillen concludes that Mississippi was a place where "the Negro could do things in the first twenty-five years of his freedom that he could not do during the second quarter of a century."[17]

The state's overlapping Black communities held a measure of promise in the 1880s and played an important role as centers of Black economic and political power, but by the early part of the twentieth century, only vestiges of this history endured. In Indianola, eating establishments allowed Black and white patrons to sit together at the same soda fountain counter, albeit with different glasses, and Minnie M. Cox, an African American woman, was appointed postmistress by President Benjamin Harrison in 1891 and by President William McKinley in 1897.[18] In nearby Clarksdale, a Black man served as an assistant cashier in a white bank, and in Holly Springs, African Americans were buried in a white cemetery.[19]

Mississippi's need for Black laborers encouraged whites to tolerate a measure of equality with Blacks, and this equality extended into the state's politics. Whether clearing land for cotton production, working land by picking cotton, or building railroads to ship timber and cotton, Black labor was needed, and the need for labor was so great in the Delta that local counties and state governments established immigration boards to draw laborers from as far away as Italy and China. By the 1890s, however, economic conditions contracted as did the price of cotton, dropping from a post war high of eleven cents per pound between 1874 and 1877 to less than five cents between 1889 and 1899.[20]

In response, cotton farmers tried to diversify their crops, but when they were unable to stem the economic shortfall, landlords sought other options and increasingly began to employ only sharecroppers hoping that laborers would accumulate debt in acquiring seed and other supplies from them for the next year's crop. Because many were illiterate and lacking in the math skills needed to track their debts, Black laborers were trapped into a cycle of debt, and Black farmers were also charged higher storage fees for their crops as well as for the goods that they purchased. Consequently, the "climb up the agricultural ladder" by African Americans stalled in the 1890s.[21]

The Mississippi Constitutional Convention of 1890 was organized with the goal of Black disenfranchisement, which was an urgent issue to many white Mississippians since Republicans controlled both houses of Congress. Throughout the South, Democrats who led state legislatures were fearful of federal intervention and pointed to Massachusetts Republican Senator Henry Cabot Lodge's bill requiring federal inspections at congressional elections. For northern Republicans, the move was essential since they had watched their political power wane following the reduction of Black voting in the 1870s. For Southerners, Lodge's legislation was dubbed the "Force Bill," and while the measure passed in the House, it failed in the Senate and was considered by many white Southerners to be an attempt to return to Reconstruction and encourage more Blacks to vote. The concern was that Democrats would lose state offices and be replaced with Republicans if there was federal oversight.[22]

The Mississippi Constitutional Convention ran from August through November of 1890, and Isaiah Montgomery of Mound Bayou, an all-Black community in the Mississippi Delta, was the loan representative of color. Montgomery sided with white delegates in stripping Blacks of their voting rights, proclaiming in his speech before the legislature, "Sirs, we are well aware that our race has not yet attained the high plane of moral, intellectual and political excellence common to yours, but it is our privilege to press onward and upward."[23]

The Constitution did not specify that Blacks would lose their right to vote, but a literacy test and an understanding clause which accomplished the same purpose were adopted through it. The literacy test barred Black Mississippians who were illiterate from voting, and the understanding clause was used to bar those who were literate by requiring them to read and explain an unusually complicated section of the state Constitution. Many white voters were allowed to simply explain a much easier section of the Constitution, and this allowed illiterate whites to vote.[24]

Moreover, new bigamy laws also curtailed the voting of many freedmen who were easily convicted since the marriages of a number of former slaves were not legally recognized. New larceny laws were also adopted, and Mississippi's pig law notoriously made pig stealing a felony, which served to harness convict labor and restrict Blacks from voting. Freedpeople often experienced poverty and hunger, and "in the lean years after emancipation," a common offense with former slaves was the stealing of a hog or chicken.[25]

Sensitized by years of experience with political and racial injustice, Anderson began to witness the kind of changes that he had experienced in Georgia and in Arkansas. In March of 1889, he sold a large portion of his land for three hundred dollars to Denton O'Dell and rented land from the Ballentine Family in Panola County. He, Lula, and their children would reside on the Ballentine land for several years before moving to Jackson, Tennessee.[26]

Tennessee was a divided state with strong supporters of secession based primarily in counties bordering the Mississippi river, and supporters of the Union living in the eastern part of the state. This division made Tennessee a seat of Union support in the heart of the confederacy and the last Southern state to join the Confederacy in June of 1861. Nearly a year later, when Union forces marched into the state, enslaved people fled to urban centers like Memphis and Nashville, and by 1864, freedpeople swelled with racial pride, pushed to serve in the army, and advocated for the extension of voting rights.

Tennessee also had a number of drawbacks: no Blacks had participated in the state's Constitutional Convention, and Democrats gained control of its legislature by 1870. Most notably, Pulaski, Tennessee, was the birthplace of the Ku Klux Klan.[27] Jackson, Tennessee was a railroad town with its share of racial violence including the lynching of Eliza Wood in 1886, John Brown in 1891, and Frank Ballard in 1894. Yet, even with the violence, adoption of Jim Crow legislation, the state held pockets of possibility for Anderson, and Jackson proved to be an ideal location. Two Black-owned newspapers, the *Afro-American Sentinel* and the *Jackson Headlight*, were published there for a short time, and though African Americans had very little involvement in Jackson's government according to the *Colored American*, many were involved in real estate, schools, churches and fraternal organizations. The town also served as the home of the CME Church until the late 1960s before relocating to Memphis, Tennessee.[28] Anderson purchased a home on Laconte Street in an all-Black neighborhood where fellow CME leaders like C. H. Phillips and Isaac Lane also resided.[29] In Jackson, he continued as a trustee of Lane College and also operated a grocery and dry goods store as well as a boarding house on Lafayette Street primarily for men who worked on the three nearby railroads.

In May 1890, just before his exodus to Tennessee, Anderson was named as publishing agent for the *Christian Index*, the official voice of the denomination, which served to highlight concerns among African Americans like public lynchings, national politics, and information helpful to locate lost relatives. Although the paper discussed the work of Black male leaders, it also was at times a venue for the issues and work of Black women throughout the 1890s. The paper frequently discussed the work of Jennie Lane, the daughter of CME Bishop Isaac Lane, who was featured prominently as a leader in the denomination. Lane was one of the first women to serve as a teacher during Lane institute's early years, and she later served as principal of Haygood School in Washington, Arkansas. The school eventually gave rise to the short lived Haygood Seminary.

The publishing agent was a powerful position within the CME, and the person who held that position was tasked with running the business side of the denomination's operations. The publishing agent served as the CME treasurer and also oversaw the denomination's publications including the weekly production of the *Christian Index*.[30] By 1894, Anderson expanded the scope of his training materials to include the history of the Negro race in addition to providing publications for congregations and preachers.[31] He fully embraced his mandate which was to make the CME's Publishing House profitable and the *Christian Index* a viable, respected, and widely read church publication. His other challenge was to supervise the denomination's finances, which involved being acutely aware of the Church's economic dependence on the Southern Methodist Church and its need to maintain a relationship with moderate white Southern Methodists.

Following her husband's elevation to publishing agent, Lula Anderson served as an occasional contributor typically contributing a poem or a song and always signing her work as "Mrs. I.H. Anderson." Her most prominent contribution, which was featured in the paper's commemoration of the denomination's twenty-fifth anniversary, emphasized the negative and positive influences of women in biblical history, and in it, she also called for married women to foster trust with their husbands and for single women to live chaste lives.[32] Her rhetoric modeled much of the politics of respectability of the Black woman who embraced the potential of Emancipation. Ida B. Wells also represented this idea, and like Anderson, she was from North Mississippi. The two women's rhetoric espoused an idea of womanhood in which ladies managed attractive homes, were companions to their husbands and nurturing mothers to their children. This image of womanhood, which was sometimes called the cult of domesticity, was normally reserved for white women, but Wells and Anderson expanded it to African American women and emphasized how they could positively influence Black men, making them into "great men."[33]

Previously, Isaac Anderson had served as the chair of the Committee on Episcopacy, and immediately following his election as publishing agent, the committee released its report, which noted that the annual CME conferences were not meeting their duties prescribed in the Church's *Book of Discipline*. The committee also recommended that no additional Bishops be added to the Church: "Members pay more per member and pay our Bishops less than any other Methodist Body and any more additions at present we believe inexpedient."[34]

The admonition by Anderson and the Episcopacy most likely angered Lucius Holsey, who was now a bishop and was already frustrated over the strains of the bishopric. The In 1891, he petitioned the General Conference to be released from his duties: "I can do some work, and expect to do it, but my physician thinks that a rest from public speaking will give me relief." His petition was rejected, and the bishops promised to lighten his duties, but the following year, he asked the conference to be released from service for two years to convalesce in New Mexico. Although his request was granted, Holsey never took the trip due to a lack of money.[35]

Holsey had always struggled financially, and as a circuit preacher with no fixed salary, was paid four dollars for his service at the end of his second year and told by a congregant, "We are glad you don't preach for money, but for souls." During his early years as a CME Bishop, Holsey was put in charge of Texas, Arkansas, Alabama, and Tennessee, and given a salary of $800, which did not include traveling expenses[36] For at least ten years, the poor financial situation created by his work burdened Holsey, his wife, and his five children, who survived on "peas, bacon, and cornbread having biscuits for Sunday morning breakfast." As he wrote, "None of them had any shoes but went barefooted, and nearly naked and lived in only a two-room house in Augusta." [37]

In 1881, Holsey traveled to Europe as a representative of the CME Church, and upon returning, he stopped in New York City, where he was forced to borrow twenty-five dollars from a Southern Methodist leader to make it home. Later, CME leaders claimed the reimbursement money should be used for educational efforts. The struggle over money plagued many CME bishops, but Holsey was the most vocal of them. For him, the lack of funding for bishops undermined the Church because these bishops were unable to focus on ministry and expand the denomination.

With long-standing differences dating back to the denomination's founding, Anderson, in his new position as publishing agent and controller of the purse, and Holsey, who was a senior bishop, entered into a public dispute.[38] During the 1890 CME General Conference, the denomination adopted a policy that presiding elders and conferences were to send all monies collected to the publishing agent rather than to individual bishops, which was the previous practice. Using a carrot-and-stick approach, Anderson hoped to encourage the payment of dues, by establishing cash awards for CME conferences that successfully submitted their reports and congregational dues, and each regional conference was awarded a prize according to the amount of their dues. He also threatened to publish the names of presiding elders in conferences who refused to send their required dues. Consequently, he faced criticism from various conferences for publicly chastising them for not submitting their reports, and several times, he nearly lost his reelection to his post.

The struggle over money and the denomination's publishing interests continued throughout his tenure as publishing agent, and the resulting public debate became known as the "paper wars" by the mid-1890s. This dispute has typically been described as a struggle between Bishop Lucius Holsey and C.H. Phillip, a CME Bishop and the previous editor of the *Christian Index*, but the dispute also included Holsey and Isaac Anderson, and the conflict eventually contributed to the end of Anderson's position as the CME Publishing Agent.[39]

By May 1893, the tension between Holsey and Anderson was evident to readers of the *Christian Index*.[40] In the paper, Holsey described Anderson's leadership actions as attempts "to scare off the Bishops of the church, and anyone else who dares to question his management of affairs pertaining to his office as Book agent and financial secretary of the church. Now I am convinced that there are not enough electric volts in that little cloud to kill a baby, so I shall proceed." In the same edition, Anderson responded, "I cannot see what Bishop Holsey is kicking about, he gets his $2000.00 every year, since the last General Conference. There are none of the other Bishops ever complain about the money; so if he had any personal objections to the Agent he should come out like a man and say so."[41]

The public argument between the two men continued well into the fall of 1893, and CME minister R. J. Johnson of Waynesboro, Georgia, wrote to the paper in dismay: "We do not like war, when it is on paper at long range. I hope the war is over. I think that both of them might adjust their difference in a private way, rather than clouding the minds of our many readers and putting our religious paper in mourning." [42]

In the spring of 1896, CME leaders began a major campaign to purchase a publishing house in order to avoid high printing costs and rent payments. After years of debating its location, church leaders decided against Nashville or Memphis and instead established the publishing house in Jackson, Tennessee, in a brick, two-story building owned by Anderson.[43] Hoping to rally the entire church, a banner ran across the August 1st edition of the *Christian Index*: "Our Publishing House Day, August 9, 1896."[44] Short pieces from prominent CME leaders also appeared in the edition urging church members to contribute to the project, and the entire denomination seemed to be behind the effort. By September, however, Holsey exposed division among CME bishops in the first edition of his new church paper, the *Gospel Trumpet*: "The trumpet has no axe to grind, no office to seek, and no favors to ask. The greatest foes the church and race have today are within and not without. These are more dangerous because their opportunities for ruin and mischief are greater."[45]

Although highly influential throughout the Deep South, Holsey's stronghold was his home state of Georgia, and he was able to get enough support for the paper and publish it in Macon.[46] Unfortunately, the *Gospel Trumpet* put Holsey at odds with his denomination as he worked out his frustrations with CME leaders such as Anderson in the paper, and ironically, as his own frustrations with white Southern Methodists grew.

* * *

The efforts of the Southern Methodist Church had always been geared toward the subordination of freedpeople, first through their establishment of Methodist slave missions, and then through their involvement in the CME Church decades later. While leaders like Holsey implicitly furthered the goals of many white Southern Methodist leaders, men such as Anderson explicitly opposed them. Michal Foucault has described racism as a state practiced and achieved by "internal colonialism," which according to Sylvester Johnson is heightened by power dynamics based on power structures.[47] Lucius Holsey had hoped to maintain his place within the power structure of the Southern Methodist Church by participating in the "internal colonialism" and playing a role that had extended from his time as a house slave into his position as one of the CME Church's early bishops.

All five of the CME's first bishops had been slaves and had been connected in some capacity to the Southern Methodist Church before the end of the Civil War. Isaac Lane was the son of his master like Holsey and Anderson, and he had been privileged not to experience the splitting up of his family during slavery. Having worked as a field hand, he described slavery as "the blackest chapter in the history of the American republic and . . . the greatest and foulest crime of the nation." William H. Miles and Joseph A. Beebe had purchased their freedom before the war, Miles, along with Richard Vanderhorst, had left the Southern Methodist Church for the AME and AME Zion Church before becoming CME leaders.[48]

Holsey decided not to leave his master after Emancipation, opting to stay for another year, and his attempt to maintain his favored status extended from slavery to his influential and important relationship with Southern Methodist Bishop George Pierce, who had been the owner of his wife, Harriet.[49] After Emancipation, Pierce provided Holsey with proximity to powerful white leaders in Georgia and in Southern Methodist circles.[50]

Holsey embraced the paternalism of Bishop Pierce and other more progressive Southern Methodist leaders, and in his autobiography, he wrote, "I have no complaint against American slavery. It was a blessing in disguise to me and to many. It has made the negro race what it could not have been in its native land." He further added regarding the ministerial training of Black men, "It was also clear to my mind that the white ministry was the only standard of excellence by which colored ministers could be inspired to reach a higher plane of fitness."[51]

Louisa Anderson and children. Courtesy of Carolyn B. Cunningham.

Holsey's role was a powerful one, and among white Southern Methodists, he served as a bridge to the CME Church and allowed Southern Methodists to influence important policies such as the restriction on political speech by CME leaders. Among CME churches, his influence provided access to funds needed to support CME efforts such as the education of freedpeople. His place within the power structure of the Southern Methodist Church explains why he would espouse a positiveness about slavery while also emphasize the need for education among former slaves and Black clergy. Although he worked to establish several schools such as Holsey Industrial, Helena B. Cobb Industrial, and the Hartwell Institute, only Paine College remains to this day.

Holsey's hope in CME and the Southern Methodist churches working together to promote the education of African Americans began to slowly ebb away in 1884 when Bishop Pierce died. For Holsey, Pierce's death was devastating, and with his long-time mentor and benefactor gone, the South's growing codification of restrictive racial laws and its increase in racial violence left him unsure of his new reality and his former commitments.

* * *

Although the *Gospel Trumpet* was similar to the *Christian Index* in its willingness to discuss political issues, the *Index* had long history of speaking out on issues such as public lynchings and political parties.[52] The *Index* was particularly critical of the Democratic party and maintained strong

Louisa Anderson, 1914. Courtesy of Carolyn B. Cunningham.

Republican leanings, but on occasion, it was willing to challenge the views of Republican leaders. The major difference between the *Index* and the *Gospel Trumpet* was the latter's tendency to focus on specific state leaders and call them out by name.

The Bourbon Democrats were a powerful group within Georgia's Democratic Party from 1872 through 1897, and Holsey described them as "shameful, degrading, and disgusting" for their support of the convict leasing system and their disregard for the working class. His comments were a direct attack on John B. Gordon, who was serving as a US Senator for Georgia and was also the lone survivor of the Bourbon Triumvirate.[53] To soften the blows of his criticism, he complimented other Democratic leaders such as Benjamin Hill and Alexander Stephens, the former vice president of the Confederacy, referring to them as "the archangel Ben Hill" and "angelic Stephens." Both men were Southern Methodists and close friends of his former benefactor, George Pierce, and by complimenting them, Holsey garnered a measure of protection from other Southern Methodists.[54] For Anderson, however, "archangel" and "angelic" were not terms he would use to describe Stephens and Hill.[55]

Ernestine Ginevra Anderson Brown, first female graduate of Lane College. Courtesy of Carolyn B. Cunningham.

By the 1890s, it was clear to Lucius Holsey that moderates in the Southern Methodist Church did not share his priority for education among African Americans. After being united for years, the CME Church had little to show in the way of support from Southern Methodists for the education of freedpeople other than Paine College. Holsey, who was weary and keenly aware of the broken promises of Southern Methodists, wrote, "For ten years we have waited, hoped, begged and prayed for almost nothing. I think it is time for us to realize that we need no longer depend on them for help in any tolerable degree."[56]

In Georgia, Holsey would remain the dominant voice in the denomination, especially after his move to Atlanta in 1897, which gave him a greater reach throughout the state. Because of his tremendous influence as a spiritual and educational leader, many CME congregants were frustrated by what they saw as attacks upon their bishop as tensions played out in the *Christian Index*, and their frustration may explain why Usher's Chapel in Fort Valley bears little memory of Isaac Anderson who was vital in giving voice to the civil rights of freedpeople in Georgia and in establishing the CME Church as a denomination in North Mississippi.

Holsey continued to serve as a fraternal delegate to the Southern Methodists, and in 1898, he attended their convention to raise funding for the training of ministers for Africa.[57] He maintained his place within the power

Isaac H. Anderson home in Jackson, Tennessee. Courtesy of Carolyn B. Cunningham.

structure of the Southern Methodist Church and continued to participate in its "internal colonialism," but this role gave him a crippling dependence on their support for Paine College and for his standing in white circles. His physical and mental health worsened, and wearing a psychological mask of sorts, he straddled lines of racial etiquette challenging white Southern Methodist leaders publicly on rare occasions, but more frequently, seeking their support with deference.

By the turn of the century, Holsey increasingly found himself on the periphery of the CME Church, which had matured and moved on in many ways. In 1899, he wrote, "From year to year, the states of the southern section have enacted laws more and more stringent, and especially adapted, not only to degrade and set bar to the progress and development of the black man, but these laws serve to destroy his civil rights, and nullify the citizenship conferred upon him, by the General Government . . . Every where the black man's privileges are abridged restricted and often annihilated."[58]

Moreover, Holsey came to believe that the problem of the oppression of Blacks by whites was best solved by "separation and segregation." As he explained, "the negro race must occupy a state or states or a territory to themselves . . . According to our theory of Government, the Negro is a free and equal citizen, but does not enjoy these rights that belong to him as such,

Anderson school in Jackson, Tennessee. Courtesy of Carolyn B. Cunningham.

largely because there is a deep-seated prejudice against him because of his color and other racial attributes and racial peculiarities. And because, also of his previous condition of bondage and servitude." During a symposium on the status of the Negro, Holsey concluded that "the Union of the States will never be fully and perfectly recemented with tenacious integrity until black Ham and white Japheth dwell together in separate tents."[59]

* * *

As the new century dawned, a generation of CME leaders arose who were particularly like the newly minted bishop of Mississippi, Elias Cottrell. These leaders were willing to take bold public stances against the Democratic Party and criticize politicians without tempering words, and with the expiration of conditional grants and the ability of CME congregations to gain full ownership of church property, little motivation remained for Black leaders to honor Holsey's alliances with white Southern Methodists.[60] By 1900, many African Americans had assumed powerful leadership roles in CME educational institutions other than Paine College, and the *Gospel Trumpet* was no longer in publication.

With the Colored Methodist Church now stabilized financially due in large part to his efforts, Anderson grew weary of public debates over bishops' salaries, church subscriptions, and annual calls for his replacement. In 1898, he lost his re-election to the position of publishing agent, yet the inheritance provided by William Jackson and his skill in establishing a business most likely allowed him to escape the crippling dependence on Southern Methodists and CME churches that had affected Holsey. In Jackson, Tennessee, he was a successful businessman, and eventually, he would become one of the wealthiest Black men in the Midsouth.

The irony is cutting: Lucius Holsey hoped that white leaders would consider the need for social progress among freedpeople to be as vital as their own welfare, yet he ended his life in poor health and, apart from the legacy of Paine College, little to show for his alliance with the Southern Methodist Church. Today, many consider him to be the dominant voice of the CME Church, and by extension, Black men and women in the rural South after Reconstruction. In contrast, Isaac Anderson was the lone advocate for not silencing the political speech of Black ministers in the CME Church as white Southern Methodists expected, yet he prospered due to an inheritance from his father and former master and from the love of his close-knit family. Until the pages of this book, his life has been all but relegated to a shroud of silence.

EPILOGUE

THE FORGETTING

IN FORT VALLEY, SHADOWS OF THE PAST INVITE VISITORS TO LOOK INTO empty storefronts and grand houses that line the heart of the town, reminding them of what once was. A train depot that once loaded cotton and signaled the economic prosperity of the town now lies in ruins with scaffolding and broken windows that hang like strands of confetti from a party that ended long ago. Iron bars form gaps like blunted, missing teeth in a visage worn by age. Across town in the time-worn house of William Jackson Anderson, shadows of the past make themselves known in a grove of peach trees at the foot of an avenue that bears his name.

My last trip to Fort Valley in the summer of 2019 was a reminder of how the lost crucible of Anderson's story was now fully uncovered. After well over a decade of research, many shadows of the past followed me through his hometown, and like many rural communities that had been built on slave labor and agriculture, time has brought tremendous change as opportunity drifted from much of the rural South. In Peach County, Fort Valley today is primarily known for peaches and pecans, and most labor comes at the hands of migrant workers. Its main employers are the Bluebird Bus company and Fort Valley State University, and the town struggles economically.

For well over a decade, the story of Isaac Anderson has been my constant companion as pieces of his life slowly come together in the pages of my notes. Both smooth and thorny places that shape Southern history have been exposed by his story, and for African Americans who come from a tradition of remembering ancestors and sharing the past, his story completes a connection broken by the trauma of slavery, the distance of time, and a gnawing shroud of silence.

Oddfellow Hall plaque. Courtesy of Marilyn N. Windham.

For descendants of former slaves, records comprised of people simply labeled Black, negro, mulatto, infant, boy, girl, man, woman, often are the only history remaining for them. Public auctions or wills vaguely point to Black men and women dispersed as property, and in the silences of these resources, Anderson's story has unfolded for me alongside hundreds of thousands of others that whisper truths about the Black experience in America. This silence speaks to why genealogy is a multibillion-dollar business with a growing clientele of African Americans who, with new DNA technology, have greater opportunity to trace the steps of their ancestors.

Anderson's story raises the question of identity in Southern society for two men with the same last name and blood. In his lifetime, Anderson could never speak publicly about his blood connection to William Jackson and the Anderson bloodline, but instead was known simply by his skin tone among whites. Making public the biracial identity of a Black person was not shocking in the 1800s, but pointedly naming his or her white parent was. In honoring Isaac Anderson publicly nearly a century later, his family made

Anderson Building in Jackson, Tennessee.
Photo by Jack D. Wood, Tennessee Room Librarian, Jackson-Madison Co. Library.

no mention of his mother but instead described him as a "descendant" of William Jackson Anderson. Today, recognizing the truth of a person's lineage has become vital to historical narrative. Only after his death in 2003 did seventy-eight-year-old Essie Mae Washington-Williams publicly identify Strom Thurmond, the South Carolina senator, Dixiecrat, presidential candidate, and virulent opponent of the 1964 Civil Rights Act, her white father.

Anderson grew into a man, started a family, established a church, and built a school for freedpeople in Fort Valley, yet a shroud of silence obscures any recognition of the first African American from Houston County to serve in the Georgia Senate. He fought for the rights of former slaves in the Georgia legislature and was exiled under threat of serving on a Houston County chain gang. Fort Valley State University, a historically Black institution, acknowledges its beginnings in the Fort Valley CME church, yet no memory of Anderson is there, and no memory of him working alongside the Freedmen's Bureau to secure funding and operate the Anderson school can be seen.

Perhaps those who remained in Georgia during the exodus of thousands of freedpeople simply failed to share their stories or fearfully refused to tell them because of the trauma of what is known as the "nadir of race relations," a hard time for Blacks in America. Perhaps CME congregations in Fort Valley

Fort Valley Railroad Depot. Courtesy of the author.

were so closely aligned Bishop Lucius Holsey that Anderson's departure and defiance angered them.[1]

In Georgia's history, there has been a general "forgetting" of local Black legislators like Anderson, and a dominant narrative has existed in which "antebellum preachers, slave and free . . . mastered the art of compromise in order to bring the Gospel message to slaves."[2] The dominant story has charged that leaders like Anderson, a minister and a politician, were not only unwilling to challenge their masters, but were inept in changing Georgia and complicit in the "Splendid Failure" that was Reconstruction. this narrative rises from the literature in dozens of public libraries and tacitly haunts venues of learning and education across the state of Georgia.

There is also a "forgetting" among Black Methodists, and much of the narrative is that of AME and AME, Zion, Churches. This belies an assumption that the Black community and African American churches were monolithic CME, AME, and AME Zion laypeople and leaders worshipped, conferenced, and voted alike. Yet, the "forgetting" exists within the CME Church, and decades after his death, very little has been written about Anderson. At Lane College, Anderson Street is named after him, but his home is gone, and the school that he established has been absorbed into the college's campus. In Isaac Lane's autobiography, scant reference is given to Isaac Anderson's contribution and support, and instead, the majority of the autobiographical

William Jackson Anderson Home. Courtesy of the author.

details other bishops and leaders. As one of the richest Black men in Jackson, Anderson's support and work as a trustee were invaluable to putting the school on a more stable financial footing.[3]

Anderson's "forgetting" is shared by many rural Black leaders of the late nineteenth century. In 1913, in his memoir, the *Facts of Reconstruction*, J. R. Lynch addressed the vilification of Black leadership during Reconstruction by deemphasizing its centrality to politics in Mississippi during the period. Lynch challenged local histories as well as the Dunning school by emphasizing Black and white cooperation, and his retelling of history to correct negative perceptions undermined the history of Black leadership experienced by thousands of African Americans.

Like Anderson, Black men and women established towns in north Mississippi where they flourished economically and politically, but when their prosperity disappeared, an unintended consequence was the disappearance of their memory and the substitution of a racially oppressive Mississippi where freedpeople never existed in thriving, vibrant communities. As Michel-Rolph Trouillet concludes in his book, *Silencing the Past*, the memory of the past is often, if not always, based on who tells it, regardless of the nobility of their purposes.[4]

I discovered a key that unlocked much of Anderson and William Jackson's story one afternoon during a visit to the local library. In the Summer of

Isaac H. Anderson. Courtesy of Carolyn B. Cunningham.

2013 during a meeting with Marilyn Windham, a Fort Valley historian, she unexpectedly found a file while I was in the local archives, and inside was an aged, pieced-together newspaper print, which was the obituary of William Jackson Anderson. As she passed me the file, she looked me in the eye and said, "I don't believe in coincidences," and for many days to follow, I remind myself of her admonition as Anderson's story took me to unexpected places at unexpected times. Genealogists say that these times are when the ancestors want us to find them, and when we listen to their stories, shrouds of silence are pierced and the life of Isaac Anderson is recovered.

Over the years, as my research progressed, Anderson's story unfolded along with the devastating stories of Alton Sterling, Tamir Rice, Sandra Bland, Eric Garner, Philando Castile, Elijah McClain, Atatiana Jefferson, Ahmad Aubrey, Breonna Taylor, and George Floyd. His story unfolded as a Black pastor and politician in Charleston, and eight of his parishioners were gunned down one summer night in their church during a Bible study, and it unfolded during the Charlottesville rally as unmasked white men walked into the night with torches and rehearsed scenes from my very own notes. Shockingly, it continued to unfold with the insurrection on the US capitol on January 6, 2021, as a mob of mainly white men stormed Congress and hunted legislators who refused to invalidate the votes of Black and Brown people in key states. Sadly, the echoes of Anderson's story have not been silenced nor has its shadow, which was cast 150 years ago, been stilled. Isaac Anderson's story surrounds us—serving as a Morse code to give voice to the generations before. It is the zeitgeist of the Black experience that is *The Recovered Life of Isaac Anderson*.

NOTES

INTRODUCTION

1. Elsa Barkley Brown, panelist, "Who is Black America" at Future of African American Past, May 20, 2016. https://futureafampast.si.edu/sessions/session-1-who-black-america accessed 6/9/2016.

2. Eric Foner, *Freedom's Lawmakers: A Directory of Black Officeholders During Reconstruction*, 2nd ed. (Baton Rouge: LSU Press, 1996) xii. More recently Justin Behrend's *Reconstructing Democracy: Grassroots Black Politics in the Deep South After the Civil War* (Athens: University of Georgia Press, 2015), follows this tradition in examining the rise of Black leadership in the South.

3. See also Thomas Holt, *Black over White: Political Leadership in South Carolina during Reconstruction* (Urbana: University of Illinois Press, 1977); Edward N. Rabinowitz ed., *Southern Black Leaders of the Reconstruction Era* (Urbana: University of Chicago Press, 1982); and Justin Behrend, *Reconstructing Democracy: Grassroots Black Politics in the Deep South After the Civil War* (Athens: University of Georgia Press, 2015), which also challenged earlier perspectives of Black leadership.

4. William A. Dunning, *Essay on the Civil War and Reconstruction* (1898; repr., New York: Harper Torchbook, 1965); William A. Dunning, *Reconstruction, Political, and Economic, 1865–1877* (New York: Harper and Brothers, 1907); C. Mildred Thompson, *Reconstruction in Georgia: Economic, Social and Political: 1865–1872* (Gloucester, Mass, Peter Smith, 1964), 78. Fellow Dunning scholar Edwin C. Woolley in *The Reconstruction of Georgia* (New York: Columbia University Press, 1901) also emphasized Black ineptitude. Although not a student of William Dunning, prominent Georgia historian, E. Merton Coulter emphasized similar perspectives in his works, *A Short History of Georgia* (Chapel Hill: UNC Press; Rev. and enl. ed edition 1933, revised, 1947, 1960) and *The South During Reconstruction, 1865–1877* (Baton Rouge: Louisiana State University Press, 1947).

5. Alan Conway, *The Reconstruction of Georgia* (Minneapolis: University of Minnesota, 1966), 226 and Edmund Drago, *Black Politicians and Reconstruction in Georgia: A Splendid Failure* (Athens: University of Georgia Press, 1992), 161.

6. Joseph P. Reidy, *From Slavery to Agrarian Capitalism in the Cotton Plantation South: Central Georgia, 1800–1880* (Chapel Hill: UNC Press, 1992) and Susan Eva O'Donovan, *Becoming Free in the Cotton South* (Cambridge: Harvard University Press, 2007). Currently

Mercer Press reissued Thompson's book in 2017 and University of Georgia Press acquired rights in 1992 to publish Drago's book which was originally published by LSU Press in 1982. The holdings in the Georgia public library system known as Pines explains why most Georgians still are influenced by the Dunning perspective through Thompson, Conway and Drago's work. As of January 8, 2020, there are roughly one hundred and seventy-two copies of Thompson's book, forty-one copies of Conway's book and thirty-nine copies of Drago's book available throughout the state of Georgia. In comparison there are four copies of Reidy's book, three of which are electronic and four copies of O'Donovan's book in the public holdings of the entire Georgia public library system.

7. According to the Georgia Department of History and Archives, with the election of Reverend Raphael Warnock a total of five Black individuals including Benham, Thurbert Baker (Attorney General), Michael Thurmond (Commissioner of Labor), Leah Ward-Sears (Georgia Supreme Court, Chief Justice) have served in statewide office in Georgia.

8. Roger L. Ransom and Richard Sutch, *One Kind of Freedom: The Economic Consequences of Emancipation* (London: Cambridge University Press, 1977); Eric Foner, *Reconstruction: America's Unfinished Revolution, 1863–1877* (New York Harper and Row, 1988) and Bruce E. Baker and Brian Kelly, "Introduction," in *After Slavery: Race, Labor, and Citizenship in Reconstruction South*, ed. Bruce E. Baker and Brian Kelly (Gainesville: University Press of Florida, 2013), 8.

9. Alex Lichtenstein, *Twice the Work of Free Labor: The Political Economy of Convict Labor in the New South* (New York: Verso; First Edition 1996); Matthew Mancini, *One Dies, Get Another: Convict Leasing in the American South, 1866–1928* (University of South Carolina Press, 1996); Douglas A. Blackmon, *Slavery by Another Name: The Re-Enslavement of Black Americans from the Civil War to World War II* (New York: Anchor; Reprint edition 2009) and Talitha L. LeFlouria, *Chained in Silence: Black Women and Convict Labor in the New South* (Chapel Hill: UNC Press, 2015). Notable work on the convict lease system in the South include David M. Oshinsky, *Worse than Slavery: Parchman Farm and the Ordeal of Jim Crow Justice* (New York: Free Press, 1997) and Michelle Alexander, *The New Jim Crow: Mass Incarceration in the Age of Colorblindness* (New York: New Press 2012).

10. https://www.sentencingproject.org/the-facts/#rankings?dataset-option=SIR accessed 1/8/2020.

11. Paul Cimbala, *Under the Guardianship of the Nation: The Freedmen's Bureau and the Reconstruction of Georgia, 1865–1870* (Athens: University of Georgia Press, 2003). More recently, Laura F. Edward's *A Legal History of the Civil War and Reconstruction* explores legal strategies used to undermine the rights of freedmen and women. *A Legal History of the Civil War and Reconstruction: A Nation of Rights* (New York: Cambridge University Press, 2015). 131, 136, 164 and *CME General Conference Minutes, 1873*.

12. Steven Hahn, *A Nation under Our Feet: Black Political Struggles in the Rural South from Slavery to the Great Migration* (Cambridge: Harvard University Press, 2003). Other recent works examining Black ministers and the state include Sylvester A. Johnson in *African American Religions, 1500–2000: Colonialism, Democracy and Freedom* (New York: Cambridge University Press) and Willie J. Jennings *The Christian Imagination: Theology and the Origins of Race* (New Haven: Yale University Press, 2010).

13. Russell Duncan, *Freedom's Shore: Tunis Campbell and the Georgia Freedman* (Athens: University of Georgia Press, 1986) Examines the life and times of Tunis Campbell Sr., a northern abolitionist who moved to Georgia during Reconstruction.

14. Work on the CME Church includes: Charles H. Phillips, *The History of the Colored Methodist Episcopal Church in America: Comprising its Organizations, Subsequent Development and Present Status* (Jackson, Tennessee: CME Publishing House, 1925); Fayette M. Hamilton, *A Plain Account of the Colored Methodist Episcopal Church in America. Being an Outline of her History and Polity; also, the Prospective Work* (Nashville, Tennessee: Southern Methodist Publishing House, 1887); Othal Lakey, *History of the CME Church*, revised ed. (CME Publishing House: Memphis, Tennessee, 1996); Glenn T. Eskew, "Black Elitism and the Failure of Paternalism in Postbellum Georgia: The Case of Bishop Lucius Henry Holsey," *Journal of Southern History* 57, no. 4, 1992 and Raymond R. Somerville, *An Ex-Colored Church, Social Activism in the CME Church, 1870–1970* (Macon, Georgia: Mercer Press, 2004). Even among the writings of CME leaders there is little to no reference of Isaac Anderson's political activity in Georgia. Lucius Holsey, *The Autobiography of Bishop L. H. Holsey (re-printed)* with Introduction by George E. Clary, Jr. (Keysville, Georgia: Briar Creek Press, 1988) and Isaac Lane, *Autobiography of Bishop Isaac Lane with a Short History of the CME Church in America and of Methodism* (Nashville, Tennessee: Publishing House of M.E. Church, South, 1916).

15. Stephen Ward Angell, *Bishop Henry McNeal Turner and African American Religion in the South* (Knoxville: University of Tennessee Press, 1992).

16. Among the notable works on the growth of Black Methodists as a group in Georgia are the following: Katherine Dvorak, *An African American Exodus: The Segregation of the Southern Churches* (Brooklyn: Carlson Publishing, 1991); Reginald Hildebrand, *The Times Were Strange and Stirring: Methodist Preachers and the Crisis of Emancipation* (Durham: Duke University Press, 1995); William E. Montgomery, *Under Their Own Vine and Fig Tree: The African-American Church in the South 1865–1900* (Baton Rouge: LSU Press, 1993); Christopher H. Owen, *The Sacred Flame of Love: Methodism and Society in Nineteenth-Century Georgia* (Athens, University of Georgia Press, 1998); Daniel Stowell, *Rebuilding Zion: Religious Reconstruction of the South, 1863–1877* (Oxford: Oxford University Press, 1998) Clarence Walker, *A Rock in Weary Land: The African Methodist Episcopal Church during the Civil War and Reconstruction* (Baton Rouge: LSU Press, 1982). The Long Civil Rights Movement was initially advanced by Jacquelyn Dowd Hall, "The Long Civil Rights Movement and the Political Uses of the Past," *Journal of American History* 91, no. 4 (March 2005).

17. The role of the Black Church as a refuge from trauma as well as the role of the minister as a comforter or therapist of sorts is based on trauma studies see Judith Herman, *Trauma and Recovery: The Aftermath of Violence—From Domestic Abuse to Political Terror* (New York, Basic Books, 2015); Veena Das, Arthur Kleinman, Mamphela Ramphele, Pamela Reynolds, *Violence and Subjectivity* (Oakland: University of California Press, 2000) and Arthur Kleinman, Veena Das, Margaret Lock, Margaret M. Lock, *Social Sufferings* (Oakland: University of California Press, 1997). For the impact of trauma on the Black community see the following: Kidada E. Williams, *They Left Great Marks on Me: African American Testimonies of Racial Violence from Emancipation to World War I* (New York: NYU Press, 2012).

18. Eddie Glaude, https://www.huffpost.com/entry/the-black-church-is-dead_b_473815 accessed 1/8/2020.

19. William Cohen, *At Freedom's Edge: Black Mobility and the Southern White Quest for Racial Control, 1861–1915* (Baton Rouge: LSU Press, 1991) and Ira Berlin, *The Making of African America: The Four Great Migrations* (New York: Penguin Books, 2010). Most recently Story Matkin-Rawn's "'The Great Negro State of the Country': Arkansas's Reconstruction and the Other Great Migration," *Arkansas Historical Quarterly* 72, no. 1, Spring 2013, explores Black agency, the Freedmen's Bureau and Black emigration within the Deep South following emancipation. For emigration outside the South, see Nell Painter, *Exodusters: Black Migration to Kansas after Reconstruction, The First Major Migration to the North of Ex-slaves* (New York: W.W. Norton and Company; reprint edition 1992) and Isabel Wilkerson, *The Warmth of Other Suns: The Epic Story of America's Great Migration* (New York: Vintage; Reprint edition, 2011).

20. John William Graves, *Town and Country: Race Relations in the Urban-rural Context, Arkansas, 1865–1905* (Fayetteville: University of Arkansas Press, 1990), Fon Louise Gordon, *Caste and Class: The Black Experience in Arkansas, 1880–1930* (Athens: University of Georgia Press, 1995) and Kenneth Barnes, *Who Killed John Clayton? Political Violence and the Emergence of the New South 1861–1893* (Durham, North Carolina: Duke University Press, 1998).

21. Ruth Watkins, "Reconstruction in Marshall County" Publications of the Mississippi Historical Society, vol. 12 (University, University of Mississippi, 1912); John W. Kyle, "Reconstruction in Panola County," Publication of Mississippi Historical Society ed. Franklin Riley, vol. 13 (University, University of Mississippi, 1913). Other works examining Blacks in Mississippi include the following: Vernon Lane Wharton, *The Negro in Mississippi 1865–1890* (New York: Harper Torchbooks, 1948); Buford Satcher, *Blacks in Mississippi Politics 1865–1900* (Washington, DC University Press of America, 1978); Neil McMillen, *Dark Journey; Black Mississippians in the Age of Jim Crow* (Urbana, University of Illinois Press, 1989); Janet Sharp Hermann, *The Pursuit of a Dream* (1981 Oxford University Press, Jackson: University Press of Mississippi, 1999). Monographs focusing on the Mississippi Delta include the following: James C. Cobb, *The Most Southern Place on Earth: The Mississippi Delta and the Roots of Regional Identity* (New York: Oxford University Press, 1992); John C. Willis, *Forgotten Time: The Yazoo Mississippi Delta after the Civil War* (Charlottesville: University Press of Virginia, 2000); John M. Giggie, *After Redemption Jim Crow and the Transformation of African American Religion in the Delta, 1875–1915* (Oxford: Oxford University Press, 2008) and Karlos K. Hill, *Beyond the Rope: The Impact of Lynching on Black Culture and Memory* (New York: Cambridge University Press, 2016).

CHAPTER ONE

1. *The Weekly Intelligencer*, January 15, 1868 (Quondam means former or onetime). James Maurice Thompson was born in Indiana, but his family relocated to Rome, Georgia, by the 1850s. He served for three years in the Confederate army and moved back to Indiana to work as an engineer in 1868. He later served in the Indiana legislature, penned a number of novels and poems and wrote for the *New York Independent*. http://ghs.galileo.usg.edu/ghs/view?docId=ead/MS%200798-ead.xml;query=Mary%20Telfair%20papers;brand=default accessed 1/20/2020.

2. Robert L. Dabney, *Discussions of Robert L Dabney.*, ed. C. R. Vaughn, vol. 4 Secular (Harrisburg, Virginia: Sprinkle Publications, 1994) 179.

3. *Newton Herald*, April 18, 1868.

4. John M. Matthews, *The Negro in Politics* Department of History Duke University, 1967 MA thesis, 10–13, 16. Georgia's Constitutional Convention did pass the Thirteenth Amendment but only a fraction of the electorate passed the new Georgia Constitution. The Georgia legislature meeting on December 4, 1865, selected Alexander Stephens the former vice president of the Confederacy and Herschel Johnson a senator in the Confederate States of America to serve in the US Senate representing the state. Alan Conway, *Reconstruction in Georgia* (Minneapolis: University of Minnesota Press, 1966), 52–53. Enraged Republicans in Congress refused to allow Stephens and Johnson to take their seats in December 1865. Ethel Maude Christler, "Participation of Negroes in the government of Georgia, 1867–1870" (master's thesis, Atlanta University, 1933).

5. General John Pope was born in Louisville, Kentucky. The Union general was best known for his defeat at the Second Battle of Bull Run or the Second Manassas.

6. "Cuffee" was a general name for a person of African descent considered to be an offensive term, see *Oxford English Dictionary*. According to the *Oxford English Dictionary*, the term first documented use in 1713. *Southern Recorder*, November 26, 1867. Newspaper accounts portrayed Black leaders and inept. In the *Georgia Weekly*, the convention's proceedings were fictitiously reported by white journalists as if being written by a "representative" Black radical: "The 'Knights of the Razor and Strap' offered an additional amendment that 'de white brudders' hav[sic] their hair frizzed and kinked at his shop in Savannah; but his colored brethren objected on the ground that people couldn't tell 'de diffrus 'tween'em, an' dey wanted'em to stay in dere-places, and not elevate demselves on a level wid us." *Southern Recorder*, November 26, 1867 and *Georgia Weekly*, March 13, 1868.

7. *Southern Recorder*, October 15, 1867.

8. *Southern Recorder*, November 19, 1867, Edward Barham Young, "The Negro in Georgia Politics, 1867–1877" (Master's Thesis, Emory, 1955), 5.

9. *Southern Recorder*, November 19, 1867. Governor Jenkins was adamant in his opposition to the Fourteenth Amendment and appealed to the Supreme Court to issue an injunction of the Reconstruction Acts. He was later removed from office by Georgia's third military general, Thomas Ruger, after refusing to pay $40,000.00 for another Constitutional Convention. See James F. Cook, *The Governors of Georgia, 1754–2004*, 3d ed. (Macon, Ga.: Mercer University Press, 2005) and Olive H. Shadgett, "Charles Jones Jenkins, Jr.," in *Georgians in Profile: Historical Essays in Honor of Ellis Merton Coulter*, ed. Horace Montgomery (Athens: University of Georgia Press, 1958).

10. *Southern Recorder*, November 19, 1867 and Alan Conway, *Reconstruction in Georgia* (Minneapolis: University of Minnesota Press, 1966), 149.

11. *Atlanta Daily Opinion*, February 1, 1868. Also arrested was the county coroner, who was accused of, "failing to discharge his duty when an inquest was held." Eventually Digby was cleared of charges and Provisional Governor Ruger issued a $200.00 bounty for Barnes arrest. For more details on the story see *Georgia Daily Opinion*, March 3, 1868 and *Southern Recorder*, March 17, 1868.

12. The three white delegates were Posey Maddox, O. H. Walton, and William P. Edwards.

13. *Georgia Weekly Telegraph*, March 20, 1868.
14. *Georgia Weekly Telegraph*, September 11, 1868.
15. *Georgia Weekly Telegraph*, May 8, 1868.
16. *Georgia Weekly Telegraph*, March 20, 1868.
17. Henry McNeal Turner was from Bibb County; Samuel A. Cobb and Isaac H. Anderson were from Houston County.
18. Joseph P. Reidy, *From Slavery to Agrarian Capitalism in the Cotton South: Central Georgia, 1800–1180* (Chapel Hill: UNC Press, 1992), 194 and *Georgia Weekly Telegraph*, April 10, 1898.
19. *Federal Union*, October 29, 1867.
20. Georgia initially rejected the Fourteenth Amendment on November 9, 1866. On July 21, 1868, the state adopted the amendment officially adding the Fourteenth Amendment to the Constitution.
21. *Georgia Weekly Telegraph*, May 8, 1868.
22. *Georgia Weekly Telegraph*, May 8, 1868.
23. After the elections, one correspondent from Houston County would victoriously report, "Our old men—our young men—all came and all put their shoulders to the wheel. And those of us who were disenfranchised attended the election constantly, and we felt that as we were not allowed to vote ourselves, each one of us would if possible, by fair meant, have deposited in the ballot-box ten votes by honest negroes in the place of the one we were disallowed the privilege of depositing for ourselves... Old men residing in distant parts of the county, that do not come to Perry once in five years, were here, aiding in the good cause, and this too, whether allowed to vote themselves or not." *Georgia Weekly Telegraph*, May 8, 1868.
24. *Georgia Weekly Telegraph*, May 8, 1868.
25. *Joel R Griffin, Houston County Contested Election May 2, 1868*, RG 2-02-110, Georgia Archives. Records of the Assistant Commissioner for Georgia, Bureau of Refugees, Freedmen and Abandoned Lands. Register of letter received vols. 3–5 June 1867–May 1869 and John M. Matthews, *The Negro in Politics 1865–1880*, Duke MA, 1967, 261–62.
26. *Georgia Weekly*, March 25, 1873.
27. After the elections, he used his social and political position to petition the military governor and congressional leaders in Washington concerning the mistreatment of Blacks living in and around Fort Valley and Houston County. Griffin later went on to deed land on which Shiloh Baptist Church, and later St. Peter's A.M.E., were established as all Black congregations in a Black section of Fort Valley near Vinevale, which became known as Griffin Lane. *First One Hundred and Ten Years Houston County* (Warner Robins: Georgia, Central Georgia Genealogical Society, 1983), 115; Joseph P. Reidy, *From Slavery to Agrarian Capitalism in the Cotton Plantation South: Central Georgia 1800–1880* (Chapel Hill: University of North Carolina Press, 1992), 188; Gilda E. Stanberry, *Images of America Fort Valley* (Mount Pleasant, South Carolina: Arcadia Publishing, 2013), 54 and *North East Georgian*, October 21, 1874.
28. *Georgia Weekly Telegraph*, May 8, 1868.
29. *Joel R Griffin, Houston County Contested Election May 2, 1868*, RG-SG-S 2-02-110, Georgia Archives. Records of the Assistant Commissioner for Georgia, Bureau of Refugees, Freedmen and Abandoned Lands. Register of letter received vols. 3–5 June 1867–May 1869 and John M. Matthews, *The Negro in Politics 1865–1880*, Duke MA, 1967, 261–62.

30. *Records of the Assistant Commissioner for Georgia Bureau of Refugees, Freedmen, Abandoned Lands, Register of Letters Received*, vol. 4, 262–63.

31. *Georgia Weekly Telegraph*, March 20, 1868.

32. *Georgia Weekly Telegraph*, May 1, 1868. Election results from Upson County located in west central Georgia, one county over from Houston County.

33. The passage of the Fourteenth Amendment was essential to overturning the Supreme Court's 1857 Dred Scott decision by which "Negroes," whether slave or free, were not citizens and consequently held no standing in court.

34. Edmund L. Drago, *Black Politicians and Reconstruction in Georgia: A Splendid Failure* (Athens: University of Georgia Press, 1992), 45.

35. This argument derives from the fact that the most vocal Black leaders like Henry McNeal Turner were not explicit in adding language that Black men had the right to vote. Many of them "suffered from misplaced faith in good intentions of their white opponents." Edmund L. Drago, *Black Politicians and Reconstruction in Georgia: A Splendid Failure* (Athens: University of Georgia Press, 1992), 45. This line of thought has the benefit of hindsight. I would agree with John M. Matthews, that, "delegates assumed it to be clear that all those citizens eligible to vote were also eligible to hold office, for they voted down a section which stated explicitly who that all electors were qualified to hold office." "Negro in Georgia Politics, 1865–1880" (master's thesis, Duke University, 1967), 41. I would argue that many of these Black delegates believed in the possibility of fairness, that they wanted to have language that was broad enough to apply to anyone. For example, when Georgia passed the Thirteenth Amendment in December 1865, language did not specifically say African Americans but was broad enough in its application to apply to all African Americans. It is also important to recognize that even if the men had pushed to have specific language would it have passed the convention in light of the opposition from Democrats and some Republicans to the convention extending Black rights outright. Ethel Maude Christler, "Participation of Negroes in the Government of Georgia, 1867–1870" (master's thesis, Atlanta University, 1932) 6; John M. Matthews, "*Negro in Georgia Politics, 1865–1880*" (master's thesis, Duke University, 1967), 137 and Edmund L. Drago, *Black Politicians and Reconstruction in Georgia: A Splendid Failure* (Athens: University of Georgia Press, 1992), 45.

36. US Bureau of Census, *Ninth Census of the United States: Statistics of Population*. (Washington, DC: Government Printing Office, Population Schedule, 1870).

37. US Bureau of Census, *Ninth Census of the United States: Statistics of Population*. (Washington, DC: Government Printing Office, Population Schedule, 1870).

38. *Christian Index*, May 11, 1895.

39. *Journal of the Proceedings of the Constitutional Convention of the People of Georgia*, 1868, 611. Joel Anderson citation and Eric Foner, *Freedom's Lawmakers: A Directory of Black Officeholders During Reconstruction*, 2nd ed. (Baton Rouge: LSU Press, 1996), 7.

40. William Jasper Cotter, *My Autobiography*, ed. Charles Jones (Nashville: Publishing House Methodist Episcopal Church South, 1917), 155.

41. James Dunwoody, *Reminiscences of Rev. James Dunwoody of the South Georgia Conference* (Milledgeville, Georgia: Boyd Publishing Company, 1995), 44.

42. James Dunwoody, *Reminiscences of Rev. James Dunwoody of the South Georgia Conference* (Milledgeville, Georgia: Boyd Publishing Company, 1995), 44.

43. "Report of the Committee on Church Organization of the Organizing General Conference of the Colored Methodist Episcopal Church in America," submitted December 16, 1870, by I. H. Anderson in Othal Hawthorne Lakey, *The History of the CME Church, Revised* (Memphis: CME Publishing House, 1996), 733–34.

44. "Report of the Committee on Church Organization of the Organizing General Conference of the Colored Methodist Episcopal Church in America," submitted December 16, 1870, by I. H. Anderson in Othal Hawthorne Lakey, *The History of the CME Church, Revised* (Memphis: CME Publishing House, 1996), 733. Anderson, along with other CME leaders, required Black Methodist clergy an identical course of study as white Southern Methodist ministers, but by the turn of the twentieth century the course of study for Black Methodist leaders included a study of African American history.

45. *Christian Index*, December 7 1889.

46. While serving as a Colored Methodist presiding elder in Mississippi, Anderson gave the following instructions to leaders of his circuit, which encompassed the Mississippi Delta: "Several questions will be asked of different delegates or Sabbath schools as follows: Senatobia [circuit] will define the word Holy Bible. Mt Moriah [circuit] will give the meaning of the word Holy Scripture . . . Johnson and Crystal Springs [station], tell the number of books forming the Pentateuch and the number of books forming the Historical part." *Christian Index*, August 27, 1887.

47. *Christian Index*, September 29, 1888. Hollywood, Mississippi is located in the Mississippi Delta in Tunica County roughly 22 miles south of Memphis.

48. Eric Foner, *Freedom's Lawmakers: A Directory of Black Officeholders During Reconstruction*, 2nd ed. (Baton Rouge: LSU Press, 1996), xxi and Edmund L. Drago, *Black Politicians and Reconstruction in Georgia: A Splendid Failure* (Athens: University of Georgia Press, 1992), appendix.

49. Edmund L. Drago, "Black Voter Registrars during Reconstruction," *Georgia Historical Quarterly* 78, no. 4, (1994) 771–72. Drago believes that Isaac Anderson was the unidentified "colored" minister who was praised in the *Savannah Daily News Herald*, August 22, 1867, as the "colored preacher, until recently under rebel influence. His eyes are now open and he is making amends for his past indifferences."

50. William Jasper Cotter, ed. Charles O. Jones, *My Autobiography* (Nashville: Publishing House Methodist Episcopal Church South, 1917), 156 and US Bureau of Census, *Ninth Census of the United States: Statistics of Population* (Washington, DC: Government Printing Office, Population Schedule).

51. During the Constitutional Convention in 1867, the only resolution that Anderson is listed as introducing in the journal minutes was a resolution providing relief to slave owners for the loss of property, and the resolution never came to a full vote. Yet according to the *Weekly Atlanta Intelligencer*, the resolution was introduced by O. H. (Overton Harrison) Walton who was mistakenly listed as G. H. Walton in the state journal. Walton was also a delegate representing the Twenty-Third District along with Isaac Anderson, and before the war, Walton lived in Crawford County, owned at least thirty slaves, and operated a grocery store. It is likely that the newspaper account is more accurate as Walton, a former slaveholder, had reason to advocate for compensation for slaves. In 1868, Walton was named penitentiary keeper by Governor Bullock but would be ousted a year later following a

state investigation which found that he had grossly mismanaged the prison. *Journal of the Proceedings of the Constitutional Convention of the People of Georgia, Held in the City of Atlanta in the Months of December 1867, and January, February and March 1868 and Ordinances and Resolutions Adopted* (Augusta, Georgia: E. H. Pughe Book and Job Publisher, 1868) 94; US Bureau of Census, *Eighth Census of the United States: Statistics of Population* (Washington, DC: Government Printing Office, Population Schedule). James C Bonner, "The Georgia Penitentiary at Milledgeville 1817–1874," *The Georgia Historical Quarterly* 55, no. 3 (Fall, 1971), 303–28.

52. Joel Griffin's father, Cyrus Griffin, served as the first vice president of the Continental Congress of Virginia, and Griffin served in the Confederate army as the captain of the Macon volunteer militia, or the "Macon Guards." He was eventually named colonel of the Third Georgia Regiment and returned home to Houston County after the war. Governor Treutlen Chapter Daughters of the American Revolution, *History of Peach County with Addenda and Errata* (Atlanta: Cherokee Publishing Company, 1972), 80.

53. Robert Scott Davis, *Ghost and Shadows of Andersonville: Essays on the Secret Social Histories of America's Deadliest Prison* (Macon: Mercer University Press, 2006), 37.

54. *General Proceedings of the Constitutional Convention of the People of Georgia: Held in the City of Atlanta in the months of December, 1867 and January, February, and March 1868, and Ordinances and Resolutions Adopted.* Published order of the Convention, 66, 155.

55. *General Proceedings of the Constitutional Convention of the People of Georgia: Held in the City of Atlanta in the months of December, 1867 and January, February, and March 1868, and Ordinances and Resolutions Adopted.* Published order of the Convention, 66, 155.

56. *Georgia Weekly*, March 13, 1868. Among those listed were Tunis Campbell representing McIntosh, Romulus Moore of representing Columbia County, Thomas Crayton representing Stewart County, Malcolm Claiborne representing Burke County, and Isaac Anderson representing Houston County.

57. Susan O'Donovan, *Becoming Free in the Cotton South* (Cambridge: Harvard University Press, 2007), 258 and Joseph P. Reidy, *From Slavery to Agrarian Capitalism in the Cotton South: Central Georgia, 1800–1180* (Chapel Hill: UNC Press, 1992), 204.

58. *Cuthbert Appeal*, April 14, 1870. Initial reports of chapters of the Grant Club were appearing in Georgia newspapers by January 1868 first appearing in the Atlanta-based New Era newspaper. Frustrated by the lack of details the *Georgia Weekly* questioned if the clubs were on par with the "Dark Lantern." *Georgia Weekly Telegraph*, January 8, 1868.

59. Richard Abbott, *Black Ministers and the Organization of the Republican Party in the South in 1867: Letters from the Field*. http://www.rbhayes.org/research/hayes-historical-journal-black-ministers-and-the-republican-party/accessed 8/6/2014.

60. Houston County Tax Record 1869 and William Jackson Anderson, Obituary March 1890 clipping from Thomas Memorial Library, Fort Valley, Georgia.

CHAPTER TWO

1. Warren lived in Perry, south east of Fort Valley. Founded before Fort Valley, Perry was a smaller community and county rival to Fort Valley, which had beat the community in wooing a railroad depot further spurring Fort Valley's economic growth and population growth.

2. *Georgia Weekly Telegraph*, May 8, 1868.

3. The first migrations into the frontier occurred between 1800 and 1820, and a second happened between the 1820s and 1840s. Joseph P. Reidy, *From Slavery to Agrarian Capitalism in the Cotton Plantation South: Central Georgia, 1800–1880* (Chapel Hill: UNC Press, 1995).

4. "Then a frontier county and at one time owned the land upon which a car shed in Atlanta now stands." William Jackson Anderson, Obituary March 1890 clipping from Thomas Memorial Library, Fort Valley, Georgia; US Bureau of Census, *Sixth Census of the United States: Statistics of Population* (Washington, DC: Government Printing Office, Population Schedule); Bruce S. Allardice, *More Generals in Gray* (Baton Rouge: LSU Press, 2006), 19–20 and Mildred W Goodlett, *Waterloo: A History of the Anderson Family of Old Laurens District of South Carolina* (Greenville, S.C: Hiott Press, 1961), 36.

5. William Jackson Anderson, Obituary March 1890 clipping from Thomas Memorial Library, Fort Valley, Georgia.

6. William Jackson Anderson, Obituary March 1890 clipping from Thomas Memorial Library, Fort Valley, Georgia.

7. William Jackson Anderson, Obituary March 1890 clipping from Thomas Memorial Library, Fort Valley, Georgia.

8. *History of Peach County Georgia with Addenda and Errata, Compiled by Governor Treutlen Chapter of Daughters of the American Revolution Fort Valley, Georgia* (Atlanta: Cherokee Publishing, 1972), 170–71.

9. William Jackson Anderson, Obituary March 1890 untitled clipping from Thomas Memorial Library Fort Valley, Georgia.

10. Louise Ayer Vandiver, *Traditions and History of Anderson County* (Anderson, S.C.: Anderson Daily Independent, 1928), 64–68.

11. Early national period is typically considered from the period of George Washington's presidency until Andrew Jackson's presidency, roughly 1789 through 1837. Alexis De Tocqueville, *Democracy in America*, translated by George Lawrence and ed. J. P. Mayer (New York: Harper Perennial, 1988), 585.

12. Steven Mintz, *Huck's Raft: A History of American Childhood* (Cambridge, Mass: Belknap Press of Harvard University Press, 2004), 87.

13. John Ellisor, *The Second Creek War: Interethnic Conflict and the Collusion on a Collapsing Frontier* (Lincoln: University of Nebraska Press, 2010), 36.

14. Louise Ayer Vandiver, *Traditions and History of Anderson County* (Anderson, South Carolina: Anderson Daily Independent, 1928), 64–68.

15. Arriving in Georgia around 1815, James Abington Everett worked tirelessly trading among the Creek Indians. By 1818 he established a trading relationship with Timothy Barnard, a white trader and well-respected diplomat to the Creek Nation. See *History of Peach County Georgia with Addenda and Errata, Compiled by Governor Treutlen Chapter of Daughters of the American Revolution Fort Valley, Georgia* (Atlanta: Cherokee Publishing, 1972), 68.

16. John Ellisor, *The Second Creek War: Interethnic Conflict and the Collusion on a Collapsing Frontier* (Lincoln: University of Nebraska Press, 2010), 145. For firsthand accounts of life on the frontier, see also: Mills Lane, ed., *The Rambler in Georgia: Desultory Observations on the Situation, Extent, Climate, Population, Manners, Customs, Commerce, Constitution, Government, etc., of the State from the Revolution to the Civil War Recorded by Thirteen*

Travelers (Savannah, Ga.: Beehive Press, 1973). For scholarly discussion of frontier life, see Joshua D. Rothman, *Flush Times and Fever Dreams: A Story of Capitalism and Slavery in the Age of Jackson* (Athens: University of Georgia Press, 2014). Columbus Georgia is immediately east of Phenix City, Alabama.

17. John Ellisor, *The Second Creek War: Interethnic Conflict and Collusion on a Collapsing Frontier* (Lincoln: University of Nebraska Press, 2010), 64.

18. Elliott J. Gorn, "Gouge and Bite, Pull Hair and Scratch: The Social Significance of Fighting in the Southern Backcountry," *American Historical Review* 90, no. 1, 35.

19. Intermarriage between white traders and Native American women occurred for a number of reasons: Native American women proved essential to their husband's livelihood as traders; they were knowledgeable of how to acquire ideal trading goods like furs or were skilled in dressing and preparing furs themselves; they were able to introduce their husbands to local chiefs and clans with whom they were familiar. With the Creek, inheritance rights were determined by the mother, and because their societies were matrilineal, Creek women held significant social influence. The US government, however, recognized the rights of males as heads of household; consequently, marriage gave white men control of the land set aside for the Creek at the first Treaty of Indian Springs in 1821. Charles J. Kappler edit and compiler, *Indian Affairs. Laws and Treaties Vol II. (Treaties)* (Washington: Government Printing Office, 1903). Document: TCC526 [Survey report on the land of] Cussena Barnard, 1821 June 6, Georgia / Wilson Lumpkin http://neptune3.galib.uga.edu/ssp/cgi-bin/tei-natamer-idx.pl?sessionid=7f000001&type=doc&tei2id=tcc526; Louise Frederick Hays, *History of Macon County* (Spartanburg, S.C.: The Reprint Company Publishers, 1979), 47) and Jimmy Smith, The Name Begins, 1970s, unpublished manuscript. Fort Valley, Georgia June 2012 and John T. Ellisor, *The Second Creek War: Interethnic Conflict and Collusion on a Collapsing Frontier* (Lincoln: University of Nebraska, 2010), 51–52.

20. Calvin Schermerhorn, "'The Time Is Now Just Arriving When Many Capitalist Will Make Fortunes': Indian Removal, Finance, and Slavery in the Making of the American Cotton South," in *Linking the Histories of Slavery: North America and Its Borderlands*, edited Bonnie Martin and James F. Brooks (Santa Fe: School for Advanced Research Press, 2015), 157.

21. William Jackson Anderson, Obituary March 1890 untitled clipping from Thomas Memorial Library Fort Valley, Georgia. Fantasy blended with reality in the backwoods of frontier life as settlers lived on the edge of society and "the abandonment of 'civilized' ways that led to the ultimate expansion of civilized society." Elliott J. Gorn, "Gouge and Bite, Pull Hair and Scratch: The Social Significance of Fighting in the Southern Backcountry," *American Historical Review* 90, no. 1, 33.

22. Everett Dick, Forward by John D. W. Guice, *The Dixie Frontier, A Social History* (University of Oklahoma Press, 1993), 140.

23. Everett Dick, Foreword by John D. W. Guice, *The Dixie Frontier, A Social History* (University of Oklahoma Press, 1993), 140, and Elliott J. Gorn, "Gouge and Bite, Pull Hair and Scratch: The Social Significance of Fighting in the Southern Backcountry," *American Historical Review* 90, no. 1, 41.

24. *Journal of the Proceedings of the Constitutional Convention of the People of Georgia, Held in the City of Atlanta in the months of December 1867, and January, February, and March, 1868. And ordinances and resolutions adopted.* Published by order of the convention (Augusta,

Georgia, E.H. Pughe, Book and Job Printer, 1868), 611 and Census Bureau, *Twelfth Census of the United States: Statistics of Population* (Washington, DC: Government Printing Office, Population Schedule). In the 1880 census, Isaac Anderson's mother and father's birthplace as Georgia, which speaks to some of the challenges using census records as sometimes neighbors and others not sure about an individual's background can provide incorrect information, especially if Isaac for whatever reason cared not to share the details of where his mother was born with the person providing information to the census taker. Isaac Anderson's father, William Jackson Anderson, was born in South Carolina. His mother was most likely also born in South Carolina. If she bore Isaac at the age of twelve in 1835, the earliest typically a young girl could bear a child, it would have been in 1823, and at that time Monroe County was still Creek land with few if any Black women slave or free lived in the area. It is likely she was brought to the county with the influx of settlers moving into Georgia in the mid-1820s many of which like his father were from South Carolina.

25. William Jackson Anderson, Obituary March 1890 clipping from Thomas Memorial Library, Fort Valley, Georgia.

26. James H. Stone, "Economic Conditions in Macon, Georgia in the 1830s," *Georgia Historical Quarterly* 54, no. 2, 214.

27. James H. Stone, "Economic Conditions in Macon, Georgia in the 1830s," *Georgia Historical Quarterly* 54, no. 2, 216, and William Thomas Jenkins, *Antebellum Macon and Bibb County, Georgia*, PhD diss., University of Georgia 1966, 19.

28. William Thomas Jenkins, *Antebellum Macon and Bibb County, Georgia*, PhD diss., University of Georgia 1966, 245.

29. W. H. Russell, *My Diary North and South* (Boston: T.O.H.P. Burnham, 1863), 162. The slave market in Macon was not large as those in Baltimore, Richmond, St. Louis, or Charleston but much larger than the market found in Augusta primarily because of its central location in the state.

30. Michael Tadman, *Speculators and Slaves: Masters, traders, and Slaves in the Old South* (Madison: University of Wisconsin Press, 1996), 8, and Winfield H. Collins, *The Domestic Slave Trade of the Southern States* (New York: Broadway Publishing Company, 1904), 27–28.

31. Frederic Bancroft, *Slave Trading in the Old South*, New York: Frederic Ungar Publishing, 1931), 95–96.

32. Mary Lane, "Macon: An Historical Retrospect," *Georgia Historical Quarterly* 5, no. 3 (September 1921), 27, 28–32.

33. Joseph P. Reidy, *Masters and Slaves, Planters and Freedmen: The Transition from Slavery to Freedom in Central Georgia, 1820–1880*, PhD diss., Northern Illinois University 1982, 16, and William Thomas Jenkins, *Antebellum Macon and Bibb County, Georgia*, PhD diss., University of Georgia 1966, 229–30.

34. William Jackson Anderson, Obituary March 1890 clipping from Thomas Memorial Library, Fort Valley, Georgia.

35. Joseph P. Reidy, *Masters and Slaves, Planters and Freedmen: The Transition from Slavery to Freedom in Central Georgia, 1820–1880*, PhD diss., Northern Illinois University 1982, 34.

36. William Jackson Anderson, Obituary March 1890 clipping from Thomas Memorial Library, Fort Valley, Georgia. *Semi-Centennial Exercises Memorials of Methodism in Macon, Georgia from 1828-1878 Held at Mulberry Street Church, December 5th to 8th 1878* Macon

Georgia: J. W. Burke and Co., Printers and Binders, 1878, 26, 89. Mulberry Street Methodist Church, Church Minute Book, 1838–1878 Bibb County, Georgia accessed 12/20/2018 https://www.familysearch.org/search/catalog/226133?availability=Family%20History%20Library.

37. *Georgia Messenger* (Ft Hawkins) August 31, 1837 and *Chronicle and Sentinel* (Augusta) May 1, 1838.

38. Harold Woodman, *King Cotton and His Retainers: Financing and Marketing the Cotton Crop of the South 1800–1925* (Washington, DC: Beard Books, 2000), 13–14, 114.

39. William Jackson Anderson, Obituary March 1890 clipping from Thomas Memorial Library, Fort Valley, Georgia; Mildred W Goodlett, Waterloo: *A Family History of the Anderson Family of Old Laurens District of South Carolina* (Greenville, S.C., Hiott Press, 1961), 41; Governor Treutlen Chapter Daughters of the American Revolution, *History of Peach County with Addenda and Errata* (Atlanta: Cherokee Publishing Company, 1972), 76; *Chronicle and Sentinel*, Augusta Georgia, May 1, 1838, and *Georgia Telegraph*, January 21 1840. The Ocmulgee Bank was backed by leading Macon businessmen despite a number of misgivings as the bank was to supply funding for the Georgia Female Seminary. By 1841 it was bankrupt. A number of powerful Georgians invested in the bank including Henry G. Lamar, a Macon attorney who would serve two terms in the US House of Representatives before becoming a Superior Court judge for the Macon circuit which included Fort Valley and Houston County.

40. William Thomas Jenkins, *Antebellum Macon and Bibb County, Georgia*, PhD diss., University of Georgia 1966, 231 and 248.

41. The Panic of 1837 spread throughout the nation. The agricultural sector was devastated by the depression. Cotton prices dropped dramatically from record high of eighteen cents a pound in 1836 to barely reaching five cents a pound between 1839 and 1845. William Thomas Jenkins, *Antebellum Macon and Bibb County, Georgia*, PhD diss., University of Georgia 1966, 247–48.

42. *Chronicle and Sentinel* (Augusta) May 1, 1838, and Semi-Centennial Exercises Memorials of Methodism in Macon, Georgia from 1828 through 1878 held at Mulberry Street Church, December 5th to 8th (Macon Georgia: J. W. Burke and Co., Printers and Binders, 1878), 26, 89.

43. *Edgefield Advertiser* December 6, 1838; James W. Hagy, *Directories for the City of Charleston, South Carolina Years 1830–31, 1835–36, 1836, 1837–1838 and 1840–1841* (Baltimore, Md.: Clearfield, 1997), 101; Samuel Hazard, *Hazard's United States Commercial and Statistical Register, Containing Documents, Facts, and other Useful Information Illustrative of the History and Resources of the American Union, and Each State: Embracing Commerce–Manufacturers–Agriculture–Internal Improvements–Banks–Currency–Finances–Education, &c, &c. Vol VI.* (Philadelphia: WM. F. Geddes, 1842), 15 and Donnie D. Bellamy, "Macon Georgia, 1832–1860: A Study in Urban Slavery," *Phylon* 45, no. 4, 305 and 308. It is not clear from records, but the two men may have been brothers as both men were from North Carolina and also worked in Charleston. Collins was heavily involved in railroad construction, serving on the Board of Directors of the Macon and Western Railroad Company.

44. Robert Collins is listed as a speculator in the 1850 census with real estate valued at $60,000. Robert H. Gudmestad defines speculators as slave traders. See his book, *A Troublesome Commerce: The Transformation of the Interstate Slave Trade* (Baton Rouge: LSU Press, 2003), 1 and Michael Tadman, *Speculators and Slaves: Masters, Traders, and Slaves in*

the Old South (Madison: University of Wisconsin Press, 1989), 8. It was common for slave traders to be "citizens of standing" as described by Michael Tadman, *Speculators and Slaves: Masters, Traders, and Slaves in the Old South* (Madison: University of Wisconsin Press, 1989), 192–200; Seventh Census of the United States, 1850; National Archives microfilm publication M452, 1009 rolls Records of the Bureau of the Census, Record Group 29; National Archives, Washington, DC The 1860 census lists Robert Collins as a banker. See Eighth Census of the United States, 1860; National Archives Microfilm publication M653, 1,438 roll. Washington, DC: National Archives and Records Administration and Barbara McCaskill, *Love, Liberation, and Escaping Slavery: William and Eliza Craft in Cultural Memory* (Athens: University of Georgia Press, 2015) 22–23.

45. Robert Collins, Essay on the Treatment and Management of Slaves. Written for the Seventh Annual Fair of Southern Central Agricultural Society, 2nd ed. (Boston: Eastburn's Press, 1853), 5–7.

46. Ellen Craft, William Craft, and R. J. M. Blackett, *Running a Thousand Miles for Freedom: Or, The Escape of William and Ellen Craft from Slavery* ([1860] Baton Rouge: Louisiana State University Press, 1999).

47. Ellen Craft, William Craft, and R. J. M. Blackett, *Running a Thousand Miles for Freedom: Or, The Escape of William and Ellen Craft from Slavery* ([1860] Baton Rouge: Louisiana State University Press, 1999).

48. *Southern Federal Union*, April 9, 1861.

49. Edward J. Balleisen, "Vulture Capitalism in Antebellum America: the 1841 Federal Bankruptcy Act and the Exploitation of Financial Distress" *Business Review* 70, no. 4, Winter 1996, 474.

50. Mildred W Goodlett, *Waterloo: A Family History of the Anderson Family of Old Laurens District of South Carolina* (Greenville, S.C.: Hiott Press, 1961), 41; Edward J. Balleisen, *Navigating Failure: Bankruptcy and Commercial Society in Antebellum America* (Chapel Hill: UNC Press, 2001); and Macon City Tax Digest 1839 and 1840. Debtors were allowed to keep $300 in personal property after their goods were sold off. According to Balleisen 40 percent of all bankruptcies were able to recover economically. Roughly 41,000 people nationally filed for bankruptcy. See *Macon Georgia Telegraph*, January 21, 1840, for advertisement for W. J. Anderson & Co.

51. William Jackson Anderson, Obituary March 1890 clipping from Thomas Memorial Library, Fort Valley, Georgia.

52. Houston County Superior Court Deed Record 1846–1850, 495–96.

53. *Georgia Telegraph*, November 3, 1846, and Houston County Superior Court Deed Records 490–92.

54. Donnie D. Bellamy, "Macon Georgia, 1832–1860: A Study in Urban Slavery," *Phylon* 45. no. 4, 305 and *Macon Messenger*, October 10, 1839. See Robert Collins is listed as a speculator in the 1850 census with real estate valued at $60,000. Seventh Census of the United States, 1850; National Archives microfilm publication M452, 1009 rolls Records of the Bureau of the Census, Record Group 29; National Archives, Washington, DC. The 1860 census lists Robert Collins as a banker. See Eighth Census of the United States, 1860; National Archives Microfilm publication M653, 1,438 roll. Washington, DC: National Archives and Records Administration. Barbara McCaskill, *Love, Liberation, and Escaping Slavery: William and*

Eliza Craft in Cultural Memory (Athens: University of Georgia Press, 2015) 22–23. It is not clear, but both Robert and Charles Collins were likely relatives as records indicate they were both from Charleston, South Carolina.

55. Bibb County Georgia Superior Court Deed and Mortgages Book 6 No. F-G 1839–1842, 4, 571.

56. *Georgia Telegraph*, January 21, 1840, and *Chronicle and Sentinel*, Augusta, Georgia, May 1, 1838.

57. Jessica M. Lepler, *The Many Panics of 1837: People, Politics, and the Creation of a Transatlantic Financial Crisis* (New York: Cambridge University Press, 2013), 12. For additional discussion of the slave trade and the economic impact on the United States see: Edward Baptist, *The Half Has Never Been Told: Slavery and the Making of American Capitalism* (New York: Basic Books, 2014); Sven Beckert, *Empire of Cotton: A Global History* (New York: Alfred A. Knopf, 2014); Caitlin Rosenthal, *Accounting for Slavery: Masters and Management* (Cambridge: Harvard University Press, 2018); Walter Johnson, *River of Dark Dreams: Slavery and Empire in the Cotton Kingdom* (Cambridge: The Belknap Press of Harvard University Press, 2013); Joshua D. Rothman, *Flush Times and Fever Dreams: A Story of Capitalism and Slavery in the Age of Jackson* (Athens: University of Georgia Press, 2012) and Calvin Schermerhorn, *The Business of Slavery and the Rise of American Capitalism 1815–1860* (New Haven: Yale University Press, 2015).

58. Bonnie Martin, *Slavery's Capitalism: A New History of American Economic Development*, ed. Sven Beckert and Seth Rockman. (Philadelphia: University of Pennsylvania Press, 2016), 108.

59. Houston County Superior Court Deed Record 1846–1850, 282–83, *History of Peach County Georgia with Addenda and Errata, Compiled by Governor Treutlen Chapter of Daughters of the American Revolution Fort Valley*, Georgia (Cherokee Publishing: Atlanta, 1972), 49.

60. *History of Peach County Georgia with Addenda and Errata, Compiled by Governor Treutlen Chapter of Daughters of the American Revolution Fort Valley, Georgia* (Atlanta: Cherokee Publishing, 1972), 49. *First One Hundred and Ten Years Houston County* (Warner Robins: Georgia, Central Georgia Genealogical Society, 1983), 114, 122, and 125. US Census Records Macon County, 1840–retrieve printed census info.

61. Houston County Superior Court Deed Record 1846–1850, 282–83.

62. Tom Downy, "Ker Boyce" South Carolina Encyclopedia http://www.scencyclopedia .org/sce/entries/boyce-ker/ accessed 6/26/2019.

63. Discussion of family history with Blanche E. Johnson, Summer 2006.

64. Bertram Wyatt-Brown, *Southern Honor: Ethics and Behavior in the Old South, Twenty-fifth Anniversary Edition* (Oxford: Oxford University Press, 2007), 295–96. Wyatt makes it clear that not all sexual liaiso54.ns between white men and black or white women was condoned but a man never acknowledged such a relationship with a black or white woman in mixed company" 297–308.

65. Joseph P. Reidy, *Masters and Slaves, Planters and Freedmen: The Transition from Slavery to Freedom in Central Georgia, 1820–1880* PhD diss., Northern Illinois University, May 1982, 21

66. By 1850, the couple had a daughter named Ophelia born a couple years after their marriage. Sometime before 1860 Ophelia Anderson died, and by 1860 the couple had an

eight-year-old son, Walter Raleigh Anderson. US Bureau of Census, *Seventh Census of the United States: Statistics of Population* (Washington, DC: Government Printing Office); US Bureau of Census, *Eighth Census of the United States: Statistics of Population* (Washington, DC: Government Printing Office).

67. Governor Treutlen Chapter Daughters of the American Revolution, *History of Peach County with Addenda and Errata* (Atlanta: Cherokee Publishing Company, 1972), 50.

68. William Jackson Anderson, Obituary March 1890 untitled clipping, Thomas Memorial Library Fort Valley, Georgia.

69. Joseph P. Reidy, *From Slavery to Agrarian Capitalism in the Cotton Planation South: Central Georgia, 1800–1880* (Chapel Hill: University of North Carolina Press, 1992), 21.

70. John P Campbell, *The Southern Business Directory and General Commercial Adviser First Part I*: (Charleston: Steam Power Press of Walker and James, 1854), 259.

71. Governor Treutlen Chapter Daughters of the American Revolution, History of Peach County with Addenda and Errata (Atlanta: Cherokee Publishing Company, 1972), 75–78.

72. Tax Digest Houston County 1856 and 1858.

73. 1850 US Federal Census–Slave Schedules Seventh Census of the United States, 1850. Washington, DC: National Archives and Records Administration, 1850, M432.

74. US Bureau of Census, *Eighth Census of the United States: Statistics of Population* (Washington, DC: Government Printing Office, Population Schedule) and John P Campbell, *Southern Business Directory and General Commercial Advertiser* (Charleston: Steam Power Press of Walker and James, 1954), 259. Most likely Cotton States Insurance also insured slaves.

75. Harold Woodman, *King Cotton and His Retainers: Financing and Marketing the Cotton Crop of the South 1800–1925* (Washington, DC: Beard Books, 2000.) 13–14, 114.

76. Robert H. Gudmestad, *A Troublesome Commerce: The Transformation of the Interstate Slave Trade* (Baton Rouge: LSU Press, 2003), 32.

77. Slave Narrative, Washington Dukes, WPA Interview, Little Rock Arkansas, 46.

78. Frederic Bancroft, *Slave-Trading in the Old South* (Baltimore: J. H. Furst and Company, 1931), 375.

79. Steven Deyle, *Carry Me Back: The Domestic Slave Trade in American Life* (Oxford: Oxford University Press, 2005), 97.

80. Houston County Tax Records 1858 William Jackson Anderson is listed as an agent for a foreign bank and by 1860 he was an agent for the People's Bank of Charleston. See Houston County Tax Records for 1860.

81. Frederic Bancroft, *Slave-Trading in the Old South* (Baltimore: J. H. Furst and Company, 1931), 145.

82. Jonathan D. Martin, *Divided Mastery: Slave Hiring in the American South* (Cambridge: Harvard University Press, 2004) 18–19; Calvin Schermerhorn, *Money over Mastery, Family over Freedom: Slavery in the Upper South* (Baltimore: John Hopkins University Press, 2011),4; Eric Foner, *Freedom's Lawmakers: A Directory of Black Officeholders During Reconstruction*, 2nd ed. (Baton Rouge: LSU Press),7; Joseph P. Reidy, *From Slavery to Agrarian Capitalism in the Cotton Plantation South: Central Georgia 1800–1880* (Chapel Hill: University of North Carolina Press, 1992), 204 and Joel Anderson "Anderson and folk" http://www.joelanderson.org/blog/2014/02/28/isaac-harold-anderson-happy-birthday-born-march-1-1835/ 10/26/2017.

83. Donnie D Bellamy, "Macon Georgia, 1823–1860: A Study in Urban Slavery," *Phylon* 45, no. 4, 303; Houston County, Georgia Tax Records; Wilma A. Dunaway *Slavery in the American Mountain South* (London: Cambridge, 2003), 99–102 and Edward Baptist, *The Half Has Never Been Told: Slavery and the Making of American Capitalism* (New York: Basic, 2014), 180.

84. Howell Cobb, *Analysis of the statutes of Georgia, in General use: with the forms and precedents necessary to their practical operation, and an appendix, containing the Declaration of Independence; the Constitution of the United States; the Constitution of the State of Georgia' General Washington's farewell address, and the naturalization laws passed by Congress* (New York: Edward O. Jenkins, 1846), 487.

85. Kent Anderson Leslie, *Woman of Color, Daughter of Privilege: Amanda America Dickson, 1849–1893* (Athens: University of Georgia Press, 1996), 41.

86. 1860; Census Place: District 9, Houston, Georgia; Roll: M653_127; Page: 963; *Family History Library Film*: 803127.

87. Advertisements indicate that William J and Company was the largest store in Fort Valley. See John P Campbell, *The Southern Business Directory and General Commercial Adviser First Part I* (Charleston: Steam Power Press of Walker and James, 1854), 259. Typically, if slaves were emancipated it was upon the death of their masters or for some heroic action. Amrita Meyers, *Forging Freedom: Black Women and the Pursuit of Liberty in Antebellum Charleston* (Chapel Hill: UNC Press, 2014), 159.

88. Howell Cobb, *Analysis of the statutes of Georgia, in general use: with the forms and precedents necessary to their practical operation, and an appendix, containing the Declaration of Independence; the Constitution of the United States; the Constitution of the State of Georgia' General Washington's farewell address, and the naturalization laws passed by Congress* (New York: Edward O. Jenkins, 1846), 487.

89. For more discussion of this tension, see Amrita Meyers, *Forging Freedom: Black Women and the Pursuit of Liberty in Antebellum Charleston* (Chapel Hill: UNC Press, 2014), 160, 175.

90. Mildred W. Goodlett, *Waterloo: A History of the Anderson Family of Old Laurens District of South Carolina*, Greenville, S.C.: Hiott Press, 1961), 41.

91. *First One Hundred and Ten Years Houston County* (Warner Robins: Georgia, Central Georgia Genealogical Society, 1983),47, and Governor Treutlen Chapter Daughters of the American Revolution, *History of Peach County with Addenda and Errata* (Atlanta: Cherokee Publishing Company, 1972), 5, 78.

92. Mildred W Goodlett, *Waterloo: A Family History of the Anderson Family of Old Laurens District of South Carolina* (Greenville, S.C.: Hiott Press, 1961), 41 and author interview with Blanche E. Johnson.

93. Discussion of Anderson family history with Blanche E. Johnson.

94. Frank J. Byrne, *Becoming Bourgeois: Merchant Culture in the South 1820–1865* (Lexington: University of Kentucky Press, 2009), 27 and 47. It is likely that William Jackson's support for the Whig party began as a result of the Panic of 1837. It was during that time that they began to emphasize economic opportunity that focused on, among other things, federally subsidized internal improvements and a national bank. Despite falling apart as national party in 1854 their ideology continued. This may explain why Whigs and Democrats were virtually equal in political influence in Fort Valley as late as 1857. Among listed Whig leaders in Houston County were Eli Warren and W. A. Matthews. *Fort Valley Leader Tribune*, December 7, 1939.

95. Wendell D. Croom, *The War-History of Company "C" (Beauregard Volunteers) Sixth Georgia Regiment (Infantry) With a Graphic Account of Each member* (Fort Valley: Advertiser Office, 1879), 7–8.

96. A. B. Caldwell, "Charles David Anderson" William J Northern, ed., in *Men of Mark in Georgia: A Complete and Elaborate History of the State from its settlement to the present time, chiefly told in the biographies and autobiographies of the most eminent men of each period of Georgia's progress and development.* Vol. 3 (Atlanta: A. B. Caldwell Publisher, 1911), 110–11 and Thelma Wilson, "Fort Valley a Century of Progress," *Georgia Review* 12, no. 3, Fall 1958, 337–38. According to Wilson Fort Valley residents used local facilities to care for wounded Confederates.

97. Mildred W Goodlett, Waterloo: *A Family History of the Anderson Family of Old Laurens District of South Carolina* (Greenville, S.C.: Hiott Press, 1961), 41. Cotton had been protected from various raids as by war's end as Georgia had more cotton than an any other state. In southwestern Georgia the bulk of the cotton harvest the was estimated to be 10,000 to 300,000 bales of cotton. C. Mildred Thompson, *Reconstruction in Georgia: Economic, Social, Political 1865–1872* (Gloucester, Mass.: Peter Smith, 1964), 96.

98. William Jackson Anderson, Obituary March 1890 clipping from Thomas Memorial Library, Fort Valley, Georgia.

99. William Jackson Anderson, Obituary 1890 clipping from Thomas Memorial Library, Fort Valley, Georgia.

100. William Jackson Anderson, Obituary 1890 clipping from Thomas Memorial Library, Fort Valley, Georgia.

CHAPTER THREE

1. *Georgia Weekly Telegraph*, March 20, 1868.

2. http://www.joelanderson.org/blog/2014/02/28/isaac-harold-anderson-happy-birthday-born-march-1-1835/ accessed 1/6/2017. William Jasper Cotter, *My Autobiography*, ed. Charles Jones (Nashville: Publishing House Methodist Episcopal, 1917), 156. Houston County Deed Book 1874. According to deed records, the land was sold to Anderson by his father, William Jackson, on December 4, 1867, but was not recorded until 1874. At the same time the land was being sold, Anderson was serving as an AME minister.

3. Donald Matthews, *Slavery and Methodism: A Chapter in American Morality 1780–1845* (Princeton: Princeton University Press, 1965), 63.

4. Albert J. Raboteau, *Slave Religion: The Invisible Institution in the Antebellum South, Updated* (Oxford: Oxford University Press, 2004) 136–37.

5. Donald G. Mathews, "The Methodist Mission to the Slaves, 1829–1844," *Journal of American History* 51, no. 4, 618.

6. Stephen Ward Angell, *Bishop Henry McNeal Turner and African American Religion in the South* (Knoxville: University of Tennessee Press, 1992), 16–21 and Albert J. Raboteau, *Slave Religion: The Invisible Institution in the Antebellum South, Updated* (Oxford: Oxford University Press, 2004), 137. According to Raboteau, in Savannah Georgia and Petersburg Virginia Black Baptist organized churches before white Baptists. Stephen Ward Angell, *Bishop*

Henry McNeal Turner and African American Religion in the South (Knoxville: University of Tennessee Press, 1992), 17–18; Donald G. Mathews, *Slavery and Methodism: A Chapter in American Morality* (Princeton: Princeton University Press, 1965), 64–65 and Kathryn Dvorak, *An African American Exodus: The Segregation of the Southern Churches* (Brooklyn: Carlson Publishing, 1991), 45–48.

7. Jimmy Smith, New Hope, Unpublished manuscript, 1970s Thomas Memorial Library, Fort Valley, Georgia.

8. Stephen Ward Angell, *Bishop Henry McNeal Turner and African American Religion in the South* (Knoxville: University of Tennessee Press, 1992), 16–17.

9. The building was modest, unpainted, and defined most by its rectangular shape and shuttered windows; inside were benches which served as pews "for women on one side and pews for men on the other," a tradition that prevailed until around 1870. History of the Fort Valley Methodist Church, Fort Valley Georgia: Homecoming Day–120th Anniversary November 13, 1960, 20, Washington Library, Macon Georgia.

10. In 1849, the new Methodist church's congregation had 567 white and 114 "colored" worshippers listed in its membership rolls, which may not signify the total number of slaves attending worship there since Methodist Conference minutes listed only members on record. In contrast, the Fort Valley slave mission at Old Pond Church served only "colored" worshippers and had a membership of 348. *Annual Conferences of the Methodist Episcopal Church South, for the Years 1848–1849* (John Early publisher, 1849).

11. Marynell S. Waite, ed., *History of the South Georgia Conference, The United Methodist Church 1866–1984: With Historical Sketches of the 713 Active Churches, South Georgia Conference Commission on Archives and History for the Bicentennial of American Methodism 1784–1984* (Dallas Texas: Taylor Publishing Company, 1984), 58 and Governor Treutlen Chapter Daughters of the American Revolution, *History of Peach County with Addenda and Errata* (Atlanta: Cherokee Publishing Company, 1972), 44. Many white congregants there typically did not bring their slaves to services with them; the gallery designated for Blacks would have been unable to seat the large number of slaves owned by the congregation's leading slaveholding families. Everett owned 248 slaves at the time of his death; the Matthews family owned 93; the Tooke family, 129; William Jackson, 37 by 1864, including Isaac Anderson. Ralph B. Flanders, "Two Plantation and County of Antebellum Georgia" *Georgia Historical Quarterly*, 12 no. 1, 1928, 5 and 13 and First *One Hundred- and Ten-Years Houston County* (Warner Robins: Georgia, Central Georgia Genealogical Society, 1983), 114–16.

12. The congregation of Usher's Chapel is still in existence. Now called Usher's Temple, the church is housed in a new building after fires destroyed the original structures.

13. History of Ushers Chapel http://www.utcme.org/about_us.aspx accessed 7/2/2019.

14. Ralph B. Flanders, "Two Plantation and County of Antebellum Georgia" *Georgia Historical Quarterly* 12, no. 1, 1928, 23 and Minutes of Superior Court 1846–1851.

15. There was no documented slave insurrection near or in Fort Valley until November 8, 1860, two days after the election of Abraham Lincoln as president in nearby Knoxville, Georgia in Crawford County. A local correspondent responding to the story days later questioned any idea of a slave insurrection describing the whole story as an, "exaggeration" but that in reality there had been among some local slaves, "a manifest intention to rebel." Local investigators found that Pennsylvania native and accused abolitionist, Amos V. Dreher,

a resident of Fort Valley, "converse[ed] freely with the negroes, at his own house about their [slaves] friends in at [sic] the north." In response, local investigators informed Dreher that "upon the next offense they would hang him from the nearest limb." Most likely the whole event was overstated and was a result of the election of Lincoln and the heightened anxiety in the South about what American slavery under Lincoln would look like. See *Weekly Georgia Telegraph*, November 16, 1860.

16. Christopher H. Owen, *The Sacred Flame of Love: Methodism and Society in Nineteenth Century Georgia* (Athens: University of Georgia Press, 1998), 79, 80–81 and Stephen Ward Angell, *Bishop Henry McNeal Turner and African American Religion in the South* (Knoxville: University of Tennessee Press, 1992), 18.

17. Christopher H. Owen, *The Sacred Flame of Love: Methodism and Society in Nineteenth Century Georgia* (Athens: University of Georgia Press, 1998), 79, 87.

18. William May Wightman, *Life of William Capers D.D., One of the Bishops of the Methodist Episcopal Church, South: Including An Autobiography* (Nashville: M.E. Church, South Publishing House, 1902), 294.

19. Donald G. Matthews, *Slavery and Methodism: A Chapter in American Morality 1780–1845* (Princeton: Princeton University Press, 1965), 69, 72.

20. Christopher H. Owen, *The Sacred Flame of Love: Methodism and Society in Nineteenth Century Georgia* (Athens: University of Georgia Press, 1998), 39.

21. *Of the Annual Conferences of the Methodist Episcopal Church South, for the Years 1845–1846*. John Early for the Methodist Episcopal Church, South. T. K. & P. G. Collins Printers, 1846, 84–85.

22. James Dunwoody, *Reminiscences of Rev. James Dunwoody of the South Georgia Conference* (Milledgeville, Georgia: Boyd Publishing Company, 1995), 44.

23. James Dunwoody, *Reminiscences of Rev. James Dunwoody of the South Georgia Conference* (Milledgeville, Ga.: Boyd Publishing Company, 1995), 43–44. Dunwoody was given the designation of superannuated for one year while he worked on his farm. Ministers that were too old, worn out from ministry or plagued with infirmity were given this designation by their conferences.

24. James Dunwoody, *Reminiscences of Rev. James Dunwoody of the South Georgia Conference* (Milledgeville, Ga.: Boyd Publishing Company, 1995), 44.

25. *Of the Annual Conferences of the Methodist Episcopal Church South, for the Years 1845–1846*. John Early for the Methodist Episcopal Church, South. T. K. & P. G. Collins Printers, 1846, 84–85. William Capers, Catechism for the use of the Methodist Missions First Part. Third Edition (Richmond: John Early, 1852), 22. https://docsouth.unc.edu/church/capers/capers.html 6/25/2019.

26. Donald G. Matthews, *Slavery and Methodism: A Chapter in American Morality 1780–1845* (Princeton: Princeton University Press, 1965), 77.

27. *Of the Annual Conferences of the Methodist Episcopal Church South, for the Years 1845–1846*. John Early for the Methodist Episcopal Church, South. T. K. & P. G. Collins Printers, 1846, 85; and Albert J. Raboteau, *Slave Religion: The "Invisible Institution" in the Antebellum South, Updated* (Oxford: Oxford University Press, 2004), 137.

28. Probationary members were candidates for membership for a six-month period while "inquiry is [was] made into their spiritual condition, their acquaintance with and

willingness to keep rules of the church and also into the genuineness of their faith," a practice that ended in 1866.

29. Charles Colcock Jones, *Suggestions on the Religious Instruction of the Negroes in the Southern States together with an Appendix Containing Forms of Church Registers, Form a Constitution, and Plans of Different Denominations of Christians* (Philadelphia: Presbyterian Board of Publications 1847) 7, 14 and 18. Italics in original text.

30. Charles Colcock Jones, *Suggestions on the Religious Instruction of the Negroes in the Southern States together with an Appendix Containing Forms of Church Registers, Form a Constitution, and Plans of Different Denominations of Christians* (Philadelphia: Presbyterian Board of Publications 1847) 7, 14 and 18. Italics in original text.

31. Charles Colcock Jones, *Suggestions on the Religious Instruction of the Negroes in the Southern States together with an Appendix Containing Forms of Church Registers, Form a Constitution, and Plans of Different Denominations of Christians* (Philadelphia: Presbyterian Board of Publications 1847), 18. Born in Liberty County, Georgia the Reverend would become a plantation owner and a staunch supporter of ministering to the slave population in his native Georgia and throughout the region. Italics not added in original text.

32. Donald G. Matthews, *Slavery and Methodism: A Chapter in American Morality 1780–1845* (Princeton: Princeton University Press, 1965), 64.

33. *Fort Valley First Methodist Church Fort Valley (Peach Co), Ga. May 1859 Dr. No. 53*, Box 62. Source number 1096, Georgia Department of Archives and History and Usher's Temple Christian Methodist Episcopal Church, "History" http://utcme.org/History.asp accessed 8/5/2019.

34. *Of the Annual Conferences of the Methodist Episcopal Church South, for the Years 1858* (Nashville: Southern Methodist Publishing House, 1859), 62 and *Annual Conferences of the Methodist Episcopal Church South, for the Years 1859* (Nashville: Southern Methodist Publishing House, 1860), 156.

35. *Annual Conferences of the Methodist Episcopal Church South, for the Year 1858* (Nashville: Southern Methodist Publishing House, 1859). 62; *Annual Conferences of the Methodist Episcopal Church South, for the Year 1859* (Nashville: Southern Methodist Publishing House, 1860), 156 and *Annual Conferences of the Methodist Episcopal Church South, for the Year 1860* (Nashville: Southern Methodist Publishing House, 1861), 259.

36. William Jasper Cotter, *My Autobiography*, ed. Charles Jones (Nashville: Publishing House Methodist Episcopal Church South, 1917), 155–56 and US Bureau of Census, *Ninth Census of the United States: Statistics of Population* (Washington, DC: Government Printing Office, Population Schedule).

37. Later, he would present an arguably well-crafted written report at the CME Church's establishment in 1870. Othal Hawthorne Lakey, *The History of the CME Church, Revised* (Memphis: CME Publishing House, 1996), 733–34.

38. Othal Hawthorne Lakey, *The History of the CME Church, Revised* (Memphis: CME Publishing House, 1996), 205–7.

39. Hunter Dickinson Farish, *The Circuit Rider Dismounts: A Social History of Southern Methodism 1865–1900* (New York: DA Capo Press) 234–35. According to Farish since, "From its earliest days American Methodism had been committed to the work of education." The domination created its first school in 1784 Cokesbury College was established in Abingdon,

Maryland. Around the same time several academies or prep schools were also established. The importance of education within Methodist circles may explain why there are a number of HBCU's created as Methodist institutions in contrast with Black Baptist schools. In review of HBCUs established there are roughly fourteen Baptist-affiliated institutions of higher education created in the nineteenth century and roughly thirty-two Methodist-affiliated institutions. Included in this list are AME, AME Zion, CME, and United Methodist Institutions. See https://en.wikipedia.org/wiki/List_of_historically_black_colleges_and_universities accessed 6/10/2019.

40. William Jackson Anderson served on the Board of Trustees for the Fort Valley Female Seminary, which was chartered in 1852. He was also likely a supporter of the Wesley annual Labor School of Houston County, the school was for the training of ministers as churches often did not have the resources to train clergy. History of Peach County Governor Treutlen Chapter DAR Cherokee Publishing. 27, 76. Helen Luce Stumbo ed., *Fort Valley Methodist History 1840–1990: A History of the Methodist Church in Fort Valley, Georgia* (Fort Valley Methodist Church, 2000) 22, 27 and 147.

41. Glenn T. Eskew," Black Elitism and the Failure of Paternalism in Postbellum Georgia," *Journal of Southern History* 58 (November 1992): 643 and William E. Montgomery, *Under Their Own Vine and Fig Tree: African American Church in the South 1865–1900* (Baton Rouge: LSU Press, 1993), 118.

42. *Annual Conferences of the Methodist Episcopal Church South, for the Year 1866* (Nashville: Southern Methodist Publishing House, 1870).

43. Clarence E. Walker, *A Rock in a Weary Land: The African Methodist Episcopal Church During the Civil War and Reconstruction* (Baton Rouge: LSU Press, 1982), 96 and 98.

44. Stephen Ward Angell, *Bishop Henry McNeal Turner and African American Religion in the South* (University of Tennessee Press, Knoxville, 1992), 74–75.

45. During the Civil War, Henry McNeal Turner befriended several influential Republicans, including Thaddeus Stevens and Charles Sumner, and helped organize the first regiment of the United States Colored Troops (USCT), where he also served as a chaplain. He organized Georgia's Republican Party and served in the State's Constitutional Convention in the winter of 1867. He mobilized support among the city's sizeable Black population and was elected as a representative in the Georgia state legislature in the spring of 1868. Stephen Ward Angell, *Bishop Henry McNeal Turner and African-American Religion in the South* (Knoxville: University of Tennessee Press, 1992), 18, 20–21. See also Eric Foner, *Freedom's Lawmakers; A Directory of Black Officeholders During Reconstruction*, revised (Baton Rouge: Louisiana State University Press, 1996).

46. Othal Hawthorne Lakey, *The History of the CME Church, Revised* (Memphis Tennessee: CME Publishing House, 1996), 143–44.

47. William Jasper Cotter, ed. Charles O. Jones, *My Autobiography* (Nashville: Publishing House Methodist Episcopal Church South, 1917), 156.

48. William Jasper Cotter, ed. Charles O. Jones, *My Autobiography* (Nashville: Publishing House Methodist Episcopal Church South, 1917), 155.

49. Historian Clarence E. Walker writes, "Emancipation enabled the ex-slaves to establish their own churches and to worship as they pleased but to a number of the freedmen the AME Church presented a threat to this process. "Clarence E. Walker, *Rock in a Weary Land:*

The African Methodist Episcopal Church During the Civil War and Reconstruction (Baton Rouge: LSU Press, 1982), 105-6.

50. Stephen Ward Angell, *Bishop Henry McNeal Turner and African American Religion in the South* (Knoxville: University of Tennessee Press, 1992), 74-75.

51. Hunter Dickinson Farish, *The Circuit Rider Dismounts: A Social History of Southern Methodism 1865-1900* (New York: Da Capo Press, 1969), 217, taken from *New Orleans Christian Advocate*, September 7, 1867.

52. *American Union*, August 16, 1867. *Minutes of the South Georgia Conference, M.E. Church South, 1867, Held in Savannah Georgia*, Burke, Boykin, and Company, Steam book and Job Printers, 1868. *Minutes of the South Georgia Conference, M.E. Church South, 1868 Held in Albany*, Burke, Boykin, and Company, Steam book and Job Printers. There is no clear date for when Anderson decided to join the AME Church, but William J. Cotter was pastor in Fort Valley in 1866 where he led a theology school and program that Isaac Anderson participated in before he was replaced as pastor by E. A. H. McGeehee in 1867. See Helen Rhea Stumbo, ed. *Fort Valley Methodist History 1840-1990: A History of the Methodist Church in Fort Valley, Georgia*, (Fort Valley: Fort Valley United Methodist Church, 2000), 150.

53. *Southern Christian Advocate* March 29, 1898, and April 19, 1868, taken from Stephen W. Angell, *Bishop Henry McNeal Turner and African American Religion in the South* (Knoxville: University of Tennessee Press, 1992), 100.

54. Hunter Dickinson Farish, *The Circuit Rider Dismounts: A Social History of Southern Methodism 1865-1900* (New York: Da Capo Press, 1969), 217, taken from *New Orleans Christian Advocate*, September 7, 1867.

55. Macon American Union, April 16, 1869 taken from Stephen Angell, *Bishop Henry McNeal Turner and African-American Religion in the South* (Knoxville: University of Tennessee Press, 1992), 102 and Clarence E. Walker, *Rock in a Weary Land: The African Methodist Episcopal Church During the Civil War and Reconstruction* (Baton Rouge: LSU Press, 1982), 106.

56. *Christian Index*, October 20, 1894.

57. *Charleston Daily News*, September 12, 1868.

CHAPTER FOUR

1. Richard Abbott, "Black Ministers and Organization of the Republican Party in the South 1867: Letters from the Field," *Hayes Historical Journal* 6, no. 1, Fall 1986.

2. Georgia was founded in 1732 by Trustees who wanted to provide a refuge for European Protestants facing persecution, incarceration and unemployment. Slavery was prohibited as trustees feared it would undermine the economic conditions of white Europeans if they had to compete with slave labor. As the population of Georgia grew, landholders soon violated the restriction. Desiring to move away from the indentured system the prohibition on slavery was reversed, and by 1752 as a royal colony Georgia began open importation of African slaves.

3. Paul Cimbala, *Under the Guardianship of the Nation: The Freedmens' Bureau and the Reconstruction of Georgia, 1865-1870* (Athens: University of Georgia Press, 2003), xiv. Cimbala's book is a masterful work that provides an overview of the challenges facing the

Freedmen's Bureau, which lasted from 1865 through 1868 in Georgia although a few efforts would continue until 1870.

4. J. D. Harris to Col. Lambert, Freedmen's Bureau Records Unregistered Letters RG 105 Roll 27 February 20, 1866 (microfilm slide 738).

5. Paul Cimbala, *Under the Guardianship of the Nation: Freedmen's Bureau and Reconstruction of Georgia 1865-1870* (Athens: University of Georgia Press, 2003), xiii–xix.

6. Eric Foner, *Reconstruction America's Unfinished Revolution: 1863-1877*, with new introduction (New York: Harper Collins, 2005), 199. Alan Conway argues that "Georgia's legislature refrained from passing a 'black code' of laws for the regulation of freedmen as such other Southern states as Mississippi had. Negroes were given the right to sue and be sued; to make and enforce contracts; to be parties to agreements and give evidence; to inherit, purchase, lease, sell, hold, and convey real and personal property." His argument ignores the fact that Blacks could not serve on juries or testify against whites, nor did they have the right to vote. Alan Conway, *Reconstruction of Georgia* (Minneapolis: University of Minnesota Press, 1966) 55-56. Susan Eva O'Donovan believes that Georgia lawmakers planned to pass harsh measures like other white Southern legislatures but removed language specifically targeting Blacks after the outrage by northern leaders over black codes passed in Mississippi and South Carolina: "The codes [that Georgia legislators] drafted were hardly less discriminatory in practice, construed as they were by men wed to the notion that capital must control labor . . . Georgia simply assigned black men and women to the margins of civil life." Susan O'Donovan, *Becoming Free in the Cotton* (Cambridge: Harvard University Press, 2007), 152–56, 210 and 318n43.

7. Alan Conway believes that this reclassification was "done out of consideration for the ignorance of freedmen who would have made the severer penalties imposed by earlier laws unjust if applied to them." Alan Conway, *Reconstruction of Georgia* (Minneapolis: University of Minnesota Press, 1966) 55-56.

8. Peter S. McGuire, "The Railroads of Georgia, 1860-1880," in *Georgia Historical Quarterly* 16, no. 3, September 1932, 183.

9. Alan Conway, *Reconstruction of Georgia* (Minneapolis: University of Minnesota Press, 1966), 104.

10. Matthew Mancini, *One Dies, Get Another: Convict Leasing in the American South 1866-1928* (Columbia: University of South Carolina Press, 1996) 42, 82.

11. *Macon Telegraph*, April 10, 1898, 1870 census. In 1837, Cole was a stockholder in the Central Railroad owning 129 shares in the Georgia based railroad and in 1855 was on the Board of Directors of the Manufacturers Bacon located in Macon, also owning 50 shares of stock. In 1849 an ad was placed in the *Georgia Telegraph* suggesting that Cole run for governor. See *Georgia Telegraph*, May 22, 1849; September 11, 1855 and *Macon Telegraph* May 16, 1837.

12. J. D. Harris to Brigadier General Tillson, Freedmen's Bureau Records Unregistered Letters RG 105 Roll 27 March 21, 1866 (microfilm slide 741-42). In a separate case, a Bureau agent reported that "Justices of the Peace and the little country lawyers . . . takes any cases, and has the freedmen committed to jail. Wherein they will have to remain for six months before they can be taken to the Superior Court and charging them enormous fees, and requiring them (as I understand) to labor on their farm to pay their fines at their great loss and detriment." J. D. Harris to Brigadier General Tillson, Freedmen's Bureau Records Unregistered Letters RG 105 Roll 27 March 26, 1866 (microfilm slide 750-53).

13. Daniel Losey to Captain N. S. Hill, Freedmen's Bureau Records Unregistered Letters RG 105 Roll 27 June 16, 1866.

14. In the 1850s, L. M. Houser moved from South Carolina to Houston County where he became a prosperous cotton planter and went from owning fourteen to forty-one slaves by 1864. In 1860, he owned $36,400 in personal property, including nearly fifty slaves and 24,000 in real estate. The 1850 Census of Georgia Slaveowners compiled by Jack F. Cox (Baltimore, Maryland: Clearfield, 1999), 151; Houston County First One Hundred years, 47, 121; US Bureau of Census, Ninth Census, District 11, Houston County, Georgia, M653_127, 1040; *Georgia Telegraph*, June 29, 1858 and *Macon Daily Telegraph*, April 27, 1869. Letter from Daniel Losey to Captain N. S. Hill, April 8, 1868, Bureau of Freedmen and Abandoned Lands at Fort Valley, Georgia, Roll 74.

15. Labor contract between John G. Davis Agent of the Bureau of Freedmen and Abandoned Lands at Fort Valley, Georgia, Roll 74. *State of Georgia vs. Houston County*, August 3, 1868. The case was filed on behalf of Sam Gilbert, a freedman against C. M. Lester by Agent Losey for violation of contract.

16. Apprentice positions were frequently listed in the newspaper seeking young people of "good moral character." During the Antebellum period in middle Georgia, apprentices were skilled positions See *Macon Telegraph*, September 22, 1828; *Macon Telegraph* June 9, 1832; *Macon Georgia Telegraph* January 22, 1838 and *Georgia Telegraph*, November 2, 1847. There were occasions where apprentices did runaway from service for example in April 11, 1854, an advertisement was placed in the *Georgia Telegraph* seeking information on Andrew Tolliard an apprenticed "boy" described as Irish who was an apprentice in the tin business. See also Herbert Gutman, *The Black Family in Slavery and Freedom, 1750–1925* (New York: Pantheon Books, 1976), 207–9, 366, 402–12.

17. Mary Nail Mitchell, *Raising Freedom's Child: Black Children and Vision of the Future of Slavery* (New York: NYU Press), 144 and 150. The Georgia apprentice law, ratified in 1866 by the Georgia legislature, applied to children and youth under twenty-one years of age who were "apprenticed" or bound over to a "master" by parents or, if orphaned, a local probate judge or ordinary; it stated that a "master shall teach the apprentice the business of husbandry, house service, or some other useful trade or occupation."

18. Barbara J Fields, *Slavery and Freedom on the Middle Ground: Maryland during the Nineteenth Century* (New Haven: Yale University Press, 1985), 140.

19. Volume 4 Records of the Assistant Commissioner for Georgia Bureau of Refugees, Freedmen and Abandoned Lands, Registers of letters Received vols. 3–5 June 1867–1869, 83–84. See also Heather Andrea Williams, *Help Me to Find My People: The African American Search for Family Lost in Slavery* (Chapel Hill: UNC Press, 2012).

20. Eventually, apprenticeship laws were overturned in US Supreme court in a case from Maryland because the Maryland laws listed African Americans as the focus of the laws. See Barbara J Fields, *Slavery and Freedom on the Middle Ground: Maryland during the Nineteenth Century* (New Haven: Yale University Press, 1985, 140 and *General Assembly of the State of Georgia Passed in Milledgeville at the Annual Session in December 1865 and January, February, and March 1866* (Milledgeville, Georgia: Boughton, Nisbet, Barnes, Moore State printers, 1866).

21. Mary Nail Mitchell, *Raising Freedom's Child: Black Children and Vision of the Future after Slavery* (New York: NYU Press, 2008), 148.

22. As a slave owner, L. M. Houser would most likely not be sympathetic to Johnson's mistreatment. The 1850 Census of Georgia Slaveowners compiled by Jack F. Cox (Baltimore, Maryland: Clearfield, 1999), 151; *Houston County First One Hundred Years*, 47, 121; US Bureau of Census, Ninth Census, District 11, Houston County, Georgia, M653_127, 1040; *Georgia Telegraph*, June 29, 1858 and *Macon Daily Telegraph*, April 27, 1869.

23. RG-Sg-S 1-1-5 Governor's Subject Files, 1868–1871, Governor Bullock ordered an investigation of Swift.

24. Letter to Brigadier general C.C. Sibley January 6, 1868 Bureau of Freedmen and Abandoned Lands at Fort Valley, Georgia, Roll 74.

25. Houston County State of Georgia, Court of Ordinary, Indenture of Apprenticeship 1866–1930.

26. Houston County State of Georgia, Court of Ordinary, Indenture of Apprenticeship 1866–1930.

27. See Freedmen's Bureau Roll 74 Contract, vol. 332 Sept. 1867–Dec 1868. For guidelines that "allowed" whipping, see *General Assembly of the State of Georgia Passed in Milledgeville at the Annual Session in December 1865 and January, February, and March 1866* (Milledgeville, Ga.: Boughton, Nisbet, Barnes, Moore State printers, 1866), 7.

28. See Freedmen's Bureau Roll 74 Target 1 Perry Letters Sent, vol. 332 Sept. 1867–Dec. 1868.

29. Acts of the General Assembly of the State of Georgia (Milledgeville, Ga.: Boughton, Nisbet, Barnes and Moore, 1866), 6–8.

30. Vol. 3 Records of the Assistant Commissioner for Georgia, Bureau of Refugees, Freedmen and Abandoned Lands. Register of Letters Received vols. 3–5 June 1867–May 1869. The three white witnesses to Johnson's beatings were J. G. Postea, Jesse Brock, and James Love. Postea was a school teacher living in nearby Crawford County. Jesse Brock was a farm laborer living in nearby Hawkinsville located in Pulaski County. James Love was a merchant in Houston County. Most likely J. G. Postea and Jesse Brock were at Love's store when they witnessed the beating of then sixteen-year-old Warren Johnson. Johnson is listed as a mulatto and an illiterate farm laborer in the 1870 census. US Bureau of Census Decennial Census Houston County; Roll M593_158; Page 6B, 41B, 397B and 471B.

31. Swift in 1864 owned 600 acres of land and 21 slaves and is listed in the 1860 census as a farmer with a property value of $7,000 and personal property mainly comprised of slaves and worth $16,000. *Houston County First One Hundred years*, 50, 121; US Bureau of Census Ninth, District 11, Houston County, Georgia, M653_127, 1009; *Acts of the General Assembly of the State of Georgia* (Milledgeville, Ga.: Boughton, Nisbet, Barnes and Moore, 1866), 239–40.

32. Freedmen's Bureau Roll 74 Target 1 Perry Letters Sent vol. 332 Sept. 1867–Dec. 1868. Houston County State of Georgia, Court of Ordinary, Indenture of Apprenticeship 1866–1930. Washington Hughes was born in South Carolina and was bound out to J. R. Haddock to learn the business of farming and provided educated to learn to read. 1870 United States Federal Census Place: Houston, Georgia; Roll: M593_158; Page: 38A.

33. Daina Ramey Berry's, *The Price for Their Pound of Flesh: The Value of the Enslaved from Womb to Grave in the Building of a Nation* (Boston: Basic Books, 2017), 58–60. Houston

County State of Georgia, Court of Ordinary, Indenture of Apprenticeship 1866–1930. 1870 United States Federal Census Place: Houston, Georgia; Roll: M593_158; Page: 38A.

34. Houston County State of Georgia, Court of Ordinary, Indenture of Apprenticeship 1866–1930 and 1870 United States Federal Census Place: Houston, Georgia; Roll: M593_158; Page: 31B. Freedmen's Bureau Roll 74 Target 1 Perry Letters Sent vol. 332 Sept. 1867–Dec. 1868.

35. H.B. Holloway, *Born in Slavery, Slave Narratives form the Federal Writer's project, 1936–1938*: Arkansas Narratives, vol. 2, part 3, 290. 1860 Census Houston County Roll M653_127 and Treutlen Chapter Daughters of the American Revolution, *The History of Peach County Georgia with Addenda and Errata* (Atlanta: Cherokee Publishing Company, 1972), 277.

36. In looking at the 1860 Houston County Slave Schedule, Clarke owned four slaves including a sixty-two-year-old man, a twenty-three-year-old woman, and two girls who were two and three years old respectively. The three-year-old may be Harriet Everett, and the two-year-old, Mary Everett. See United States of America, Bureau of Census, Eighth Census of the United States 1860, Washington, DC: National Archives and Records Administration, 1860, Freedmen's Bureau Roll 74 Target 1 Perry Letters Sent vol. 332 Sept. 1867–Dec. 1868 and 1870 US census, population schedules. NARA microfilm publication M593, 1,761 rolls. Washington, DC: National Archives and Records Administration, n.d., *General Assembly of the State of Georgia Passed in Milledgeville at the Annual Session in December 1865 and January, February, and March 1866* (Milledgeville, Georgia: Boughton, Nisbet, Barnes, Moore State printers, 1866) and Barbara J Fields, *Slavery and Freedom on the Middle Ground: Maryland during the Nineteenth Century* (New Haven: Yale University Press, 1985), 151. Not all request for family reunions were endorsed by the Bureau as was the case involving Major James Culpepper, who had served in the Sixth Georgia Infantry Regiment and a well-respected member of the Fort Valley Community. With a farm, a wife and two small children, and caring for his sixty-seven-year-old mother and matriarch Jane Culpepper, the service of an apprenticed child was helpful to the family. Agent Losey referred the matter to Captain N. S. Hill, his sub assistant commander, and Hill concluded that "the child is probably as well off with the woman as with the parties who seeks restoration to them." Years later, the Culpepper household was void of a domestic servant, which most likely was a clear indication that the apprenticed child either ran away to rejoin or was reclaimed by his or her family. Freedmen's Bureau Roll 74 Target 1 Perry Letters Sent vol. 332 Sept. 1867–Dec. 1868, Culpepper Family Papers, Emory University Stuart A. Rose Manuscript, Archives, and Rare Book Library https://findingaids.library.emory.edu/documents/culpepper638/printable/ and 1870 US and 1870 Census Houston County Roll M593_158.

37. 1870 US census, population schedules. NARA microfilm publication M593, 1,761 rolls. Washington, DC: National Archives and Records Administration.

38. *History of Peach County Georgia: Compiled by Governor Treutlen Chapter Daughters of the American Revolution Fort Valley* Georgia (Atlanta: Cherokee Publishing, 1972), 51, 81. In 1880, after J. H. Usher took over the pastorate of the church a new edifice was built across the street from Blind Academy building which was eventually torn down in 1972. During the Civil War, the Blind Academy in Macon was being used for a hospital, and nearly one hundred children housed in the facility were sent to Fort Valley. When the war ended, the children returned to Macon.

39. William Jasper Cotter, *My Autobiography*, ed. Charles Jones (Nashville: Publishing House Methodist Episcopal Church South, 1917), 155–56.

40. Freedmen's Bureau, September 14, 1868, page 157 and Sub-Assistant Commissioner's (or agents) Monthly Report on the Education of Freedmen and Refugees in Sub-District of Georgia in charge of Daniel Losey for January 1868.

41. Freedmen's Bureau, Teacher's Monthly School Report for the Month of August 1868, Anderson, Fort Valley Georgia, Adeline Wallace, Teacher. Usher's Chapel is today named Usher's Temple. The church was the first church for freedpeople in Fort Valley. The upper level served as the church, and the lower level served as a school. The school became the antecedent to the Fort Valley High and Industrial School. Gilda E. Stanbery and James Khoury, *Images of America Fort Valley* (Charleston, South Carolina: Arcadia Publishing, 2013), 53.

42. Freedmen's Bureau, Adeline E. Wallace, Teacher's Monthly School Report for the Month of April 1868, Anderson School, Fort Valley Georgia and Christopher M. Span, *From Cotton Field to Schoolhouse: African American Education in Mississippi, 1862–1875* (Chapel Hill: UNC Press, 2009), 67. Similarly, the New Hope School in Perry, east of Fort Valley, was supported by freedpeople, and George Ormond, who was a Grant Club leader, served as its main teacher. A Sabbath school at New Hope served 145 to 165 adult students. Freedmen's Bureau, George Ormond Teacher's Monthly School Report for the Month of April 1868, New Hope School, Perry, Georgia; Donald Lee Grant, *The Way It Was in the South: The Black Experience in Georgia* (Athens: University of Georgia Press, 2001), 241 and Gilda E. Stanbury and James E. Khoury, *Images of America Fort Valley* (Charleston, South Carolina: Arcadia Publishing, 2013), 8.

43. Heather Andrea Williams, *Self-Taught, African American Education in Slavery and Freedom* (Chapel Hill: UNC Chapel Hill, 2005), 125.

44. As head of the Georgia Bureau, Tillson stated his racial views before the Freedmen's' Convention proclaiming, "Do not suppose that I am advocating social equality which has never existed among colored people. All persons white and black, have the right to select their associates, and to live on terms of intimacy and social equality with those only whom they may choose and who may have like convictions, feelings, and taste with themselves." *Loyal Georgian*, January 20, 1866, and Paul Cimbala, "The 'Talisman Power': David Tillson, "The Freedmen's Bureau, and Free Labor in Reconstruction Georgia, 1865–1866," in *Civil War History* 28, no. 2, June 1982.

45. Joseph P. Reidy, *From Slavery to Agrarian Capitalism in Cotton Plantation South: Central Georgia 1800–1860* (Chapel Hill: UNC Press, 1992), 147 and *The Loyal Georgian*, January 20, 1866.

46. David Irwin, Revised Edition Georgia Code, 1866, 869–70. The code reads: "If any person, by himself or agent, shall be guilty of employing the servant of another, during the term for which he, she or they may be employed, knowing that such servant was so employed, and that his term of service was not expired—or, if any person or persons shall entice, persuade, or decoy, or attempt to entice, persuade or decoy, any servant to leave his employer either by offering higher wages, or in any way whatever during the term of service, knowing that said servant was so employed shall be deemed guilty of a misdemeanor, and upon conviction thereof, shall be fined any sum not more than two hundred dollars, or be confined in the common jail of the County, in the discretion of the Court, not to exceed

three months." In 1873, the statue was amended to apply only to written contracts with one or more witnesses. In 1882, the term "cropper" or "farm laborers" was added to "servant," and the contract was no longer required to be written. In 1876, the legislature required all agents to purchase a $100 license, and by 1877, the license increased to $500.00. See William F. Holmes, Labor Agents and the Georgia Exodus, 1899-1900 in the *South Atlantic Quarterly* 79, no. 4, Autumn 439-40 and Horace Calvin Wingo, *Race Relations in Georgia 1872-1908*, University of Georgia PhD diss., 1969, 221.

47. C. Mildred Thompson, *Reconstruction in Georgia: Economic, Social, Political 1865-1872* (Gloucester, Mass.: Peter Smith, 1964), 91; and Freedmen's Bureau Roll 74, Monthly Report of Contracts October 1867-February 1868; and William Cohen, "Black Immobility and Free Labor: The Freedmen's' Bureau and the Relocation of Black Labor, 1865-1868, in *Civil War History* 30, no. 3, September 1984, 221-22. In Southwest Georgia, homesteading was still occurring, and the Georgia legislature approved homesteading in the 1868 Georgia State Constitution, which surely encouraged African Americans to hope to acquire land. James T. Mitchell et al., ed. *The American Law Register*, new vol. 10, old series vol. 19, from January to December 1871 (Philadelphia: D. B. Canfield and Company, 1871), 4-10. http://scholarship.law.upenn.edu/cgi/viewcontent.cgi?article=2414&context=penn_law_review

48. Paul Cimbala, "The 'Talisman Power': David Tillson, the Freedmen's Bureau and Free Labor in Reconstruction Georgia, 1865-1866," in *Civil War History* 28, no. 2, June 1982, 166-67. *Loyal Georgian*, January 20, 1866.

49. By 1867, the land was made available to everyone, including former Confederates. Paul Cimbala, "The 'Talisman Power': David Tillson, the Freedmen's Bureau, and Free Labor in Reconstruction Georgia, 1865-1866," in *Civil War History* 28, no. 2 June 1982, 166-67 and Michael Lanza, "'One of the Most Appreciated Laborers of the Bureau' The Freedmen's Bureau and the Southern Homestead Act," in *The Freedmen's Bureau and Reconstruction: Reconsiderations*, ed. Paul Cimbala and Randall Miller (New York: Fordham University Press, 1999), 74.

50. After Tillson, the Freedmen's Bureau was reorganized with Colonel Caleb Sibley as its new head. For more discussion of Tilison's departure and Sibley's tenure, see Paul A. Cimbala, *Under the Guardianship of the Nation: The Freedmen's Bureau and Reconstruction of Georgia, 1865-1870* (Athens: University of Georgia Press, 1997), 42-45.

51. Freedmen's Bureau Roll 74, Monthly Report of Contracts October 1867-February 1868. White leaders used the *Georgia Weekly Telegraph* to appeal to the Freedmen's Bureau for intervention in the growing labor shortage: "We are glad that Lieut. Howard . . . urges negroes to form contracts. It is the duty to instruct the ignorant blacks . . . an eye should be had to the interest of whites. For we need not remind Lieut. Howard, nor any one else, that almost every planter has lost money by the wages he [gave] last year." *Georgia Weekly Telegraph*, January 31, 1868.

52. *Georgia Weekly Telegraph*, February 28, 1868.

53. Daniel Losey to Brigadier General C. C. Silbey, Agent of the Bureau of Freedmen and Abandoned Lands September 7, 1868.

54. Roll 74 Monthly report of Contracts filed, registered and c. in the office of Agent of the Bureau of Freedmen and Abandoned Lands at Fort Valley, Georgia November and December 1868.

55. *Fort Valley Leader and Tribune*, July 21, 1938.

56. Local historian Warren Grice's characterization of the Freedmen's Bureau is audacious in its neglect of the perspectives of most freedpeople during this period: "The Freedmen's Bureau was established and no white man could contract with a negro unless the officials of the Bureau approved the agreement. A horde of unprincipled carpetbaggers moved in and joining the few renegades, organized the ex-slaves into secret clubs, called the 'Loyal League Clubs.' They taught the negroes to hate their former masters. They led them to believe that the lands would be taken from their white owners and parceled out among the Blacks, each negro to get forty acres and a mule. The blacks refused to work, left the plantations and congregated in the towns . . . The negroes were insolent as well as dolent. White women could not move without problems from them. The lowest type of white men went among the negroes urging them to insist on social equality." Warren Grice, ed. *A History of Houston County*, Perry Georgia, 1934, 233–34.

57. In December 1866, the Georgia legislature ever mindful of Black efforts to seek better pay passed legislation making it illegal "for any person to employ any servant in the employment for and during his term of service. any person, by himself or agent shall be guilty of employing the servant during the term for which he or she may be employed knowing that such servant was so employed, and this his term of service was to expire, or if any person or persons shall entice, persuade, or decoy any servant to leave his employer, either by offering higher wages, or in any other way whatever during the term of service, knowing that said servant was so employed, shall be deemed guilty of a misdemeanor, and upon conviction thereof shall be fined any sum not more than two hundred dollars, or confined in the common jail of the county in the discretion of the court, and not to exceed three months. *Georgia Weekly*, January 21, 1867. The law would also be applied to whites, but Blacks were most often targeted.

58. Houston County, Superior Court Records, August Adjournment Term 1869.

59. Houston County, Superior Court Records, August Adjournment Term 1869.

60. Alex Lichenstein, *Twice the Work of Free Labor: The Political Economy of Convict Labor in the New South* (New York: Verso, 1996), 28–29.

61. US Census, "Defective and Dependent Delinquent Classes, 480 and Alan Conway, *Reconstruction in Georgia* (Minneapolis: University of Minnesota, 1966), 209.

62. *Macon Telegraph*, April 10, 1898, 1870 census. In 1837 Cole was a stockholder in the Central Railroad owning 129 shares in the Georgia based railroad and in 1855 was on the Board of Directors of the Manufacturers Bacon located in Macon, also owning 50 shares of stock. In 1849 an ad was placed in the *Georgia Telegraph* suggesting that Cole run for governor. See *Georgia Telegraph* May 22, 1849; September 11, 1855 and *Macon Telegraph* May 16, 1837.

63. Alex Lichtenstein, *Twice the Work of Free Labor: The Political Economy of Convict Labor in the New South* (New York: Verso, 1996), 44; and Matthew J. Mancini, *One Dies, Get Another: Convict Leasing in the American South, 1866–1928* (Columbia: University of South Carolina Press, 1996), 85.

64. Alex Lichtenstein, *Twice the Work of Free Labor: The Political Economy of Convict Labor in the New South* (New York: Verso, 1996), 51.

65. *Macon Daily Telegraph*, April 15, 1869.

66. *Executive Documents Printed By the Order of The House of Representatives During the Session of the Forty-first Congress 1869–1870*, vol. 12, no. 265 (Washington Government Printing Office, 1870), 64–68. https://books.google.com/books?id=lpoFAAAAQAAJ&pg=RA4-PA60&lpg=RA4-PA60&dq=f+h+fyall+georgia&source=bl&ots=Idtyg8JCga&sig=ACfU3UoA7IpX3nSZ5ro7FcZHA9hNfhHnCA&hl=en&sa=X&ved=2ahUKEwioiZuEke_jAhVFmKoKHV-gC-AQ6AEwCXoECA4QAQ#v=onepage&q=f%20h%20fyall%20georgia&f=false 8/7/2019. Willard E. Wight, "Negro in the Georgia Legislature: The Case of F. H. Fyall of Macon County," *The Georgia Historical Quarterly* 44, no. 1, 97. Fyall was the son of a French slave woman and a French dance master who moved to Charleston, South Carolina, from Santo Domingo and was a slave at a billiards parlor in Macon according to Eric Foner's Freedom's Lawmakers" (Baton Rouge: LSU Press, 1996), 80. Fyall was released by July 1869 as Georgia governor Rufus Bullock passed on a letter from Fyall requesting an investigation. See *Executive Documents Printed By the Order of The House of Representatives During the Session of the Forty-first Congress 1869–1870*, vol. 12:265 (Washington Government Printing Office, 1870), 56, 59. https://books.google.com/books?id=lpoFAAAAQAAJ&pg=RA4-PA60&lpg=RA4-PA60&dq=f+h+fyall+georgia&source=bl&ots=Idtyg8JCga&sig=ACfU3UoA7IpX3nSZ5ro7FcZHA9hNfhHnCA&hl=en&sa=X&ved=2ahUKEwioiZuEke_jAhVFmKoKHV-gC-AQ6AEwCXoECA4QAQ#v=onepage&q=f%20h%20fyall%20georgia&f=false accessed 8/7/2019.

67. Grant Clubs were originally known as the Loyal League, which had originated in the North during the Civil War as a patriotic organization and eventually established chapters in the South as Union troops marched southward. After the war, the League focused on freedpeople and began recruiting members to the Republican Party. The organization was of particular interest to the Republican Party, which had little if any support in the South, and a handful of Republicans like Henry Wilson and William D. Kelley traveled to the South to speak in large cities where they found support. Their greatest challenge was in rural areas where there was often open hostility to northerners and Republicans, but it was in these areas that the majority of Blacks lived. In April of 1868, the Republican congressional committee began raising funds, sending mass pro-Republican mailings and paying speakers to travel throughout the South. Because they served as leaders in their communities, Isaac Anderson was likely among the other Black ministers who served on the committee and would serve as league organizers. See Richard Abbott, "Black Ministers and the Organization of the Republican Party in the South in 1867: Letters from the Field," *Hayes Historical Journal* 6, no. 1, Fall, 1986.

68. *Christian Index*, May 1, 1868.

69. Daniel Losey to Brigadier General Sibley, July 6, 1868 Governor's Subject Files, Governor's Office, RG 1-1-5, Georgia Archives.

70. Daniel Losey to Brigadier General Sibley, July 6, 1868, Governor's Subject Files, 1868–1871, Governor's Office, RG 1-1-5, Georgia Archives. By 1870 Ballard and his family relocated to Macon, Georgia.

71. Daniel Losey to Brigadier General Sibley, July 6, 1868, Governor's Subject Files, 1868–1871, Governor's Office, RG 1-1-5, Georgia Archives. Kidada Williams, *They Left Great Marks on Me: African American Testimonies of Racial Violence from Emancipation to World War I* (New York: NYU Press, 2012), 23.

72. Joel Griffin to Governor Bullock, August 17, 1868, Governor's Subject Files, 1868–1871, Governor's Office, RG 1-1-5, Georgia Archives.

73. Shep Rogers to Daniel Losey, September 4, 1868, Governor's Subject Files, 1868–1871, Governor's Office, RG 1-1-5, Georgia Archives.

74. Paul Cimbala, *Under Guardianship of the Nation: The Freedmen's Bureau and the Reconstruction of Georgia, 1865–1870* (Athens: University of Georgia Press, 2003) 209.

75. George Ormond to Captain Hill, July 21, 1868, Governor's Subject Files, 1868–1871, Governor's Office, RG 1-1-5, Georgia Archives.

76. Joel Griffin to Governor Bullock August 24, 1868, and Joel Griffin to Governor Bullock August 30, 1868, Governor's Subject Files, 1868–1871, Governor's Office, RG 1-1-5, Georgia Archives.

77. George Ormond to Captain Hill, July 21, 1868, Governor's Subject Files, 1868–1871, Governor's Office, RG 1-1-5, Georgia Archives.

78. Richard Abbott, "Black Ministers and Organization of the Republican Party in the South 1867: Letters from the Field," *Hayes Historical Journal* 6, no. 1, Fall 1986.

79. *Atlanta Weekly Sun*, February 11, 1873.

CHAPTER FIVE

1. Nelson Tift, *The Condition of Affairs in Georgia: Statement of Hon. Nelson Tift to the Reconstruction Committee of the House of Representatives, Washington, February 18, 1869* (United States, 1869) 1–4.

2. Nelson Tift, *The Condition of Affairs in Georgia: Statement of Hon. Nelson Tift to the Reconstruction Committee of the House of Representatives, Washington, February 18, 1869* (United States, 1869), 52.

3. Nelson Tift, *The Condition of Affairs in Georgia: Statement of Hon. Nelson Tift to the Reconstruction Committee of the House of Representatives, Washington, February 18, 1869* (United States, 1869), 52–55.

4. Nelson Tift, *The Condition of Affairs in Georgia: Statement of Hon. Nelson Tift to the Reconstruction Committee of the House of Representatives, Washington, February 18, 1869* (United States, 1869), 234.

5. Forty-First Congress 1st Session, House of Representatives, Mis. Doc 34. Conditions of Affairs in Georgia. Nelson Tifts Rejoinder to the Letter of Governor Bullock Relative to the Condition of the affairs in Georgia in Nelson Tift, *The Condition of Affairs in Georgia: Statement of Hon. Nelson Tift to the Reconstruction Committee of the House of Representatives, Washington, February 18, 1869* (United States, 1869), 5. Nelson Tift would later finish out his second year of his two-year term in March 3, 1869. When he ran for office again, he won, but because of strong ties to the Confederacy in supporting the war effort he was not allowed to be seated. Republican Richard Whitley would end up being elected and representing Southwest Georgia in the House. John D. Fair, "Nelson Tift: A Connecticut Yankee in King Cotton's Court," *Georgia Historical Quarterly* 88 (fall 2004) Susan O'Donovan, ed., "The Journal of Nelson Tift," *Journal of Southwest Georgia History* 3–8, 10–12, Fall 1985–Fall 1993, Fall 1995–Fall 1997. Nelson Tift, "Dougherty County: Historical Address," *Journal of Southwest Georgia*

History 4, Fall 1986. "Nelson Tift," Biographical Directory of the United States Congress, http://bioguide.congress.gov/scripts/biodisplay.pl?index=T000269 accessed 6/7/2019.

6. Russell Duncan, *Freedoms' Shore: Tunis Campbell and the Georgia Freedmen* (Athens: University of Georgia Press, 1986), 69. In Georgia, the most well-known AME Zion leader certainly was Tunis Campbell Sr., the same man who had challenged the legality of William Jackson Anderson and at least four other white members of the Georgia Senate in January 1870 for their support of the Confederacy. A freeborn native of New Jersey, Tunis Campbell Sr., at the war's end, oversaw land claims and land resettlement on the Georgia Sea Islands. He also served as vice-president of the Republican Party, registrar, justice of the peace, and delegate to the 1868 Georgia state constitutional convention. The AME Zion elder had been a staunch abolitionist opposing colonization of Blacks and in the 1850s had shared the speaker's stage with Frederick Douglass. In the spring of 1868, Campbell, like Isaac Anderson, ran for office, but unlike Anderson, Campbell won his election to the Georgia Senate, where he represented the Second District, comprising Mcintosh, Tattnall, and Liberty Counties with sizeable Black majorities. Glenn Eskew, "Paternalism among Augusta's Methodist: Black, White, and Colored," in *Race, Religion, and Gender in Augusta, Georgia: Paternalism in a Southern City*, ed. Edward J. Cashin and Glenn T. Eskew (Athens: University of Georgia Press, 2001), 96. Campbell was also known as, "preacher to prostitutes and thieves" as he lived and worked in New York City as a head waiter. Jaqueline Jones, *Saving Savannah: The City and the Civil War* (New York: Vintage, 2008), 179.

7. Congressional Globe, Senate, 40th Congress, 3rd Session.

8. *Journal of the Senate of the State of Georgia, at the Annual Session of the General Assembly, Atlanta January 10, 1870* (Public Printer: Atlanta, Georgia, 1870), 4–6.

9. Tunis G. Campbell, *The Sufferings of Rev. T. G. Campbell and His Family in Georgia* (Washington, DC: Enterprise Publishing Company, 1877), 12.

10. Tunis G. Campbell, *The Sufferings of Rev. T. G. Campbell and His Family in Georgia* (Washington, DC: Enterprise Publishing Company, 1877), 11.

11. Tunis G. Campbell, *The Sufferings of Rev. T. G. Campbell and His Family in Georgia* (Washington, DC: Enterprise Publishing Company, 1877), 12.

12. *Atlanta Intelligencer*, January 11, 1870.

13. Tunis G. Campbell, *The Sufferings of Rev. T. G. Campbell and His Family in Georgia* (Washington, DC: Enterprise Publishing Company, 1877).

14. *Journal of the Senate of the State of Georgia at the Annual Session of the General Assembly, Atlanta, January 10, 1870* (Atlanta: Public Printer) 4–7. and Duncan, *Freedom's Shore*, 69–70.

15. *Journal of the Senate at an Extra Session of the General Assembly of the State of Georgia, Convened under the Proclamation of the Governor, March 25th, 1863* (Milledgeville, Ga.: Boughton, Nisbet, And Barnes, State Printers, 1863) http://www.docsouth.unc.edu/imls/gaextr63/georgia.html accessed 8/26/2010. In the Georgia House twenty-one members were dismissed.

16. William Jackson was appointed notary public to aid in conducting the affairs of a bank and was never sworn. *Georgia Weekly Telegraph* and *Georgia Journal and Messenger*, January 25, 1870. See also *Georgia Before the Senate Judiciary Committee* (Washington, DC) February 9, 1870. Under Farrow's definition commissioners and state librarians could also

be charged. See C. Mildred Thompson, *Reconstruction in Georgia: Economic, Social, Political 1865–1872* (Gloucester, Mass: Peter Smith, 1964), 263.

17. Dr. William Asbury Matthews was notably actively in his position on the South seceding the Union, "seeking redress through Congress for the wrongs against the South." Governor Treutlen Chapter, D.A.R. *History of Peach County Georgia*, Cherokee Publishing Company, 37.

18. Edward Barham Young, *The Negro in Georgia Politics, 1867–1877*, Emory, Masters of Science, 1955, 42–45.

19. *Journal of the House of Representative of the State of Georgia at the Annual Session of the General Assembly Commenced at Atlanta January 10, 1870* (Atlanta: Public Printer, 1870), 366–68.

20. *Journal of the House of Representatives of the State of Georgia at the Annual Session of the General Assembly Commenced at Atlanta, January 10, 1870* (Atlanta: Public Printer, 1870), 366–67.

21. *Journal of the House of Representatives of the State of Georgia at the Annual Session of the General Assembly Commenced at Atlanta, January 10, 1870* (Atlanta: Public Printer, 1870), 368.

22. Hoping to remind readers of Griffin's historic pedigree, in a letter to the editor of the *American Union*, James Swayze, a former Freedmen's Bureau agent turned newspaperman highlighted Griffin's notable father and connection to the nation's founding, highlighting his service in the first continental convention of Virginia and his "longstanding residen[ce] in the county." *American Union*, January 14, 1870, *American Union*, February 11, 1870.

23. Christopher H. Owen, *The Sacred Flame of Love: Methodism and Society in Nineteenth Century Georgia* (Athens: University of Georgia Press, 1998), 129.

24. W. Fitzhugh Brundage, "The Roar on the Other Side of Silence: Black Resistance and White Violence in the American South, 1880–1940," in W. Fitzhugh Brundage, *Under the Sentence of Death: Lynching in the South* (Chapel Hill: UNC Press, 1993), 277.

25. H. B. Holloway, *Born in Slavery, Slave Narratives form the Federal Writer's Project, 1936–1938*: Arkansas Narratives, vol. 2, part 3, H. B. Holloway, 293–94.

26. Hymn published in the CME hymnal published in 1891 and written by Lucius H. Holsey and F. M. Hamilton. Lucius H. Holsey, *The Autobiography of Bishop L. H. Holsey*, intro. by George E. Clary (Keysville Georgia: Briar Creek Press, 1988), 5.

27. E. Franklin Frazier, *The Negro Church in America*, 45.

28. *American Union*, August 16 1867.

29. Edward L. Wheeler, *Uplifting the Race: The Black Minister in the New South 1865–1902* (Lanham: University Press of America, 1986), 17.

30. Judith Herman, *Trauma and Recovery: The Aftermath of Violence—From Domestic Abuse to Political Terror* (New York: Basic Books, 2015), 1.

31. Judith Herman, *Trauma and Recovery: The Aftermath of Violence—From Domestic Abuse to Political Terror* (New York: Basic Books, 2015), 207.

32. Judith Herman, *Trauma and Recovery: The Aftermath of Violence—From Domestic Abuse to Political Terror* (New York: Basic Books, 2015), 177.

33. Judith Herman, *Trauma and Recovery: The Aftermath of Violence—From Domestic Abuse to Political Terror* (New York: Basic Books, 2015), 207.

34. S. B. Wallace, *What the National Government is Doing for Our Colored Boys: The New System of Slavery in the South*. Two Sermons delivered at the Israel CME church Washington, DC: by its pastor Rev. S. B. Wallace, MD, August 19 and September 9, 1894. African American Perspectives: Pamphlets from the Daniel A. P. Murray Collection, 1818–1907, 36–38.

35. Edmund Drago, *A Splendid Failure: Black Politicians and Reconstruction in Georgia* (Athens: University of Georgia Press, 1992), 28.

36. Hunter Dickerson Farish, *The Circuit Rider Dismounts: A Social History of Southern Methodism 1865-1900* taken from *New Orleans Christian Advocate*, September 7, 1867, and November 7, 1868. (New York: Da Capo Press, 1969), 221-22. Years after the establishment of the CME Church, Bishop Atticus Haygood, future president of Emory College and editor of the *Nashville Christian Advocate*, known as moderate among Southern Methodist leaders, in his book, *Our Brothers in Black*, clarified his ultimate belief in Black inferiority and harkened back to a centuries-old perspective: "They spend their money freely while it last, much as children do. Instance, a colored man, who lives near me and who has no income but his wages as a common laborer, recently gave seven dollars for a flashy bound family Bible, being overcome by the arrangement at the back of it for receiving family photographs . . . The wisdom of providence is justified in an improved and better race. They needed for a time, the guidance and protection of a stronger people, They found such a race in the Southern whites as they could have found it nowhere else in the United States." Atticus Haygood, *Our Brother in Black: His Freedom and His Future* (New York: Phillips and Hunt, 1889), 12 and 34. Haygood was not alone in his sentiment. Bishop Charles B. Galloway, who was also a moderate, condemned the mob lynching of African Americans while arguing that "whites will retain political supremacy, for intelligence and wealth and should control the administration of governmental affairs." I. A. Newby, *Jim Crow's Defense: Anti-Negro thought in America, 1900-1920* (Baton Rouge: LSU Press, 1965), 86-87 and Glenn Eskew, "Black Elitism and Failure of Paternalism in Postbellum Georgia: The Case of Bishop Lucius Henry Holsey," *Journal of Southern History* 58, no. 4, November 1992, 649.

37. *Christian Advocate*, January 7, 1871.

38. The former issue elicited a spirited debate in which one Reverend from Mississippi argued that an educational requirement was a "high notion." To this, Anderson responded, "In his District there was a rush to become preachers. All the Lord's people felt called. The Presiding Elder [Anderson] could hardly keep them down if they didn't look out, the new bishops would be run over. Must put up the fence." Ultimately, William H. Miles of Kentucky, the first elected CME bishop brought the debate to an end when he pronounced, "Any man that has sense enough to preach, can learn to read, if he want to, in six months . . . Let these persons be exhorters–there is no such rule for exhorters; and that is their place. Say to them, when they apply for a license to preach go back and learn to read; stay as you are till you learn to read. And this will stimulate them." *Christian Advocate*, January 7, 1871. An exception was made for those already licensed but the rule applied for future ministers in the denomination.

39. *Christian Advocate*, January 7, 1871.

40. *Christian Advocate*, January 7, 1871.

41. Anderson's successful run for office may have inspired Little John Scurlock who, served as assistant editor at the *Christian Index*, to resign his post and run for the Mississippi legislature in 1872. Anderson would eventually face local opposition to his political activity by 1873.

42. W. Fitzhugh Brundage, "The Roar on the Other Side of Silence: Black Resistance and White Violence in the American South, 1880-1940." W. Fitzhugh Brundage, *Under the Sentence of Death: Lynching in the South* (Chapel Hill: UNC Press, 1993), 277.

43. As a Southern-based denomination comprised primarily of rural freedpeople, the CME Church followed six core tenets described by Katherine Dvorak in *An African American Exodus: The Segregation of the Southern Churches: Initiative*, or a challenge to any notion of passivity in CME leaders as well as a rebuttal to any notion that they were cast out by Southern whites; *religious legitimation*, which validated their recognition as a distinct, all-Black, religious body like the AME and AME Zion Churches which formed as religious bodies distinct from the Northern Methodist Church in the 1790s; *congregational polity*, which fostered a connection and a measure of support from the Southern Methodist Church; *religious revivalism* leading to a surge in Black membership in the Methodist Church and an expansion of Black religious leadership in Houston County; *internal church politics* which existed in Black churches during slavery and became visible after Emancipation; and *segregation and separation* which were vital to autonomy and essential to Southern Blacks who were living out their faith. Katherine Dvorak, *An African American Exodus: The Segregation of the Southern Churches* (Brooklyn, N.Y.: Carlson Publishing, 1991), 114–19.

44. According to Edmund Drago, there were roughly twenty-three of the sixty-nine men who served in the Georgia Constitutional Convention and state legislature between 1867 and 1872 that were ministers, twenty of which were Methodist or likely Methodist in their affiliation. See Edmund Drago, *A Splendid Failure: Black Politicians and Reconstruction in Georgia* (Athens: University Press of Georgia, 1992), 20 and Appendix Black Legislators and Convention Delegates, 1867–1872.

45. Lucius H. Holsey, "The Colored Methodist Episcopal Church" in *Afro-American Religious History: A Documentary History*, Milton C. Sernett ed. (Durham: Duke University Press, 1985), 237

46. Lucius H. Holsey, *The Autobiography of Bishop L. H. Holsey (Re-printed)* Introduction by George E. Clary, Jr., (Keysville, Georgia: Briar Creek Press, 1988), 17.

47. Lucius H. Holsey, *The Autobiography of Bishop L.H. Holsey (Re-printed)* Introduction by George E. Clary, Jr., (Keysville, Georgia: Briar Creek Press, 1988), 24–27 and Glenn Eskew, "Black Elitism and Failure of Paternalism in Postbellum Georgia: The Case of Bishop Lucius Henry Holsey," *Journal of Southern History* 58, no. 4, November 1992, 638–45.

48. Othal Lakey, *The History of the CME Church (Revised)* Memphis, Tennessee: CME Publishing House, 1996), 737–38.

49. John Brother Cade, *Holsey–The Incomparable* (New York: Pageant Press, 1969), 60–61.

50. 1870 census population schedules. NARA microfilm publication M593, 1761 Washington, DC National Archives and Records Administration.

51. *Houston Home Journal*, December 17, 1870, and *Weekly Sumter Republican*, December 23, 1870.

52. John Brother Cade, *Holsey, the Incomparable* (New York: Pageant Press, 1969), 21.

53. Eric Foner, *Freedom's Lawmakers: A Directory of Black Officeholders During Reconstruction*, 2nd ed. (Baton Rouge: LSU Press, 1996), xxi.

54. Edward L. Wheeler, *Uplifting the Race: The Black Minister in the New South 1865–1902* (Latham: University Press of America, 1986), 15. Alabama had a sizable CME population in 1890 with 18,940 followed by Tennessee with 18,906, but in both states the AME had a comparable membership of 18, 398 in Alabama and 23,718 in Tennessee. *Report on the Statistics*

of Churches in the United States at the Eleventh Census, Henry K. Carroll, Washington, DC Government Printing Office, 1894, 605–6.

55. Stephen Ward Angell, *Bishop Henry McNeal Turner and African American-Religion in the South* (Knoxville: University of Tennessee Press, 1992), 71–76.

56. I. H. Anderson was among attendees at the Presiding Elders Georgia Conference held in the summer of 1870. *Journal, General Conference, M.E. South, 1870*, pp. 227–28. *The Doctrines and Discipline of the Methodist Episcopal Church, South* (Nashville: E. Stevenson & F. A. Owen, Agents for the Methodist Episcopal Church, South, 1856), 52–55. There are no known early editions of the CME book of discipline from the 1870s. Because the CME church closely followed the Southern Methodist *Book of Discipline* it is most likely that CME adopted similar policies for duties of presiding elders within their denomination.

57. It was in correspondence to National Republican leaders that Henry McNeal Turner described his political activity in Georgia being facilitated under the garb of a presiding elder. See Richard Abbott, *Black Ministers and the Organization of the Republican Party in the South in 1867: Letters from the Field* 6, no. 1, Fall, 1986. https://www.rbhayes.org/research/hayes-historical-journal-black-ministers-and-the-republican-party/ accessed 2/20/2020.

58. *Third Annual Minutes of the Colored Georgia Conference held with the Colored Methodist Church of Augusta, Georgia., January 4th, 5th, 6th, 7th, and 9th, 1871* (Augusta, Ga.: Georgia Republican Printing Company, 1871), 11.

59. Albert Raboteau, *Slave Religion: The "Invisible institution" in the Antebellum South*, (Oxford: Oxford University Press, 2004), 177 and Marriage Licenses vol. F 1865–1871 Houston County Court House, pg. 193.

60. The Methodist Episcopal Church in the North found its most visible proponent in John C. Caldwell, who was native to Georgia and a former pastor of one of the larger Southern Methodist churches in Savannah. In the summer of 1865, Caldwell offered two sermons to his church in Newman, Georgia, espousing his belief that condemned slavery and argued it corrupted the Church. Shocked by the former Confederate supporter his congregation appealed to church leaders who removed him. After appeals to Bishop Pierce and to the military commander at the time Major General George H. Thomas in the fall of 1865 Caldwell was reinstated to his position as pastor of the Newman church. He would travel north where MEC leaders hailed him as a hero for his stanch against slavery and he would join the northern based denomination shortly after. Caldwell would make inroads into the Black community in supporting Black education and politics as an organizer of the Loyal League/ Union League chapters. By promoting civil and political rights along with the provision of buildings for Black worshippers there was a significant draw to the denomination by freedmen and women. With an established and well-funded missionary organization the denomination made inroads into the South most notably in South Carolina. Daniel W. Stowell, *Rebuilding Zion: The Religious Reconstruction of the South, 1863–1877* (Oxford: Oxford University Press, 1998), 9, 60–61, 138, 150–53 and William E. Montgomery, *Under Their Own Vine and Fig Tree: African American Church in the South 1865–1900* (Baton Rouge: LSU Press, 1993), 72–73.

61. Edmund Drago, *A Splendid Failure: Black Politicians and Reconstruction in Georgia* (Athens: University of Georgia Press, 1992), 2; Reginald F. Hildebrand, *The Times Were Strange and Stirring: Methodist Preachers and the Crisis of Emancipation* (Durham: Duke

University Press, 1995), 50–72 and Gayraud S. Wilmore, *Black Religion and Black Radicalism: An Interpretation of Religious History of Afro-American People* Second edition (New York, Orbis, 1993), 122–24. For an in-depth study of the AME Church and the denomination's history of activism, see Richard S. Newman, *Freedom's Prophet: Bishop Richard Allen, the AME Church, and the Black Founding Fathers* (New York: NYU Press, 2008) and Denis C. Dickerson, *The African Methodist Episcopal Church: A History* (Cambridge: Cambridge University Press, 2019).

62. Stephen Ward Angell, *Bishop Henry McNeal Turner and African American-Religion in the South* (Knoxville: University of Tennessee Press, 1992), 104; Governor Treutlen Chapter Daughters of the American Revolution, *History of Peach County with Addenda and Errata*, (Atlanta: Cherokee Publishing Company, 1972), 57–58; Daniel W. Stowell, *Rebuilding Zion: The Religious Reconstruction of the South 1863–1877* (Oxford: Oxford University Press, 1998), 95–97 and Edward L. Wheeler, *Uplifting the Race: The Black Minister in the New South 1865–1902* (Latham: University Press of America, 1986), 15. Alabama had a sizable CME population in 1890 with 18,940 followed by Tennessee with 18,906, but in both states, the AME had a comparable membership of 18, 398 in Alabama and 23,718 in Tennessee. Henry K. Carroll, *Report on the Statistics of Churches in the United States at the Eleventh Census* (Washington, DC Government Printing Office, 1894), 605–6.

63. William B. Campbell was also a CME pastor who worked to establish the denomination in Georgia. According to Stephen Angell, once the CME Church was established, the AMEs saw a drop from roughly five thousand members a year to fewer than five hundred members a year. Stephen Ward Angell, *Bishop Henry McNeal Turner and African American Religion in the South* (Knoxville: University of Tennessee Press, 1992), 102–3.

64. Othal Hawthorne Lakey, *The History of the CME Church*, revised (Memphis: CME Publishing House, 1996), 214–16.

65. J. W. Hood, *One Hundred Years of the African Methodist Episcopal Church; or the Centennial of African Methodism* (New York City: A.M.E. Zion Book Concern, 1895), 364–36 and Daniel W. Stowell, *Rebuilding Zion: The Religious Reconstruction of the South 1863–1877* (Oxford: Oxford University Press, 1998), 97.

66. Daniel W. Stowell, *Rebuilding Zion: The Religious Reconstruction of the South 1863–1877* (Oxford: Oxford University Press, 1998), 96.

67. *Houston Home Journal*, January 5, 187.

68. There is no evidence explaining why Samuel Anthony Cobb opted not to run for office the fall of 1870, but surely the violence he would face as well as that of his family was a consideration. It is not even clear if Cobb still lived in Houston County by November 1870, but either way there were familiar faces running for office on the Republican ticket. The census for Houston County was taken in June 1870, and there is no clear Samuel or Anthony Cobb listed in the census, which is why it is unclear if Cobb was living in Houston County during the election.

69. Joseph P. Reidy, *From Slavery to Agrarian Capitalism in Cotton Plantation South: Central Georgia 1800–1860* (Chapel Hill: UNC Press, 1992), 212.

70. Edmund Drago, *A Splendid Failure: Black Politicians and Reconstruction in Georgia* (Athens: University of Georgia Press, 1992), 162.

71. *Testimony taken by the Joint Select Committee to inquire into The Conditions of Affairs in the Late Insurrectionary States Georgia vol. 2* (Washington: Government Printing Office, 1872), 1034–1035.

72. *Testimony taken by the Joint Select Committee to inquire into The Conditions of Affairs in the Late Insurrectionary States Georgia vol. 2* (Washington: Government Printing Office, 1872), 1182–94 and 1034–1142.

73. Judge Cole was extremely critical of Henry McNeal Turner, a candidate for office from Macon. In a letter written to the court by James Fitzpatrick, an Irishman and a Republican candidate running for office with Turner, described Judge Cole, "He is a bitter enemy of Turner's in fact he is a bitter enemy of republicanism . . . He was a rampant reb., and ready and willing at all times to respond to the wished of rebs." *Testimony taken by the Joint Select Committee to inquire into The Conditions of Affairs in the Late Insurrectionary States Georgia vol. 2* (Washington: Government Printing Office, 1872), 1036–1038 and 1182–92.

74. Stephen Angell, *Bishop Henry McNeal Turner and African American Religion in the South* (Knoxville: University of Tennessee Press, 1992), 95; *Georgia Weekly Telegraph*, June 4, 1869 and *Macon Daily Telegraph*, June 10, 1869.

75. *Houston Home Journal*, January 5, 1871.

76. *Houston Home Journal*, January 5, 1871. See also *Houston Home Journal*, January 12th and 19th, 1871.

77. Third Annual Minutes of the Colored Georgia Conference held with the Colored Methodist Church of Augusta Georgia, January 4th, 5th, 6th, 7th and 9th, 1871 (Augusta Georgia: Georgia Republican Printing, 1871). It is not clear why all three men were selected as Isaac Anderson was a state senator and could surely make sure the denomination was recognized. In reality it may have been a way to depoliticize the newly founded church by having Brown and especially Holsey participate.

78. The pledge amount was a significant sum of $84.00 equivalent to $1,626.00 in 2017. CPI Calculator https://www.minneapolisfed.org/community/financial-and-economic-education/cpi-calculator-information.

79. Third Annual Minutes of the Colored Georgia Conference held with the Colored Methodist Church of Augusta Georgia, January 4th, 5th, 6th, 7th and 9th, 1871 (Augusta Georgia: Georgia Republican Printing, 1871).

80. Third Annual Minutes of the Colored Georgia Conference held with the Colored Methodist Church of Augusta Georgia, January 4th, 5th, 6th, 7th and 9th, 1871 (Augusta Georgia: Georgia Republican Printing, 1871).

81. Eric Foner, *Freedom's Lawmakers: A Directory of Black Officeholders During Reconstruction*, 2nd ed. (Baton Rouge: LSU Press), 38 and Russell Duncan, *Freedom's Shore: Tunis Campbell and the Georgia Freedmen* (Athens: University of Georgia Press, 1986), 108

CHAPTER SIX

1. Georgia was among seven states that succeeded from the Union by February 1861 and before the firing upon Fort Sumter. Tennessee would succeed later that year in June and end Reconstruction in 1870, a year before Georgia. Eric Foner, *Freedom's Lawmakers: A Directory of Black Officeholders During Reconstruction*, 2nd ed. (Baton Rouge: LSU Press, 1996), xiii.

2. Horace Calvin Wingo, *Race Relations in Georgia 1872–1900*, PhD diss., Emory, 1962, 12–13. Factions within the Georgia Republican party added to a split and lack of strong support within the party. *Houston Home Journal*, January 16, 1871

3. Warren Grice, ed. *A History of Houston County*, 1930, 233–34. Interestingly, Grice fails to mention Isaac Anderson, and a possible reason for this omission may have been Anderson's relation to William Jackson, which was most likely an open secret in the county. William Jackson was known to "love his children" and be "quick to resent an insult to either himself, family or friends," and influential white leaders were mindful of how far to push the powerful banker and businessman. The close connection between the two men was well known throughout Houston County, and although William Jackson was known for his support of the Confederacy and opposition to the rights of freedpeople during his tenure in the state legislature, the protection he may have provided to Anderson could have been excused by claiming that his former slave was under the influence of Northern whites and radicals. This explanation of the actions of Black leaders, though not rooted in truth, would become the basis for much "Lost Cause" rhetoric after Reconstruction. References taken from William Jackson Anderson Obituary.

4. Alan Conway, *The Reconstruction of Georgia* (Minnesota: University of Minnesota Press, 1966), 200–2. Even with the weakened status of the Republican Party during the 1871 legislative session of the State Assembly, Anderson joined with his Black counterparts in the State Senate to try and maintain the Republican agenda. One of their tasks was to hold on to Georgia's congressional seats. Twelve months earlier, Foster Blodgett, a Republican and a close associate of Governor Bullock, had declared his election to the US Senate valid, but Democrats argued that their candidate, Thomas M. Norwood, was duly elected. Norwood was a true secessionist at heart, and in *Vindication of the South in a Review of American Political History*, published after his death, he argued that the South was correct in succeeding from the Union. Thomas Mason Norwood, *The Vindication of the South: In A Review of American Political History* (Savannah, Ga.: Braid and Hutton, 1917). The *Norwood vs. Blodgett* case went before the Senate Congressional Committee on Privileges and Elections, and the committee agreed with Democrats that Norwood should be seated. A month before the case went before the Senate committee, Isaac Anderson, Tunis Campbell Sr., Thomas Crayton, James Deveaux, and George Wallace, "respectfully" entered a letter to the minutes of the Senate Journal expressing their protest of Norwood's seating. *The Compilation of Senate Election Cases From 1789–1913* (Washington, DC Government printing Office, 1913), 389–95. https://books.google.com/books?id=WN5GAQAAIAAJ&pg=PA389&lpg=PA389&dq=norwood+v+blodgett&source=bl&ots=EgDevOST8M&sig=asEgU1l6pfvZBordFtH2QiNftck&hl=en&sa=X&ved=oahUKEwjZy_e-qoXbAhWLjFQKHTpXDjUQ6AEIKTAA#v=onepage&q=norwood%20v%20blodgett&f=false accessed 6/14/2018. *Journal of the Georgia Senate*, 92.

5. Houston County Superior Court Amy Adjournment term 1871 *The State vs. George Ormond*.

6. Houston County Superior Court Amy Adjournment term 1871 *The State vs. George Ormond*.

7. Houston County Superior Court Amy Adjournment term 1871 *The State vs. George Ormond*.

8. During Ormond's trial, Democratic Party leader Andrew S. Giles also testified against Ormond. Giles was born in Houston County in 1841 and later served as a Confederate soldier in the Army of Tennessee under Generals Johnston and Bragg. He later served as Houston County Ordinary from 1873–1885. He served in a number of Democratic leadership positions including the head of the local county Democratic committee and then serving on the state Democratic committee. In 1894, he was elected to represent Houston County in the state legislature. Orville A. Park, ed., Report of the Sixteenth Session of the Georgia Bar Association Held at Warms Springs, Georgia Thursday, July 6th, and July 7th, 1899 (Atlanta: Franklin Printing and Publishing Co., 1899), 166–67. W.L. Grice was a former colonel in the Thomas Loyless ed., Confederate Army. Georgia Public Men (Atlanta: Byrd Printing Company, 1899) 123. https://books.google.com/books?id=dbpFAQAAMAAJ&pg=PA167&lpg=PA167&dq=A+S+Giles+Fort+Valley+Georgia+ordinary&source=bl&ots=zIsdd-gydM&sig=B69iOBkcaHsLlRbGS67buBefxTI&hl=en&sa=X&ved=0ahUKEwiJ87ve9ZnbAhU6FjQIHXPuD6AQ6AEImQEwDQ#v=onepage&q=A%20S%20Giles%20Fort%20Valley%20Georgia%20ordinary&f=false

9. It is not clear why Ormond was not convicted in light of other frivolous charged often directed at African Americans in addition to the standing of A.S. Giles in Houston County. Likely the reason Ormond was not found guilty was due to the growing federal oversight in state elections in the South. By May 1871 Congress had passed the last Enforcement Acts leading to a growing federal and increasingly aggressive oversight of elections.

10. *The Condition of Affairs in the Late Insurrectionary State in Georgia vols. 1 and 2* (Washington: Government printing Office, 1872).

11. H. B. Holloway, *Born in Slavery, Slave Narratives form the Federal Writer's Project, 1936–1938: Arkansas Narratives*, vol. 2, part 3, 293.

12. These organizations had existed early in the state's history and develop as a result of restrictions on whites participating in local militias. Sally E. Hadden, *Slave Patrols: Law and Violence in Virginia and the Carolinas* (Cambridge, Mass.: Harvard University Press, 2001), 205–7.

13. Sally E. Hadden, *Slave Patrols: Law and Violence in Virginia and the Carolinas* (Cambridge, Mass: Harvard University Press, 2001), 209.

14. Warren Grice, ed., *A History of Houston County* (1934 Perry, Georgia Public Library).

15. Sally E. Hadden, *Slave Patrols: Law and Violence in Virginia and the Carolinas* (Cambridge, Mass.: Harvard University Press, 2001), 208.

16. *Rome Courier*, October 27, 1871. Outdone by what he viewed as unwarranted federal intervention into Georgia, State Senator James R. Brown offered a resolution, "Whereas it has been alleged by certain politicians North and South, who esteem the success of the party to which they belong and the accomplishment of their political purposes and are in the habit of committing great outrages upon the peaceable and law aiding citizens of the country." In addition, he challenged the legitimacy of the Georgia hearings, claiming that it "greatly defames the people of the state." See also *Rome Courier*, October 27, 1871.

17. Ku Klux Klan Resolution, November 8, 1871, RG 37-01-001, Georgia Archives and *Journal of the Georgia Senate* (Atlanta: W. A. Hemphill Public Printer, 1872), 46.

18. *Journal of the Georgia Senate* (Atlanta: W.A. Hemphill Public Printer, 1872), 46.

19. Allen W. Trelease, *White Terror: The Ku Klux Klan Conspiracy and Southern Reconstruction* (New York: Harper and Row, 1971), 409–10. Local grand juries, which were often Democratic, meant that very few indictments occurred in Georgia in October 1871. In a number of cases, threats of retribution scared witnesses away from testifying and a number of indicted individuals were never arrested. In some cases, defendants found legal aid from well-respected attorneys like Benjamin H. Hill of Georgia.

20. William S. McFeely, "Amos T. Akerman: The Lawyer and Racial Justice," in *Region, Race, and Reconstruction: Essays in Honor of C. Vann Woodward*, ed. J. Morgan Kousser and James M. McPherson (New York: Oxford University Press, 1982), 396. His support for Black issues was most likely connected to his upbringing in Massachusetts, which resulted in his membership in the Republican Party and his service in Georgia's Constitutional Convention in 1867–68, where he advocated for Black suffrage and citizenship. Akerman had supported Grant during the presidential election in November 1868, and after his brief tenure as US district attorney for the state of Georgia, President Grant appointed the "lean and balding Akerman" to serve as US attorney general. William S. McFeely, *Grant: A Biography* (New York; W. W. Norton, 1981), 368 and 36 and Jean Edwards Smith, *Grant* (New York: Simon Schuster, 2001), 544. Simultaneously Congress created the Solicitor General's Office, and Benjamin H. Bristow a well-respected US attorney from Kentucky, filled it. Under Akerman and Bristow, litigation increased dramatically targeting states such as Mississippi and North and South Carolina. The violence in North Carolina was so intense that during the election in the 1870, Klan violence allowed Democrats to recapture virtually every congressional seat in the state.

21. Allen W. Trelease, *White Terror: The Ku Klux Klan Conspiracy and Southern Reconstruction* (New York: Harper and Row, 1971), 385.

22. Allen W. Trelease, *White Terror: The Ku Klux Klan Conspiracy and Southern Reconstruction* (New York: Harper and Row, 1971), 388–89. Jean Edwards Smith, *Grant* (New York: Simon Schuster, 2001), 545.

23. William S. McFeely, "Amos T. Akerman: The Lawyer and Racial Justice," in *Region, Race, and Reconstruction: Essays in Honor of C. Vann Woodward*, ed. J. Morgan Kousser and James M. McPherson (New York: Oxford University Press, 1982).), 406. Akerman opposed secession from the Union before begrudging serving as a supported reluctantly Georgia's secession from the Union.

24. Jean Edwards Smith, *Grant* (New York: Simon Schuster, 2001), 546–47. According to Smith, Akerman was directly involved in purging South Carolina of much of its Klan activity and what Grant described as "a condition of lawlessness" resulting in the President suspending the writ of habeas corpus in sending federal troops in nine upland counties. For those arrested and willing to identify leaders of the Klan Akerman often did not prosecute those individuals. See also William S. McFeely, *Grant: A Biography* (New York: W. W. Norton, 1981), 370–71.

25. William S. McFeely argues that Akerman's firing was primarily due to his rigorous oversight of the railroad industry which frustrated Jay Gould and Cellis Huntington which was exacerbated by Akerman's "obsession with the Klan." William S. McFeely, "Amos T. Akerman: The Lawyer and Racial Justice," in *Region, Race, and Reconstruction: Essays in Honor of C. Vann Woodward*, ed. J. Morgan Kousser and James M. McPherson (New York:

Oxford University Press, 1982), 405. See also William S. McFeely, *Grant: A Biography* (New York: W. W. Norton, 1981), 373.

26. *Telegraph and Messenger*, December 6, 1871. Convicts being leased typically worked on railroads and other non-mining areas. Those who were leased at this rate were considered "higher quality" convicts because of their health and skill and typically had a sentence of two years or less. Alex Lichtenstein, *Twice the Work of Free Labor: The Political Economy of Convict Labor in the New South* (Verso: London, 1996), 116.

27. *Atlanta Daily Sun*, December 7, 1871 and *Journal of the Georgia Senate*.

28. Eric Foner, *Reconstruction, American's Unfinished Revolution: America's Unfinished Revolution: 1863–1877* (New York: Francis Parkman Prize Edition History, 1988), 390; Alex Lichtenstein, *Twice the Work of Free Labor: The Political Economy of Convict Labor in the New South* (London: Verso, 1996), 60–61 and *Journal of the Senate of Georgia at the Annual Session of the General Assembly* (Atlanta: Public Printer, 1870), 158–361. After the measure to reconsider the penitentiary bill failed a resolution to appoint a "joint committee of five, from the General Assembly, to visit the Penitentiary and the several places where the convicts are employed, and report upon their manner of their treatment, and all matters connect there with" was adopted with a vote of twenty-five ayes to fifteen nays. The main reason for the passage of the measure was not so much to investigate the conditions of Blacks but was, "to audit all claims against the Penitentiary; also to inquire what disposition was made of the appropriation of $150,000 to the Penitentiary made in March 1869." *The Atlanta Daily Sun*, December 8, 1871. The following day, Senator Candler was able to successfully undermine efforts to investigate prison conditions by passing a resolution revisit the resolution by arguing that previous a special committee had sufficiently investigated the Penitentiary ultimately resulting in, "great expense and trouble." *The Atlanta Daily Sun*, December 8, 1871.

29. Francis H. Smith, reporter, *Proceedings of the National Union Republican Convention Held at Philadelphia, June 5 and 6, 1872, which Nominated for President and Vice-President Ulysses S. Grant and Henry Wilson* (Washington: Gibson Brothers, 1872), 154 and 155.

30. Othal Hawthorne Lakey, *The History of the CME Church (Revised)* (Memphis, CME Publishing House, 1996), 32, 191, 197, 222, and 296 and C. H. Phillips, *The History of the Colored Methodist Episcopal Church in America: Comprising its Organization, Subsequent Development, and Present Status* (Jackson, Tenn.: CME Publishing House, 1898), 42. Other members of the Mississippi delegation to the Republican Convention in 1872 included B.K. Bruce, only the second Black US Senator in Congress, J. J Spellman representing central Mississippi, and James Hill representing North Mississippi. At the time, Bruce, Lynch, and Hill were known in Mississippi as the Republican Triumvirate due to their power and influence. Howard N. Rabinowitz, "Blanche K. Bruce, Robert Brown Elliott, and Holland Thompson," *Black Leaders in the Nineteenth Century*, Leon Litwack and August Meier (Champagne: University of Illinois Press, 1991), 199.

31. Francis H. Smith, Reporter, *Proceedings of the National Union Republican Convention Held at Philadelphia, June 5 and 6, 1872, which Nominated for President and Vice-President Ulysses S. Grant and Henry Wilson* (Washington: Gibson Brothers, 1872), 137–39. The Commission of Immigration and States Lands was an effort to recruit Blacks to Arkansas to work in the agricultural sector with the promise of land ownership.

32. During the nomination process Isaac Anderson would receive some votes for elevation to Bishop.

33. *The Atlanta Daily Sun*, December 8, 1871 and *Journal of the Georgia Senate*, December 7, 1871, 249.

34. James Forman Jr., "Juries and Race in the Nineteenth Century," *Yale Law Review*, December 10, 2003, 910–13.

35. James Forman Jr., "Juries and Race in the Nineteenth Century," *Yale Law Review*, December 10, 2003, 915.

36. Thompson, *Reconstruction in Georgia*, 354. Charles Nordoff, *The Cotton States in the Spring and Summer of 1875* (New York: D Appleton and Company, 1876), 101–2. By 1868, the legislature passed a Jury Law that allowed the county ordinary, the superior court clerk, and three commissioners appointed for each county by the presiding superior court judge to select jurors. Because the majority of county officers were Democrats, very few Blacks were ever allowed to serve on juries.

37. James Forman Jr., "Juries and Race in the Nineteenth Century" in *Yale Law Journal* 113, no. 4, January 2004, 915.

38. *Georgia Weekly Telegraph and Journal and Messenger*, July 30, 1872.

39. Eric Foner, *Reconstruction, American's Unfinished Revolution: America's Unfinished Revolution: 1863–1877* (New York: Francis Parkman Prize Edition History, 1988), 372–72.

40. Joseph P. Reidy, *From Slavery to Agrarian Capitalism in the Cotton Plantation South Central Georgia, 1800–1880* (Chapel Hill: UNC Press, 1992), 209, 224.

41. *Journal of the Georgia Senate 1872*, 494–95. *Atlanta Daily Sun*, August 23, 1872. Other Senators voting in opposition to the measure were Brown, Bruton, Clark, Colman, Conley, Nunnally and Smith. Senator Colman moved to strike out the county of Glynn. Trying to get support from white senators the *Atlanta Daily Sun* reported of, Deveaux's appeal to their Southern honor and white nostalgia of Black subservice: "He states that he did not make the motion because it inflicted greater hardship on the colored race than the white. He moved in behalf of the men who fought your battles and those who protected your wives in the darkest hour of the war. He moved on behalf of the honest, toiling, laboring men." *Atlanta Daily Sun*, August 17, 1872.

42. *New York Times*, October 5, 1872, *Historical New York Times* accessed 8/9/2010. See also Jacqueline Jones, *Saving Savannah: The City and the Civil War* (New York: Knopf, 2008).

43. Edmund Drago, *Black Politicians and Reconstruction in Georgia: A Splendid Failure* (Athens: University of Georgia Press, 1992), 155.

44. Warren Grice, *A History of Houston County* (1934 Perry, Georgia Public Library), 234.

45. Gregory Mixon, *Show Thyself a Man: Georgia State Troops, Colored 1865–1905* (Gainesville: University Press of Florida, 2016), 82 and 84. A year after James M. Smith's inauguration Congress passed legislation allowing for the creation of a Georgia militia which were known as the Georgia Volunteers which was to be open to both races with volunteers being at least sixteen years of age. Sally E. Hadden, *Slave Patrols: Law and Violence in Virginia and Carolinas* (Cambridge: Harvard University Press, 2001), 205–7.

46. Gregory Mixon, *Show Thyself a Man: Georgia State Troops, Colored 1865–1905* (Gainesville: University Press of Florida, 2016), 83.

47. Gregory Mixon, *Show Thyself a Man: Georgia State Troops, Colored 1865-1905* (Gainesville: University Press of Florida, 2016), 83 and *Journal of the Georgia Senate Annual Session of General Assembly, Commenced in Milledgeville, Georgia November 3, 1859* (Milledgeville, Georgia: Boughton, Nisbet, and Barnes State Printers, 1859), 544.

48. Nicholas Johnson, *Negroes and the Gun: The Black Tradition of Arms* (Amherst: Prometheus Books, 2014), 92-93. A number of Blacks were willing to serve in the militias, and by 1870 Georgia had Black militias. Other states not allowed to reinstate militias were Virginia, Texas, and Mississippi. When white South Carolinians refused to join integrated militias alongside Blacks, they formed all-white units like the Carolina Rifles of Charleston, which the state identified as illegal. In response, the former militias adjusted their description to that of social club where they sponsored social events as well as acquired uniforms and guns and drilled regularly. Bruce E. Baker, *What Reconstruction Meant: Historical Memory in the American South* (Charlottesville: University of Virginia Press, 2007), 16, and 66-67.

49. J. W. Matthews, S. D. Killen, and W. L. Grice, father of Warren Grice, were among sixty-eight names listed for the militia. *Houston Home Journal*, May 3, 1872. By 1874, Andrew S. Giles, who in 1873 served as Houston County ordinary, was also listed as a member of the militia. *Houston Home Journal*, September 26, 1874.

50. Nicholas Johnson, *Negroes and the Gun: The Black Tradition of Arms* (Amherst: Prometheus Books, 2014), 94.

51. *Atlanta Daily Herald*, January 28, 1874, and *Savannah Morning News*, March 5, 1874. The *Savannah Morning News* was critical of both a *New York Times* column written by Henry McNeal Turner who supported the establishment of freedmen's militias, and a convention of Black militia companies in Georgia. According to Gregory Mixon, roughly forty-two Black militias with varied activity existed in Georgia in 1878, and the closest Black militia to Fort Valley was roughly thirty miles away in Macon. It is not clear if any were in existence in 1872. Gregory Mixon, *Show Thyself a Man: Georgia State Troops, Colored 1865-1905* (Gainesville: University Press of Florida, 2016), 93.

52. Ida Anderson was born March 11, 1872. *Christian Index*, September 1892. 1880 US Census, Marshall, Mississippi; Roll: 657; Page: 555A.

53. 1870 US Census, Fort Valley Houston County, Georgia Roll: M593_158 12A. In 1872, Henry was fourteen, Isaac, thirteen, Victoria, eleven, Jacob, seven, Jane, four, and Edie, two. Edie was named after Anderson's wife, Edith. Ida was born in 1872 as she is listed in the 1880 census as being eight years old. See 1880 US Census, Marshall, Mississippi; Roll: 657; Page: 555A.

54. Allen Trelease, *White Terror: The Ku Klux Klan Conspiracy and Southern Reconstruction* (Baton Rouge: LSU Press, 1971) 241-42. According to the New York Times, "a partisan local police were kept from intimidating voters by a competent force of deputy United States marshals." *New York Times*, November 18, 1872.

55. *New York Times*, November 18, 1872; *New York Times*, Georgia, October 5, 1872, *Historical New York Times* accessed 8/9/2010. Olive Hall Shadgett, *The Republican Party in Georgia: From Reconstruction through 1900* (Athens: University of Georgia Press, 1964), 45 and Horace Calvin Wingo, *Race Relations in Georgia 1872-1908* University of Georgia, PhD diss., 1969, 15-17.

56. The Savannah Sabre Club and Georgia Hussars were newly established state militias and joined with local law enforcement officers like Savannah's chief of police to set up a perimeter of men to stop and intimidate Black voters like Josiah Grant, who was promptly arrested for "exhorting voters to resist white intimidation." Jacqueline Jones, *Saving Savannah: The City and the Civil War* (New York: Knopf, 2008), 383.

57. *New York Times*, Georgia, October 5, 1872, *Historical New York Times* 8/9/2010; Olive Hall Shadgett, *The Republican Party in Georgia: From Reconstruction through 1900* (Athens: University of Georgia Pres, 1964), 44 and Russell Duncan, *Freedom's Shore: Tunis Campbell and the Georgia Freedmen* (Athens: University of Georgia Press, 1986), 94–97.

58. 1860; Census Place: District 11, Houston, Georgia; Roll: M653_127; Page: 1035. See https://www.findagrave.com/cemetery/2362648/feagin-cemetery#view-photo=36013553 accessed 6/8/2018. Land owned by Feagin was called Feagin and was located in and or around the Warner Robbins Airforce Base. See *Houston Home Journal*, August 17, 1884, for an example of a suit brought before Judge Feagin by a Black man hoping to recover judgment not received. The case resulted in the Black man owing the court $1.25. *Houston Home Journal*, August 15, 1874. See also History of Byron, Georgia https://www.peachchamber.com/history. accessed 6/8/2018.

59. *Atlanta Daily Sun*, August 22, 1873 and Houston *Home Journal*, November 22, 1872.

60. Story Matkin-Rawn, "The Great Negro State of the Country": Arkansas's Reconstruction and the Other Great Migration," *Arkansas Historical Quarterly* 72, no. 1, Spring 2013, 11, 21, and 22.

61. *Atlanta Weekly Constitution*, December 8, 1874.

62. Eric Foner, *Reconstruction, American's Unfinished Revolution: America's Unfinished Revolution: 1863–1877* (New York: Francis Parkman Prize Edition History, 1988), 535.

63. Joseph P. Reidy, *From Slavery to Agrarian Capitalism in Cotton Planation South: Central Georgia, 1800–1880* (Chapel Hill: University of North Carolina Press, 1992), 231.

64. Journal of the Senate of the State of Georgia of the Annual Sessions of the General Assembly Atlanta, January 8, 1873 (Atlanta, Georgia: W. A. Hemphill and Co. Printers, 1873), 38.

65. *New York Times*, January 27, 1873. Other papers across Georgia like the *Savannah Morning News* and *Cuthbert Appeal* carried the exact story about the exodus from Houston County, writing, "About two hundred negroes have left Houston County for Arkansas during the past week" with the *Savannah Morning News* adding "This reduced the radical majority." *Savannah Morning News*, January 8, 1873; and *Cuthbert Appeal*, January 17, 1873.

66. *The Atlanta Weekly Sun*, February 11, 1873.

67. As head of the Georgia Bureau, Tillson stated his racial views before the Freedmen's' Convention proclaiming, "Do not suppose that I am advocating social equality which has never existed among colored people. All persons white and black, have the right to select their associates, and to live on terms of intimacy and social equality with those only whom they may choose and who may have like convictions, feelings, and taste with themselves." *Loyal Georgian*, January 20, 1866, and Paul Cimbala, "The 'Talisman Power': David Tillson, the Freedmen's Bureau, and Free Labor in Reconstruction Georgia, 1865–1866," *Civil War History* 28, no. 2, June 1982.

68. Joseph P. Reidy, *From Slavery to Agrarian Capitalism in Cotton Plantation South: Central Georgia 1800–1860* (Chapel Hill: UNC Press, 1992), 147 and *The Loyal Georgian*, January 20, 1866.

69. David Irwin, Revised Edition Georgia Code, 1866, 869–70. The code reads: "If any person, by himself or agent, shall be guilty of employing the servant of another, during the term for which he, she or they may be employed, knowing that such servant was so employed, and that his term of service was not expired—or, if any person or persons shall entice, persuade, or decoy, or attempt to entice, persuade or decoy, any servant to leave his employer either by offering higher wages, or in any way whatever during the term of service, knowing that said servant was so employed shall be deemed guilty of a misdemeanor, and upon conviction thereof, shall be fined any sum not more than two hundred dollars, or be confined in the common jail of the County, in the discretion of the Court, not to exceed three months." In 1873, the statue was amended to apply only to written contracts with one or more witnesses. In 1882, the term "cropper" or "farm laborer" was added to "servant," and the contract was no longer required to be written. In 1876, the legislature required all agents to purchase a $100 license, and by 1877, the license increased to $500.00. See Horace Calvin Wingo, *Race Relations in Georgia 1872–1908*, University of Georgia PhD diss., 1969, 221; William F. Holmes, "Labor Agents and the Georgia Exodus, 1899–1900," *South Atlantic Quarterly* 79, no. 4, 1980 and William Cohen, *At Freedom's edge: Black Mobility and the Southern White Quest for Racial Control 1861–1915* (Baton Rouge: Louisiana State University Press, 1991).

70. Paul Cimbala, "The 'Talisman Power': David Tillson, the Freedmen's Bureau, and Free Labor in Reconstruction Georgia, 1865–1866 in *Civil War History* 28, no. 2 June 1982, 166–67. *Loyal Georgian*, January 20, 1866.

71. Story Matkin-Rawn, "'The Great Negro State of the Country': Arkansas's Reconstruction and the Other Great Migration" *Arkansas Historical Quarterly* 72, no. 1, Spring 2013, 25.

72. In 1876, Georgia passed a law imposing a tax on those who transported laborers out of the state. William F. Holmes, "Labor Agents and he Georgia Exodus, 1899–1900," *The South Atlantic Quarterly* 79, no. 4., Autumn 1980, 437 and 444.

73. Clement Richardson, *The National Cyclopedia of the Colored Race* (Montgomery, Ala.: National Publishing Company, 1919), 94. J. H. Blount was the first African American to run for governor in the state of Arkansas. See also Clement Richardson, *The National Cyclopedia of Colored Race* (Montgomery, Ala.: National Publishing Company, 1919), 94.

74. *Atlanta Daily Sun*, February 15, 1873.

75. *Acts and Resolutions of the General Assembly of the State of Georgia, Passed at the Regular Session 1873*. 1873 vol. 270.

76. David Irwin, Revised Edition Georgia Code, 1866, 869–70.

77. N. J. Hammond, reporter, Reports of Cases in Law and Equity argued and determined in the Supreme Court of Georgia at Atlanta, parts of January and July terms, 1871 vol. 43 annotated edition (Atlanta: Harrison Company, 1918), 601–5. The case was *Slater v. Howard*.

78. See Georgia's First Regiment–Company C, Sons of Confederate Veterans, Warner Robbins Georgia. http://scvcamp1399.org/units/1stGA_CoC.php accessed 6/22/2018.

79. *Houston Home Journal*, February 22, 1873.

80. *Morning News*, March 27, 1873.

81. Othal Hawthorne Lakey, *The History of the CME Church, Revised* (Memphis: CME Publishing House, 1996), 252.

82. Othal Hawthorne Lakey, *The History of the CME Church, Revised* (Memphis: CME Publishing House, 1996), 252.

83. Daniel W. Stowell, *Rebuilding Zion: The Religious Reconstruction of the South, 1863–1877* (Oxford: Oxford University Press, 1998), 15 and 151 and Othal Hawthorne Lakey, *The History of the CME Church, Revised* (Memphis: CME Publishing House, 1996), 252. CME 1873 General Conference Minutes.

84. Benjamin H. Hill Jr., *Senator Benjamin H. Hill of Georgia: His Life and His Speeches* (Atlanta Georgia: Hudgins and Company, 1891), 16 and *Georgia Weekly Telegraph*, March 20, 1868.

85. George Foster Pierce papers, 1872–1875, Emory University, Stuart A. Rose Manuscript, Archives, and Rare Book Library *Bishop Robert Pierce Journal*.

86. C. H. Phillips, *The History of the Colored Methodist Episcopal Church in America: Comprising its Organization, Subsequent Development, and Present Status* (Jackson, Tenn.: CME Publishing House, 1898), 60–61. At the 1873 General Conference in Augusta there was a large contingency of MEC South leaders at the Conference. Among them were "Bishop George Pierce; Dr. Abby, of the Mississippi Conference; Rev J. E. Evans, Rev. C. W. Key, Rev. Thomas Scals, and Dr. Hicks, of the North Georgia Conference; and several others." Isaac Lane also made note of the "goodly number of white brethren" of MEC South in attendance See *Autobiography of Bishop Isaac Lane, LL.D. with a Short History of the CME Church in American and of Methodism* (Nashville, Tenn.: Publishing House of the M.E. Church, South, 1916), 66.

87. In 1883, the Supreme Court would rule that Congress had the right to regulate the actions of the state and not individuals. Southerners bristled at the language in the Civil Rights Bill, stating, "All persons within the jurisdiction of the United States shall be entitled to the full and equal enjoyment of the accommodations, advantages, facilities, and privileges of inns, public conveyances on land or water, theaters, and other places of public amusement; subject only to the conditions and limitations established by law, and applicable alike to citizens of every race and color, regardless of any previous condition of servitude." The last provision of the bill called for all cases to be brought before federal courts with the possibility of financial restitution for violation of the law. Cornell Law School https://www.law.cornell.edu/supremecourt/text/109/3 accessed 8/30/2019.

88. *Macon Telegraph and Messenger*, March 12, 1874.

89. *New National Era*, July 11, 1872. By February 22, with the legislative session meeting, the full assembly moved to select a US Senator to represent Georgia. The candidates were well known, A. H. Stephens, Benjamin Hill, Herbert Fielder, and Amos T. Akerman. Both Anderson and Deveaux consistently supported Akerman until the final ballot, when it became clear that Akerman had no chance and with the constant shifting of support there was a real possibility that either Hill or Stephens might win. Both Anderson and Deveaux voted for Gordon. The selection of Gordon certainly was a choice of the lesser of evils as none of the candidates less Akerman held any high regard for Black Georgians. But by the 1870s, Gordon was part of Georgia's New South boosters who wanted to portray an amicable relationship between Black and white Georgians and who tried to calm Northern fears, when in 1876 state Democratic leaders threatened to write Blacks out of the Georgia Constitution. Horace Calvin Wingo, *Race Relations in Georgia 1872–1908*, University of Georgia PhD diss., 1969, 30.

CHAPTER SEVEN

1. *Acts and Resolutions of the General Assembly of the State of Georgia, Passed at the Regular January Session 1873*, vol. 1 Sequential Number 245, Law Number 266. Story Matkin-Rawn, 21–22. Isaac Anderson in a report to the *Christian Index* referenced his transfer from West Tennessee to North Mississippi. See *Christian Index*, March 1885 and Horace Savage, *Life and Times of Bishop Isaac Lane* (Nashville: National Publication Company, 1958), 96–97.

2. David Irwin, Revised Edition Georgia Code, 1866, 869–70.

3. Horace C Wingo, *Race Relations in Georgia 1872–1877*, PhD diss., Emory University, 1969, 221.

4. *The Weekly Constitution*, December 4, 1874.

5. *Daily Phoenix*, April 11, 1873.

6. Minoa D. Uffelman, Ellen Kanervo, Eleanor Williams, Smith Phyllis, *The Diary of Nannie Haskins Williams: A Southern Woman's Story of Rebellion and Reconstruction, 1863–1890* (Knoxville: University of Tennessee Press, 2014), 241n25. *Daily Intelligencer*, May 28, 1863. Peters was a doctor who served in the Tennessee legislature before the war and was a Union supporter by the end of the war. Drawn into the national spotlight in 1863 for his killing of Confederate general Van Dorn following accusations that Van Dorn had an affair with Peter's much younger second wife, Jessie Mckissic, Peters was exonerated and following the war resided in Arkansas, where he owned three plantations.

7. *Houston Home Journal*, September 12, 1874 and *Columbus Daily Inquirer*, September 18, 1874.

8. *Memphis Daily Appeal*, October 6, 1874.

9. Charles Nordhoff, *The Cotton States In the Spring And Summer of 1875* (New York: D. Appleton & Company, 1876), 35–36.

10. *The Weekly Constitution*, December 8, 1874.

11. *The Georgia Weekly*, December 8, 1874.

12. Martin Delany and Niger Valley Exploring Party, *The Condition, Elevation, Emigration, and Destiny of Colored People of the United States; and Official Report of the Niger Valley Exploring Party* (Amherst: New York, 1852) and Sylvester A. Johnson, *African American Religions, 1500-2000: Colonialism, Democracy, and Freedom* (New York: Cambridge University Press, 2015), 226–27.

13. Jesse Lawson, *How to Solve the Race problem: The Proceedings of the Washington Conference on the Race Problem in the United States, Under the auspices of the National Sociological Society. Held at the Lincoln Temple Congregational Church; at the Nineteenth Street Baptist Church and at the Metropolitan A.M.E. Church, Washington, DC, November 9, 10, 11. And 12, 1903* (Washington, DC: Beresford Printers, 1904), 42–43, and 58. After 1890, Holsey pressed for the creation of a territory excluding whites and discouraging white settlement where "the Negro would be free and a full-fledged citizen, with all the immunities, privileges and political rights that belong to American citizens without friction, envy jealousies. Then the Negro, as a man and a race would have a chance to develop his mental powers, his physical character, and his essential responsibilities as an American citizen."

14. Nell Irvin Painter, *Exodusters: Black Migration to Kansas after Reconstruction* (New York: W. W. Norton, 1986).

15. See James Cobb, *The Most Southern Place on Earth* (Oxford: Oxford University Press, 1992), 7–9. In Mississippi settlers moved onto land originally belonging to the Choctaw with the first white settlers arriving around 1825. As the years progressed, settlers followed but often served as absentee owners. John C. Willis, *Forgotten Time: The Yazoo–Mississippi Delta after the Civil War*. Charlottesville: University of Virginia, 2000), 41.

16. Story Matkin-Rawn, "'The Great Negro State of the Country': Arkansas's Reconstruction and the Other Great Migration," *Arkansas Historical Quarterly* 72, no. 1, Spring 2013, 21.

17. Charles Nordhoff, *The Cotton States In the Spring And Summer of 1875* (New York: D. Appleton & Company, 1876), 35–36. According to Nordhoff, schools were permitted to separate Blacks and whites. He observed that Arkansas' Civil Rights Law included constitutional measures that allowed a candidate running for political office in the state to "appeal to the court with proof that voters so claimed are counted as actually cast for him; and if they give him a majority, he secures thereby the office without a new election. This makes it to the interest of candidates and of each party to look after and support the rights of voters, and give them power to remedy wrongs." Nordhoff also condescendingly observed. "The negroes have shown no disposition to make the law offensive."

18. *New National Era*, June 29, 1871.

19. Tom Dillard, "Important Black Leaders in Phillips County," *Phillips County Historical Quarterly* 19, no. 1 (December 1980–March 1981), 11–12. Beverly Watkins, "Efforts to Encourage Immigration to Arkansas, 1865–1874" *Arkansas Historical Quarterly* 38, no. 1 (Spring 1979), 51–53. Watkins argues that Grey was not "energetic" as a commissioner due to the cutting of his staff and his focus on land records. By the end of his term in office, Grey's administration was wracked with accusations of bribery and corruption. Political upheaval ended his tenure and he was eventually impeached and removed from office in May 1874.

20. *Memphis Daily Appeal*, October 6, 1874 and Story Matkin-Rawn, "'The Great Negro State of the Country': Arkansas's Reconstruction and the Other Great Migration," *Arkansas Historical Quarterly* 72, no. 1, Spring 2013, 5, 28.

21. John Blassingame, *The Slave Community: Plantation Life in the Antebellum South* revised and enlarged edition (New York: Oxford University Press, 1979), 315–17. Not all slaves trusted one another. One caveat to the code of trust among slaves was that between house servants who would violates the trust of the slave community in hopes of maintaining favor with the slave master. This reality makes Isaac Anderson's story even more compelling as he had a close relationship with his father yet was able to pass legislation to protect Black rights in addition to leading a number of Blacks out of central Georgia.

22. C. H. Phillips, *The History of the Colored Methodist Episcopal Church in America: Comprising its Organization, Subsequent Development, and Present Status* (Jackson, Tennessee: CME Publishing House, 1898), 29; Llewellyn W. Williamson, *Black Footprints around Arkansas* (Hope Arkansas: Southern Printing, 2012), 45–46 and Eric Foner, *Freedom's Lawmakers: A Directory of Black Officeholders During Reconstruction*, 2nd ed. (Baton Rouge: LSU Press, 1996), 188. At the CME founding meeting, Rev. Richard Samuels represented the Clerical and Itinerary Committee for the Arkansas Methodist Conference. As a state legislator, he represented Hempstead County in the Arkansas General Assembly. In 1872 Samuels ran for superintendent of the Arkansas penitentiary.

23. Henry Carroll, *Department of the Interior Census Office Report on Statistics of Churches in the United States and the Eleventh Census (1890)* (Washington: D.C.: Government Printing Office, 1894), 605. Hempstead County, Arkansas, had the largest number of CME members out of all five counties with 1,758 members and twenty CME Churches. The next largest concentration of CME members was in St. Francis with 475, followed by Pulaski with 453, Lee with 160 and Phillips with 150. In Hempstead County, local CMEs started Haygood Academy and later Seminary in Washington, Arkansas. A CME congregation was in the county before the denomination's founding in 1870 with John Williamson as the pastor. The school existed from 1883-1930s. See Haygood Seminary in Arkansas Encyclopedia, https://encyclopediaofarkansas.net/entries/haygood-seminary-4262/ accessed 8/29/2019. The fact that there was a strong impetus for education in Washington likely encouraged Anderson's settling in the area in order to provide an education for his children.

24. Kidada Williams, *The Left Great Marks on Me: African American Testimonies of Racial Violence from Emancipation to World War I* (New York: New York University Press, 2012), 41. US Bureau of Census, *Ninth Census of the United States: Statistics of Population* (Washington, DC: Government Printing Office, Population Schedule).

25. Jacob Bor et al. "Police killings and their spillover effects on the mental health of black Americans: a population-based, quasi-experimental study," *The Lancet* 392, no. 10144, 302-10. The other mysterious notation in the census record includes a marked-out notation of Edith Anderson being deaf.

26. Story Matkin-Rawn, "'The Great Negro State of the Country': Arkansas's Reconstruction and the Other Great Migration" *Arkansas Historical Quarterly* 72, no. 1, Spring 2013, 38-39.

27. C. H. Phillips, *The History of the Colored Methodist Episcopal Church in America: Comprising its Organization, Subsequent Development, and Present Status* (Jackson, Tennessee: CME Publishing House, 1898), 107.

28. John C. Willis, *Forgotten Time: The Yazoo-Mississippi Delta after the Civil War* (Charlottesville: University of Virginia Press, 2000), 68-69. Hubert H. McAlexander, *A Southern Tapestry: Marshall County, Mississippi, 1835-2000* (Virginia Beach: Donning Publishing, 2000), 38, 40. In 1836, Chulahoma had been a stagecoach stop on the Old Memphis Road, but the community had flourished in the 1840s and 50s with roughly thirty establishments, including a mortuary, a post office, a tailor shop, a cotton and grist mill, at least two churches, and a female seminary known as Chulahoma College for Girls. Before Holly Springs was selected, Chulahoma competed with the town for Marshall county's seat. See R. B. Henderson, "Chulahoma rich in Antebellum Memories," *The South Reporter* Holly Springs Mississippi, November 25, 1965. Martha Fant, "Chulahoma was Pretentious Village" *The South Reporter* Holly Springs Mississippi. E. R. Palmer Jr., "History of Chulahoma." http://msgw.org/marshall/locales/histchul.php

29. James Cobb, *The Most Southern Place on Earth: Mississippi Delta and the Roots of Regional Identity* (New York: Oxford University Press, 1992), 82.

30. James Cobb, *The Most Southern Place on Earth: Mississippi Delta and the Roots of Regional Identity* (New York: Oxford University Press, 1992), 9. John Kyle, *Publications of the Mississippi Historical Society* ed. Franklin L. Riley, vol.13 (University: University of Mississippi, 1913), 10-11, 16, 19 and John C. Willis, *Forgotten Time: The Yazoo-Mississippi Delta after the Civil War* (Charlottesville: University of Virginia Press, 2000), 58. The prospect of rebounding

cotton market furthered economic opportunity and a growing lumber industry as lumber companies extracted timber from the land to make way for cotton cultivation, and by 1889, cotton production had multiplied to 160 percent of what it was ten years earlier. The result was significant as land prices rose in the Mississippi Delta counties. Railroads like the Central Illinois and the Louisville, New Orleans, Texas Railway Company (LNO&T) aided economic growth and transported goods outside the region. In addition, there was the Sardis and Delta, a short line that traveled twenty-two miles primarily for the timber industry. James Cobb, *The Most Southern Place on Earth: Mississippi Delta and the Roots of Regional Identity* (New York: Oxford University Press, 1992), 80–81.

31. United States Census Bureau, "Population, by Race, Sex, and Nativity," Population, by Race and by Counties: 1880, 1870, 1860, table V, http://www2.census.gov/prod2/decennial/documents/1880a_v1-13.pdf accessed 4/1/2016.

32. Michael W Fitzgerald, *The Union League Movement in the Deep South: Politics and Agricultural Change during Reconstruction* (Baton Rouge: LSU Press, 1989), 72, 90, 102. Urbain Ozanne was an active supporter of freedpeople, and he wrote to the secretary of war when a Bureau agent failed to pay Black soldiers.

John Kyle, *Publications of the Mississippi Historical Society*, ed. Franklin L. Riley, vol. 13 (University: University of Mississippi, 1913), 49–50 and Buford Satcher, *Blacks in Mississippi Politics, 1865-1900* (Washington, DC: University Press of America, 1978), 42.

33. William J. Simmons, *Men of Mark, Eminent, Progressive and Rising With An Introductory Sketch of the Author By Rev. Henry M. Turner, D.D., LL. D., Bishop A.M.E. Church* (Cleveland, Ohio: George M. Rewell & Co. 1887), 538–45; G. P. Hamilton, *Beacon Lights of the Race* (Memphis: F. H. Clarke & Brother, 1911), 474–86; Eric Foner, *Freedom's Lawmakers: A Directory of Black Officeholders During Reconstruction*, 2nd ed. (Baton Rouge: LSU Press, 1996), 192 and J. Clay Smith Jr., *Emancipation and the Making of the Black Lawyer, 1844-1944* (Philadelphia: University of Pennsylvania Press, 1999), 291. Settle would eventually see the political winds change in Mississippi and relocate to Memphis, where in private practice he would represent Mary Morrison and Benjamin Booth in challenging Tennessee State law mandating segregation in 1905. See Miriam DeCosta-Willis, *Notable Black Memphians* (Amherst, New York: Cambria Press, 2008), 274.

34. The four Black Republicans who served on Panola County's Board of Supervisors were John Wilson, Lang Hunt, Jerry Hibbler and Peter Shegog. According to Satcher, "Mindful of the fact that the Black voter was still an important factor in politics, the Democrats made an attempt to persuade Blacks to vote with their party. The earliest efforts made toward a quest for the Black vote occurred in the Democratic state convention in 1875. Those leaders who pushed for Black alliance had accepted the terms of the war, and they urged the adoption of the Black vote in the platform for that year. But another faction of the party opposed such an alliance on the grounds that it was dangerous to the party." Buford Satcher, *Blacks in Mississippi Politics, 1865-1900* (Washington, DC: University Press of America, 1978), 138–39. Another example of the vibrancy of the Black community in Mississippi was the presence of Black fraternal organizations established throughout the Delta. See John Giggie, *After Redemption: Jim Crow and the Transformation of African American Religion in the Delta 1875-1915* (New York: Oxford, 2008), 63–64.

35. Eric Foner, *Freedom's Lawmakers: A Directory of Black Officeholders during Reconstruction* Revised Edition (Baton Rouge: LSU Press, 1996), 170. Also elected to represent Panola County in the Mississippi House during the same election was Charles A Yancey who was a minister and lived in Ohio and Canada several years before the Civil War he served only a brief time after his election in 1869 died in 1870. *Freedom's Lawmakers: A Directory of Black Officeholders During Reconstruction*, 2nd ed. (Baton Rouge: LSU Press, 1996), 237.

36. *Memphis Commercial Appeal*, November 28, 1874.

37. C. H. Phillips, *History of the Colored Methodist Episcopal Church in America: Comprising its Organization, subsequent Development and Present Status* (Jackson, Tennessee: CME Publishing House, 1898), 106; M. F. Jamison, *Autobiography and Work of Bishop M. F. Jamison, D. D. Editor, Publisher, Church Extension Secretary, A Narration of His Whole Career from Cradle to Bishopric of the Colored M.E. Church in America* (Nashville: Tennessee: Publishing House of M.E. Church South, Smith and Lamar Publishing Agents, 1912). Bishops Isaac Lane and Lucius Holsey would establish schools in Tennessee and Georgia by the 1880s, but the hardship of establishing schools for freedpeople led Holsey to heavily seek economic support from white Southern Methodists.

38. CME's had the largest number of Black congregants in the tricounty area of Marshall, Panola, and Tate County with 5,080 members. The next highest was the AME Zion with 1,382 followed by AME with 991. See Department of the Interior Census Office, *Report on the Statistics of Churches in the United States at the Eleventh Census (1890)*, Henry K. Carroll, Special Agent (Washington, DC: Government Printing Office, 1894) 547,561, and 605.

39. Buford Satcher, *Blacks in Mississippi Politics, 1865–1900* (Washington, DC: University Press of America, 1978), 206–7.

40. Gill, along with other local white and Black leaders, organized Union League clubs in other communities in Marshall County including Red Bank, Byhalia and Chulahoma. Ruth Watkins, *Reconstruction in Marshall County Publications of the Reconstruction in Northern Counties of Mississippi,"* Mississippi Historical Society, vol. 12 (University: University of Mississippi, 1912), 175 and Don Harrison Doyle, *Faulkner's County: The Historical Roots of Yoknapatawpha* (Chapel Hill: UNC Press, 2001), 276. For more information on Holly Springs see, Linda O. McMurry, *To Keep the Waters Troubled: The Life of Ida B. Wells* (New York: Oxford University Press, 1998) and Mia Bay, *To Tell the Truth Freely: The Life of Ida B. Wells* New York: Hill and Wang, 2009).

41. Ruth Watkins, *Reconstruction in Marshall County Publications of the Reconstruction in Northern Counties of Mississippi,"* Mississippi Historical Society, vol. 12 (University: University of Mississippi, 1912), 174.

42. J. H. Graham, *Asbury United Methodist Church, Our Templed Hills* (Holly Springs, Mississippi, 1991), 2 and 13–35. The efforts of the educational efforts of the church certainly influenced Asbury's membership. Which according to Graham grew from 168 members in 1867 to 443 members and 189 probationary members by 1869. J. Clay Smith, Jr., *Emancipation and the Making of the Black Lawyer, 1844–1944* (Philadelphia: University of Pennsylvania Press, 1999), 57. Rust's law school was short-lived because so few students applied to the program in 1878 and 1879, which most likely was due to the yellow fever epidemic in Holly Springs. Another prominent resident of Holly Springs was former Mississippi senator Hiram Revels, who taught at Rust.

43. Stuart Grayson Noble, *Forty Years of the Public Schools in Mississippi, with Special Reference to the Education of the Negro* (New York: Teachers College, Columbia University, 1918), 89. The other was Alcorn, located nearly three hundred miles south and focused on agricultural and industrial training, and because Alcorn was created as a land-grant institution, the school received crucial federal funding. See Robert L. Jenkins, "Development of Black Higher Education in Mississippi (1865–1920)," *Journal of Mississippi History* 45, no. 4, November 1983, 278.

44. *Chickasaw Messenger*, December 8, 1887.

45. Stuart Grayson Noble, *Forty Years of the Public Schools in Mississippi, with Special Reference to the Education of the Negro* (New York: Teachers College, Columbia University, 1918), 84, 87.

46. Deanne Stephens Nuwer, *Plague Among the Magnolias: The Yellow Fever Epidemic in Mississippi* (Tuscaloosa: University of Alabama press, 2009) 128.

47. United States Census Bureau, "Population, by Race, Sex, and Nativity," Population, by Race and by Counties: 1880, 1870, 1860, table V, http://www2.census.gov/prod2/decennial/documents/1880a_v1-13.pdf accessed 4/1/2016). See also Ruth Watkins, "Reconstruction in Marshall County" in *Reconstruction in Northern Counties of Mississippi*," Mississippi Historical Society, vol. 12 (University: University of Mississippi, 1913).

48. Blanche Elizabeth Brown Johnson, *The Daughters of Samuel Guy and Ernestine Minerva Brown: A Family History as Seen through the Eyes of Blanche Elizabeth Brown Johnson* (Detroit Michigan: Desktop Publishing Albert T. Berry, 1987), 5. The 1880 census lists Louisa Allen's father from Tennessee and her mother from Alabama.

49. 1880 United States Federal Census Thyatira and Tyro, Tate Mississippi Roll 665 Page 342D Enumeration District 188 and 1880 United States Federal Census Marshall County, Mississippi; Roll 657, page 559b, Enumeration District 119.

50. *Christian Index*, March 10, 1888.

51. *Christian Index*, June 11, 1887. Reference to Edith's presentation was given during the closing exercises of the Institute May 26, 1887. See *Christian Index*, June 4, 1887.

52. J. H. Patterson, of Senatobia complained, "Therefore, I say we have very few parsonages, and the preachers have to get their own houses to live in, or else they will be out of doors. We will move but slowly brothers, unless the circuits and stations provide houses for their ministers see *Christian Index*, May 1885 and *Christian Index*, December 8, 1888.

53. *Christian Index*, June 29, 1889.

54. *Christian Index*, September 28, 1889. The congregation of Anderson Chapel was established on College Street and is still in Holly Springs but has relocated farther out of town. http://andersonchapel.org/about-us/ accessed 8/9/2018.

55. Sardis CME Church's building was overseen and constructed by the following members of the building committee: J. P. Hightower, a local blacksmith; Silas P. Patton, a local carpenter; Walton, R.D. Leake, a local school teacher; and B. M. Moore, a local farmer. *Christian Index*, July 7, 1888. Members of the Sardis CME Church included R. D. and Ida Leake, who were local educators, R. D. Leake, a Republican candidate for county sheriff in 1881 and treasurer for the Sunday School Conference, and Ida B. Leake, a local teacher and participant in the Colored Teachers Institute, which was a program created for Black and white teachers to advocate for teacher training. *Weekly Panola Star*, August 20, 1881; *Christian Index*, November

26, 1887; *The Southern Reporter*, July 8, 1887 and C. E. Lindgren, *A Historical Comparative Study of the County School Systems of North and South Panola, Mississippi*, Doctorate of Education University of South Africa, 1999, 94.

56. The Hollywood CME Church was pastored by D. F. Fielding, and by 1888, his small membership of twenty-five had acquired a modern-style building with papered walls and painted sky-blue ceilings. Although the congregation owed a hefty amount on the property, the work earned the praise of Anderson and Bishop J. A. Beebe, who oversaw the North Mississippi Conference. http://www.msrailroads.com/Towns/Hollywood.htm accessed 8/9/2018 and *Christian Index* October 20, 1888.

57. *Report on the Statistics of Churches in the United States at the Eleventh Census: 1890* Henry K. Carroll Washington, DC Government Printing Office, 1894, 607.

58. John Blasingame, "Before the Ghetto: The Making of the Black Community in Savannah, Georgia, 1865–1880." *Journal of Social History* 6, no. 4, 463.

59. Steven Hahn, *A Nation under Our Feet: Black Political Struggles in the Rural South from Slavery to the Great Migration* (Cambridge: Harvard University Press, 2003).

60. According to Jamison, CME pastors frequently preached at Asbury, a racially mixed congregation, where they often faced criticism of their preaching. M. F. Jamison, *Autobiography and Work of Bishop M. F. Jamison, D. D. Editor, Publisher and Church Extension Secretary, A Narration of His Whole Career from Cradle to Bishopric of the Colored M.E. Church in America* (Nashville: Smith Lamar Publishing, 1912). 168.

61. William Montgomery, *Under Their Own Vine and Fig Tree: African American Church in the South 1865–1900* (Baton Rouge: LSU Press, 1993), 72–73.

62. John Blasingame, "Before the Ghetto: The Making of the Black Community in Savannah, Georgia, 1865–1880," *Journal of Social History* 6, no. 4, 466.

63. John Blasingame, "Before the Ghetto: The Making of the Black Community in Savannah, Georgia, 1865–1880," *Journal of Social History* 6, no. 4, 473.

64. Sharon D. Wright, *Race, Power and Political Emergence in Memphis* (New York: Routledge 2003), 31 and 33.

65. US Reports: Williams v. Mississippi, 170 US 213 (1898). Library of Congress http://cdn.loc.gov/service/ll/usrep/usrep170/usrep170213/usrep170213.pdf Amanda Brown, "Williams v. Mississippi," *Mississippi Encyclopedia* https://mississippiencyclopedia.org/entries/williams-v-mississippi/ accessed 7/25/2019. Henry Williams was an African American man convicted of murder by an all-white jury in 1896. Williams challenged the conviction arguing it be squashed as the laws passed under Mississippi's 1890 Constitution restricted Blacks from voting through the poll tax, literacy test, and other means. By restricting Blacks from voting, they would never serve on juries as members of the jury were pulled from voting rolls.

66. Neil R. McMillen, *Dark Journey: Black Mississippians in the Age of Jim Crow* (Urbana: University of Illinois Press, 1989), 5.

67. Denton O'Dell was a white carriage maker who was originally from New York state but moved to Panola county then to Chulahoma in Marshall County, Mississippi, by 1860 and served as a Confederate soldier. See *Biographical and Historical Memoirs of Mississippi: Embracing an Authentic and Comprehensive Account of the Chief Events in the History of the State and a Record of the Lives of Many of the Most Worthy and Illustrious Families and Individuals* (Chicago: Goodspeed publishing Company, 1891), 528.

68. Mississippi Department of Archives and History, Sardis Roll 39473. Although Anderson was likely planning to move to Jackson, Tennessee, the final decision to move to the city was decided in 1894 when the CME General Conference decided to move the Publishing House to Jackson, Tennessee. There were a number of communities considered including Nashville, Tenn.

CHAPTER EIGHT

1. Milton C. Sernett, *Afro-American Religious History: A Documentary Witness* (Durham: Duke University Press, 1985), 235, 236, and 237; Lucius Holsey, *The Autobiography of Bishop L. H. Holsey (Re-printed) with an Introduction by George E. Clary, Jr. Former Professor of History at Paine College, Augusta Georgia* (Keysville, Georgia: Brier Creek Press, 1988), 33.

2. John Brother Cade, *Holsey, the Incomparable* (New York: Pageant Press, 1969), 44.

3. *Christian Index*, April 14, 1894.

4. The classic work examining the use of respectability by Black women at the end of the nineteenth century and turn of the twentieth century is found in Evelyn Brooks Higginbotham, *Righteous Discontent: The Women's Movement in the Black Baptist Church 1880-1920* (Cambridge: Harvard University Press, 1993), 196. For discussion and portrayal of women described as both mulatto and the Jezebel stereotype, see Deborah Gray White's *Aren't I a Woman: Female Slaves in the Plantation South* (New York: Norton, 1985), 37. Many of these women were described as "fancy women" who were frequently used as concubines and mistresses by white men. See also Edward Baptist, *The Half Has Never Been Told: Slavery and the Making of American Capitalism* (New York: Basic Books, 2014) 240, 242.

5. Blanche Elizabeth Brown Johnson, *The Daughters of Samuel Guy and Ernestine Ginevra Brown: A Family History as Seen through the Eyes of Blanche Elizabeth Brown Johnson* (Detroit: Albert T. Berry Desktop Publishing, 1987), 5.

6. Linda J. Higgins and Scott Parish, *Images of America Madison County* (Charleston, South Carolina: Arcadia Publishing, 2009), 82.

7. Othal Hawthorne Lakey, *The History of the CME Church, Revised* (Memphis: CME Publishing House, 1996), 270, 272, and 303. By 1890, the first constitution of the Woman's Missionary Society Board was established with the goal of raising funds for the advancement of local and general mission work of the CME Church, yet CME women's organizations were still governed by male leadership and were required to have one male officer on the board and a corresponding male secretary elected by the general conference. 1890 CME General Conference Minutes, 424.

8. L. D. McFee, *History of the Woman's Missionary Society: In the Colored Methodist Episcopal Church Comprising Its Founders, Organizations, Pathfinders, Subsequent Developments and Present Status*, revised edition (Phenix City, Alabama: Phenix City Herald, 1945), 42.

9. In the Black Methodist Church that Anderson helped to establish in Fort Valley, J. H. Usher delivered a call to recognize women in the church at the CME General Conference in 1886, and this eventually led to the establishment of the position of stewardess. *History of Peach County Georgia with Addenda and Errata, Compiled by Governor Treutlen Chapter of the Daughters of the American Revolution Fort Valley, Georgia* (Atlanta: Cherokee Publishing, 1972), 27-28 and 51.

10. Willard Range, *A Century of Georgia Agriculture 1850–1950* (Athens: University of Georgia Press, 1969) 93–95.

11. *Cuthbert Appeal*, March 15, 1872. According to the paper, "The entrance was made through the rear door by the use of a lever made of cast steel for the purpose. After opening the door, they proceeded to open the vault door. They attempted to drill out the bolts in the lock, but finding that plan too slow, prized open the vault door with their crow bars. It appears the worst job of all was the easiest performed, that was obtaining entrance to the money safe." *Delaware State Journal*, March 8, 1872.

12. Isaac Anderson leased land from Colonel J. G. Ballentine and his wife, Mary Laird Ballentine. Her father, who was a doctor and served in the Tennessee legislature, lived in Memphis and owned a plantation in Sardis area. His son-in-law would run the former plantation. See *Pulaski Citizen*, September 11, 1884, and Barney A. Laird Interview, Federal's Writers' Project Slave Narrative Project, vol. 2 Arkansas, part 4, Jackson-Lynch, 1936., 225–27. Manuscript/Mixed Material. https://www.loc.gov/item/mesn024/. accessed 5/29/2019.

13. http://www.joelanderson.org/blog/category/andersons/ accessed 5/5/2019.

14. William Jackson Anderson, Obituary March 1890 clipping from Thomas Memorial Library, Fort Valley, Georgia.

15. US Reports: Williams v. Mississippi, 170 US 213 (1898). Library of Congress http://cdn.loc.gov/service/ll/usrep/usrep170/usrep170213/usrep170213.pdf Amanda Brown, "Williams v. Mississippi," *Mississippi Encyclopedia* https://mississippiencyclopedia.org/entries/williams-v-mississippi/ 7/25/2019. Henry Williams was an African American man convicted of murder by an all-white jury in 1896. Williams challenged the conviction arguing it be squashed as the laws passed under Mississippi's 1890 Constitution restricted Blacks from voting through the poll tax, literacy test and other means. By restricting Blacks from voting they would never serve on juries as members of the jury were pulled from voting rolls.

16. Buford Satcher, *Blacks in Mississippi Politics 1865–1900* (Washington, DC, University Press of America), 143.

17. Neil R. McMillen, *Black Mississippians in the Age of Jim Crow* (Urbana: University of Illinois Press, 1989) 4.

18. Cox would eventually draw criticism following her second appointment in 1897 when in 1902 James K. Vardaman, a Mississippi Democrat drew local and regional attention questioning a Black individual holding the position. In 1903 Cox resigned her post.

19. Neil R. McMillen, *Black Mississippians in the Age of Jim Crow* (Urbana: University of Illinois Press, 1989), 5.

20. John C. Willis, *Forgotten Time: The Yazoo–Mississippi Delta after the Civil War* (Charlottesville: University Press of Mississippi, 2000), 119.

21. John C. Willis, *Forgotten Time: The Yazoo–Mississippi Delta after the Civil War* (Charlottesville: University Press of Mississippi, 2000), 119–24; Buford Satcher, *Blacks in Mississippi Politics 1865–1900* (Washington, DC, University Press of America), 154 and John C. Willis, *Forgotten Time: The Yazoo–Mississippi Delta after the Civil War (Charlottesville: University Press of Mississippi, 2000)*, 127.

22. William Alexander Mabry, "Disfranchisement of the Negro in Mississippi," *The Journal of Southern History*. 4, no. 3 (Aug., 1938), pp. 318–33. According to Mabry, the Lodge bill ended up not passing in the Senate and instead Republicans made an agreement with Democrats to pass a tariff bill instead.

23. Address by Isaiah T. Montgomery, Delegate from Bolivar Mississippi Constitutional Convention 1894) accessed 5/22/2019 http://www.mshistorynow.mdah.ms.gov/images/115.gif

24. James H. Stone, "A Note on Voter Registration Under the Mississippi Understanding Clause, 1892," *The Journal of Southern History* 38, no. 2 (May, 1972), pp. 293-96.

25. John C. Willis, *Forgotten Time: The Yazoo-Mississippi Delta after the Civil War* (Charlottesville: University Press of Virginia, 2000), 141-44 and Neil R. McMillen, *Dark Journey, Black Mississippians in the Age of Jim Crow* (Urbana: University of Illinois Press, 1990), 43. Under the new Constitution a conviction for "arson, bigamy, fraud, and petty theft, but not murder, rape or grand larceny-was tailored in the opinion of the state supreme court, to bar blacks" The Mississippi Supreme Court made it clear in *Ratliffe v. Beale* (1896) that the main purpose for the new constitution was to restrict Black voting. Writing the majority opinion Chief Justice Tim E. Cooper wrote, "Within the field of permissible action under the limitations imposed by the federal constitution, the convention swept the circle of expedients to obstruct the exercise of the franchise by the negro race ... This race had acquired certain peculiarities of habit, of temperament, and of character, which clearly distinguished it as a race from that of the whites ... and its criminal members given rather to furtive offenses than to the robust crimes of the whites. Restrained by the federal constitution from discriminating against the negro race, the convention discriminated against its characteristics and the offenses to which its weaker members were prone." See http://global.oup.com/us/companion.websites/fdscontent/uscompanion/us/static/companion.websites/9780199751358/instructor/chapter_7/ratliffvbeale.pdf accessed 7/25/2019.

26. Denton O'Dell was a white carriage maker who was originally from New York state but moved to Panola county then to Chulahoma in Marshall County, Mississippi by 1860 and served as a confederate soldier. See *Biographical and Historical Memoirs of Mississippi: Embracing an Authentic and Comprehensive Account of the Chief Events in the History of the State and a Record of the Lives of Many of the Most Worthy and Illustrious Families and Individuals* (Chicago: Goodspeed Publishing Company, 1891), 528 and Mississippi Department of Archives and History, Sardis Roll 39473. Although Anderson was likely planning to move to Jackson, Tennessee the final decision to move to the city was decided in 1894 when the CME General Conference decided to move the Publishing House to Jackson, Tennessee. There were a number of communities considered including Nashville, Tenn.

27. Judy Bussell LeForge. "State Colored Conventions of Tennessee, 1865-1866." *Tennessee Historical Quarterly* 65.3 (2006): 231-47.

28. *The Colored American*, January 6, 1900

29. 1900; Census Place: Jackson Ward 3, Madison, Tennessee; Page: 6; Enumeration District: 0110; FHL microfilm: 1241586 and 1900; Census Place: Jackson Ward 1, Madison, Tennessee; Page: 1; Enumeration District: 0103; FHL microfilm: 1241586.

30. Othal Hawthorne Lakey, *The History of the CME Church, Revised* (Memphis: CME Publishing House, 1996), 300.

31. *Christian Index*, February 14, 1894.

32. *Christian Index*, May 11, 1895. Lula Anderson wrote an Anniversary Hymn for the twenty-fifth anniversary of the denomination August 17, 1895 and a Christmas poem, December 28, 1895.

33. Mia Bay, *To Tell the Truth Freely: The Life of Ida B. Wells* (New York: Hill and Wang, 2009), 72–73 and Shirley J. Carlson, "Black ideals of Womanhood in the Late Victorian Era," *Journal of Negro History* 77, no. 2, Spring 1992, 61.

34. The Committee on Episcopacy reported that Bishops Miles, Holsey, and Lane had been examined and were "blameless," but not all the Bishops escaped criticism. Bishop Joseph Beebe was identified as having "retained" $824.44 which should have been sent to the Publishing Agent for missionary funds. Beebe explained to the committee that over $500 of the funds were loaned to the CME church in Little Rock, and the bulk of the other money was spent on CME efforts in New Orleans and on a cash reserve for other expenses. The committee required Bishop Beebe to, "give a written statement for the payment of 824.44 and in the future to be punctual in seeing all monies sent to their proper places." *Christian Index*, June 7, 1890.

35. C. H. Phillips, *The History of the Colored Methodist Episcopal Church in America: Comprising its Organization, Subsequent Development, and Present Status* (Jackson, Tennessee: CME Publishing House, 1898), 146, 149 and 176.

36. In 1869 Holsey joined Southern Methodist Bishop Robert Pierce and other future CME leaders to organize what would be the Georgia Conference of the CME. Lucius Holsey, *The Autobiography of Bishop L. H. Holsey (Re-printed) With an Introduction by George E. Clary, Jr. Former Professor of History at Paine College, Augusta Georgia* (Keysville, Georgia: Brier Creek Press, 1988), 22.

37. Lucius Holsey, *The Autobiography of Bishop L. H. Holsey (Re-printed) with an Introduction by George E. Clary, Jr. Former Professor of History at Paine College, Augusta Georgia* (Keysville, Georgia: Brier Creek Press, 1988), 29.

38. In 1886, Franklin M. Hamilton was the editor of *The Christian Index*. With the establishment that same year of a strong Book Committee that included Elias Cottrell, C. H. Phillips and Isaac Anderson, the paper stabilized, and denominational leaders mandated that all CME pastors were required to collect five cents per member in support of the *Christian Index*. With his background in business and his skill as an organizer, Anderson was an ideal choice to serve as publishing agent, and immediately, tensions arose between him and the editor. Late in 1890, Hamilton resigned as editor of the *Christian Index*, and without consulting other CME leaders, Anderson quickly replaced him with R. T. Brown. This was a decision that quickly put him at odds with Lucius Holsey, who interpreted his actions as a power play. Othal Hawthorne Lakey, *The History of the CME Church, Revised* (Memphis: CME Publishing House, 1996), 258–59.

39. During an earlier CME Conference, J. J. Hollis, who was the presiding elder in the Fort Valley District gave Lucius Holsey twenty-five dollars in dues, which was a violation of the policy requiring presiding elders to send their money to the publishing agent. In turn, Isaac Anderson deducted the amount from Holsey's salary. Frustrated by what he saw as a reduction in his salary, Holsey took to the *Christian Index* to express his anger. Othal Hawthorne Lakey, *The History of the CME Church, Revised* (Memphis: CME Publishing House, 1996), 335–36. Glenn T. Eskew, "Black Elitism and the Failure of Paternalism in Postbellum Georgia: The Case of Bishop Lucius Henry Holsey," *Journal of Southern History* 58, no. 4, November 1992, 652.

40. *Christian Index*, April 14, 1894.

41. *Christian Index*, May 27, 1893.

42. In his reply to Holsey, Anderson described their interaction as two leaders "discussing the law in a Christian spirit." *Christian Index*, July 23, 1893. During an earlier CME Conference, J. J. Hollis, who was the presiding elder in the Fort Valley District gave Lucius Holsey twenty-five dollars in dues, which was a violation of the policy requiring presiding elders to send their money to the publishing agent. In turn, Isaac Anderson deducted the amount from Holsey's salary. In October 1993, Hollis weighed in on Anderson's actions hoping to bring an end to tensions and being sympathetic to Holsey's fragile state of health. He wrote, "Now we purpose to speak plain about everything. Our curiosities have been aroused, our energies awakened and our minds startled by so much thunder, lightning and rain through the Index by the Agent for the lone sake of twenty-five dollars . . . Just Hold on Mr. Agent, we think we can settle the whole affair. We don't feel disposed to have Bishop Holsey's feelings wrought up and his mind disturbed any longer about twenty-five dollars. We are willing and will make him a present of that much money if you just don't say any more about it." *Christian Index*, October 21, 1893.

43. The new publishing house was reportedly worth $4000, and after a denominational committee had reviewed the agreement, a decision was made to pay Anderson $1000 in August 1896 with a promise to pay the outstanding amount in two years. *Christian Index*, June 20, 1896.

44. *Christian Index*, August 1, 1896.

45. John Brother Cade, *Holsey-The Incomparable* (New York: Pageant Press, 1969), 124.

46. Holsey invited R. A. Carter, a longtime mentee of his, to serve as editor of the *Gospel Trumpet*. Carter was later elected bishop in 1914. In the paper, Holsey criticized Christian Index editor, C. H. Phillips, whom he believed was "advertising Himself" to "grandstand" in hopes of being elected bishop. John Brother Cade, *Holsey, the Incomparable* (New York: Pageant Press, 1969), 122. Othal Hawthorne Lakey, *The History of the CME Church, Revised* (Memphis: CME Publishing House, 1996), 258–59.

47. Sylvester A. Johnson, *African American Religions, 1500–2000: Colonialism, Democracy and Freedom* (New York: Cambridge University Press, 2015), 2, 33–54. Johnson's discussion of Phillip Quaque provides a complementary experience that is similar to Holsey's experience but in eighteenth-century Cape Coast.

48. Autobiography of Bishop Isaac Lane, LL.D., (Nashville: Tenn.: Methodist Episcopal Church South Publishing House, 1916), 48. For more analysis of the different perspectives of Miles, Vanderhorst, Beebe, Lane, and Holsey, see Reginald F. Hildebrand, *The Times Were Strange and Stirring: Methodist Preachers and the Crisis of Emancipation* (Durham: Duke University Press, 1995), 16–21.

49. Reginald F. Hildebrand, *The Times Were Strange and Stirring: Methodist Preachers and the Crisis of Emancipation* (Durham: Duke University Press, 1995), 16–21 and Lucius Holsey, *The Autobiography of Bishop L. H. Holsey (Re-printed) with an Introduction by George E. Clary, Jr. Former Professor of History at Paine College, Augusta Georgia* (Keysville, Georgia: Brier Creek Press, 1988) 19–20.

50. Benjamin Hill and Robert Toombs were two powerful politicians in Georgia with whom Pierce acquainted Holsey. In 1868, Hill had mocked Isaac Anderson and other Black delegates to Georgia's Constitutional Convention. Toombs had served as Secretary of State

in the Confederacy under Jefferson Davis and had refused to seek a pardon. He also was heavily involved in Georgia's politics as a Democrat. Benjamin H. Hill Jr., *Senator Benjamin H. Hill of Georgia: His Life and His Speeches* (Atlanta Georgia: Hudgins and Company, 1891), 16; *Georgia Weekly Telegraph*, March 20, 1868 and George Foster Pierce papers, 1872–1875, Emory University, Stuart A. Rose Manuscript, Archives, and Rare Book Library *Bishop Robert Pierce Journal*.

51. Lucius Holsey, *The Autobiography of Bishop L. H. Holsey (Re-printed) with an Introduction by George E. Clary, Jr. Former Professor of History at Paine College, Augusta Georgia* (Keysville, Georgia: Brier Creek Press, 1988), 18 and 31.

52. By the mid-1890s, under C. H. Phillips's leadership, the *Christian Index* added a column on politics. See *Christian Index*, October 20, 1894.

53. The most prominent leaders of the Bourbon Democrats included Alfred Colquitt, John B. Gordon, and Joseph E. Brown. Brown and Colquitt had ties to the Southern Methodist Church, and Colquitt became a Southern Methodist minister not long after the Civil War and was also a prominent member of the Ku Klux Klan. Christopher H. Owen, *The Sacred Flame of Love: Methodism and Society in Nineteenth Century Georgia* (Athens: University of Georgia Press, 1998), 166, 180–82.

54. Alexander Stephens died in 1883, and Benjamin Hill in 1882. John Brother Cade, *Holsey, the Incomparable* (New York: Pageant Press, 1969), 130–31 and Glenn T. Eskew, "Black Elitism and the Failure of Paternalism in Postbellum Georgia: The Case of Bishop Lucius Henry Holsey," *Journal of Southern History* 58, no. 4, November 1992, 655–56.

55. Alexander Stephens died in 1883, and Benjamin Hill, in 1882. John Brother Cade, *Holsey, the Incomparable* (New York: Pageant Press, 1969), 130–31 and Glenn T. Eskew, "Black Elitism and the Failure of Paternalism in Postbellum Georgia: The Case of Bishop Lucius Henry Holsey" *Journal of Southern History* 58, no. 4, 655–56. In 1853, Wesley Chapel was established in Fulton County, Georgia, and was named after Benjamin Hill. According to the church's website, Hill "was a great orator of his day and brought prominence to the community." By the 1960s, African Americans became a majority in the neighborhood, and the church's membership shrank. As whites left the church, leaders decided to hire a Black assistant pastor who ushered in growth, and the congregation became predominantly Black. Ironically, it is still known as the Ben Hill Church. See https://benhillumc.org/our-history/ 5/17/2019.

56. Horace Savage, Life and Times of Bishop Isaac Anderson (Nashville: National Publication Company, 1958), 134. *Christian Index*, April 14, 1894. See also Glenn T. Eskew, "Black Elitism and the Failure of Paternalism in Postbellum Georgia: The Case of Bishop Lucius Henry Holsey," *Journal of Southern History* 58, no. 4, November 1992, 649. The attempts of the CME Church to have more trained clergy coincides with its growing efforts to be independent from the Southern Methodists, and this is demonstrated by the *Christian Index*'s Black editor and growing efforts at Lane College to choose a Black president, which would happen in 1903 with J. A. Bray, a Paine College graduate.

57. Glenn T. Eskew, "Black Elitism and the Failure of Paternalism in Postbellum Georgia: The Case of Bishop Lucius Henry Holsey," *Journal of Southern History* 58, no. 4, 652.

58. W. B. Parks, *The Possibilities of the Negro in Symposium* (Atlanta: Franklin Printing and Publishing Company, 1904), 99–119.

59. *Atlanta Constitution*, September 29, 1899. See also W. B. Parks, *The Possibilities of the Negro in Symposium* (Atlanta: Franklin Printing and Publishing Company, 1904), 99–119. For more analysis of Holsey's transformation in perspective, see, Glenn T. Eskew, "Black Elitism and the Failure of Paternalism in Postbellum Georgia: The Case of Bishop Lucius Henry Holsey," *Journal of Southern History* 58, no. 4, November 1992, 637–66. Years later, Reverend Randall Carter, who was Holsey's mentee, the editor of the *Gospel Trumpet*, and a future CME bishop, described African Americans as the "untouchables of American society." Randall A Carter, *Gathered Fragments* (Nashville: Parthenon Press, 1939), 143.

60. Anderson was instrumental in fostering the growth of the CME Church in Holly Springs, which became known as Anderson Chapel and still bears his name. Anderson likely disapproved of Elias Cottrell's decision to establish Mississippi Industrial College. It was public knowledge that Isaac Lane did not approve of the establishment of the school as it was less than eighty miles away from Jackson and competed with Lane for students and support. See Alicia Jackson, "Having Our Own: The Colored Methodist Episcopal Church and the Struggle for Black Autonomy in Education," in *Southern Religion, Southern Culture Essays Honoring Charles Reagan Wilson*, ed. Darren E. Grem, Ted Ownby, James G. Thomas Jr. (Jackson: University Press of Mississippi, 2019), 63–75.

EPILOGUE

1. Treutlen Chapter Daughters of the American Revolution, *The History of Peach County Georgia with Addenda and Errata* (Atlanta: Cherokee Publishing Company, 1972), 57–58.

2. Edmund l. Drago, *Black Politicians and Reconstruction in Georgia: A Splendid Failure* (Baton Rouge: LSU Press, 1982), 161.

3. *Christian Index*, December 8, 1906.

4. In his article on J. R. Lynch, Justin Behrend addresses the silences in the discussion of Black political life in Mississippi. Justin Behrend, "Facts and Memories: John R. Lynch and the Revising of Reconstruction History in the Era of Jim Crow," *Journal of African American History* 97, no. 4, Fall 2012, 427–48 and Michel-Rolph Trouillot, *Silencing the Past: Power and the Production of History* (Boston: Beacon Press, 2015).

INDEX

Page numbers in **bold** indicate pictures.

Abbey, Richard, 111
African Methodist Episcopal Church (AME), 9, 49, 51, 53–55, 57, 86, 88, 90–94, 140, 150, 175, 189, 191
African Methodist Episcopal Church Zion (AMEZ), 9, 49, 53, 86, 88, 90–92, 94, 140, 150, 175, 186, 189, 191
Akerman, Amos T., 100, 195, 201
Alcorn Normal School, 124, 207
Allen, Richard, 49, 91
Alpeoria, Aaron, 79
Anderson, Anna Coker, 27–28, 133
Anderson, Benjamin Franklin, 125, 132
Anderson, Celestine Lucy, 125, 131
Anderson, Charles David, 27, 42–43, 119, 171
Anderson, Edith, 47, 103, 105, 119–20, 124, 204
Anderson, Edith "Edella," 131, 198, 207
Anderson, Ernestine Minerva, 125, 131–32, **143**
Anderson, Ida, 105, 131
Anderson, Isaac, 3–4, 6–9, 11, 15–16, 20, 23, **24**, 24–25, 30, 37–38, 41–43, 45–58, 67–69, 70, 72–73, 81, 84, 86, 96, 98, 101, 103, 107, 114, 118–19, 124–25, **128**, 128–30, 133, 136–37, 139–40, 143–44, 146–50, **152**, 152–53, 156n14, 159n117, 161n56, 165n24, 171n2, 172n11, 176n52, 184n67, 188n38, 215n60
Anderson, Jake, 97–98
Anderson, James Christian, 125, 131, **141**
Anderson, John Ernest, 125, 131–32, **141**
Anderson, Louisa "Lula" Allen Byrd, 124–25, 130–31, 132, 135, 137, **141**, **142**, 207n48
Anderson, Rebecca Hollinshead, 37–38, **44**, **45**, 132
Anderson, Rebecca Louisa, 125, 131, **131**
Anderson, William Jackson, 4, 6–7, 11, 24–43, **44**, 44–48, 51, **56**, 56–59, 64, 66, 72, 77, 79–83, 89, 92, 105–6, 110, 119, 132–33, 146–47, 149, 151–52, 164n21, 170n94, 175n40, 186n6, 193n3
Anderson, William Robert, 27–28
Anderson School, 67–68
apprenticeship, 62–67
Asbury, Francis, 33, 48
Asbury Methodist Episcopal "Asbury Chapel," 123, 127, 208n60
Ashburn, George W., 100

Bacon, A. O., 96, 177, 183
Ballard, Frank, 136
Ballard, Jack, 73–74, 83, 119
Ballard, Mary, 73–74, 83, 119
Ballentine, J. G., 120–21, 129, 135, 210n12
Ballentine, Mary Laird, 210n12
Bancroft, Frederic, 40–41
bank agent, 39–40, 169n80
Barnett, Paul, 52, 67
Beebe, Joseph, 140, 208, 212, 213n48
black codes, 60–62, 72, 76, 103, 177

INDEX

Black newspapers: *Afro-American Sentinel*, 136; *Colored American*, 136; *Jackson Headlight*, 136
Black Voting: 1868, 7, 11, 16–19, 24, 26, 47, 57, 59, 72–73, 90, 186n6; 1870, 86, 88, 89, 92, 94, 96–99, 159n23, 191n68, 194n9; 1872, 104–7, 113; Arkansas, 117; Georgia, 6, 100, 155n7; Mississippi, 122; Suppression, 78, 82, 83, 93, 152
Blassingame, John, 118, 126, 203n21
Blount, J. H., 10, 109, 200n73
Boley, Oklahoma, 117
Boyce, Ker, 38, 168
Brock, Jesse, 179n30
Brown, Bertram Wyatt, 38, 158n64
Brown, Brad, 78
Brown, James R., 99, 194n16
Brown, John, 136
Brown, Morris, 49
Brown, R. J., 94
Brundage, Fitzhugh, 83, 87–88
Bullock, Rufus, 16, 18, 77, 79, 97, 184n66

Cain, Richard, 61, 72
Caldwell, John C., 190n60
Cameron Place, Alabama, 117
Camilla Massacre, 19, 58
Campbell, Tunis, Sr., 9, 20, 77, 79–80, 88, 94–95, 99, 101–4, 106, 110, 156n13, 162n56, 186n6, 193n4
Candler, M. A., 80, 196
Capers, William, 48–50
Carter, R. A., 213n46, 215n59
Cimbala, Paul, 8, 60, 75, 176n3
Civil Rights Bill of 1875, 103, 113, 117, 201n87
Clarke, George C., 55, 66, 84
Cleveland, J. F., 34
Clinton, J. J., 92
Cobb, George, 74
Cobb, James, 74
Cobb, Samuel, 15–16, 23, 81, 159n17, 191n68
coffles, 32
Cole, Carlton B., 61, 71–73, 93, 97, 110
Coleman, Thomas, 50–51
Collier, John J., 80

Collins, Robert, 34–35, 38, 166n43, 167n44, 168n54
Colored Convention of 1874, 107, 114, 116
Colored Methodist Episcopal (CME), 9, 10–11, 21–22, 54, 85–92, 94, 102, 108–9, 111–12, 114, 119–20, 122–23, 125–28, 130–31, 133, 136–41, 143, 144–46, 149, 150, 155, 156, 161, 175n39, 187n43, 188n36, 188n38, 189n43, 189n54, 190n56, 191nn62–63, 201n86, 203n22, 204n23, 206n38, 207n55, 208n56, 209n7, 209n9, 211n26, 212n34, 212n36, 212n38, 213n42, 214n56, 215nn59–60; beginning in central Georgia, 48–57
Colquitt, Alfred, 214n53
Conley, Benjamin, 97
convict leasing, 7–8, 60–62, 71–73, 81, 85, 94–95, 101, 103, 109, 113–14, 135, 142, 155n9, 183n57, 196n26, 200n69
Cooper, Tim E., 211n25
Cotter, William Jasper, 20, 22, 52, 54, 64, 67, 176n52
cotton commissioner (cotton factor), 33–34, 38–40, 43
Cotton Planters Convention, 62
Cotton States Insurance, 81, 132, 169n74
Cottrell, Elias, 86, 123, 127, 145, 212n38, 215n60
Courtney, Alice, 131
Cox, Minnie M., 134, 210n18
Craft, Ellen, 35
Crayton, Thomas, 99, 102, 106, 162n56, 193n4
Creek Indians, 27–29, 163n15
Croom, Wendell, 44
Crump, E. H., 129
Culpepper, James, 180n36

Dabney, Robert, 12
Davis, Jefferson, 112, 214n50
Dean, Hugh, 73–74, 83
Delany, Martin, 116
De Tocqueville, Alexis, 28
Deveaux, James, 99, 104, 106, 113, 193n4, 197n41, 201n89

Deyle, Steven, 40
Dooly County, Georgia, 49, 57, 61, 65, 72–75, 83, 97
Dorn, Van, 202n6
Dorsey, Matthew, 48
Douglas, Frederick, 118, 186n6
Drago, Edmund, 5, 92, 104, 155n6, 161n49, 189n44
Duncan, C. C., 82
Dunning school, 4–6, 151, 154n4, 155n6
Dunwoody, James, 20–21, 48, 50

Eatonville, Florida, 117
Eldridge, Felix, 122
Enforcement Acts, 100, 102, 104, 117, 194
Erskine, Judge, 62
Evans, Lucius G., 46
Everett, Fanny, 66, 83, 180n36
Everett, Harriet, 180n36
Everett, James Abington, 29, 48, 50, 66, 83, 163
Everett, Mary, 66, 83, 180n36

Fagan, Jack, 61, 72
Farrow, H. P., 81, 186n16
Feagin, George M. T., 106, 113, 199n58
Felder, Bob, 91
Felder, Charlotte McCas, 91
Felder, H. R., 82
Fielding, D. F., 208n56
Fields, Barbara, 63
Foner, Eric, 4, 7, 41, 60, 184n66
Fort Valley Black Churches: Shiloh Baptist, 159n27; St. Peter's AME, 159n27. *See* Usher's Chapel
Fort Valley Methodist Church, 20, 22, 37, 39, 48, 51–54, 64, 81, 83–84, 89, 90, 106, 172n9; Old Pond Church, 39, 48
Fort Valley Slave Mission, 20–22, 48, 50–52, 55, 84, 172n10
Foucault, Michel, 140
Fourteenth Amendment, 8, 13–14, 16–17, 19, 77, 79, 81, 100, 103–4, 158n9, 159n20, 160n33
Foy, Amanda, 65

Frazier, E. Franklin, 84
Freedmen's Bureau, 6, 8, 59, 99, 117; Georgia, 13, 18, 26, 54, 58, 61–64, 66–68, 70–71, 74–77, 108, 149, 177n3, 181n42, 182n50, 183n56, 187n22; Mississippi, 121–23
Fyall, F. Y., 73, 83, 184n66

Gallagher, Frank M., 70
Galloway, Charles B., 188n36
Georgia Constitutional Convention of 1865, 13
Georgia Constitutional Convention of 1867–1868, 4, 9, 12, 14–16, 19, 22, 23, 30, 55, 70, 100, 112, 175n45, 186n6, 189n44, 195n20, 213n50
Georgia Equal Rights and Educational Association (GERA), 85
Georgia Female College. *See* Wesleyan College
Georgia Grange, 107
Gill, Nelson G., 123, 206n40
Glover, Taylor, 61, 72
Gordon, John B., 16, 19, 58, 99, 142, 214n53
Gorn, Elliot, 29, 164n21
Gospel Trumpet, 139, 141–42, 145, 213n46, 215n59
Grant, Ulysses S., 73, 75, 100–102, 118, 195n20
Grant Clubs, 23, 62, 73–75, 91, 162n58, 181n42, 184n67; Loyal League, 89, 123, 183n56, 184n67, 190n60; Union League, 68, 78, 118, 121–23, 206n40
Gray, C. G., 45–46, 133
Greene, Myles, 66, 83
Grey, William H., 102, 109, 118, 203n19
Grice, Warren, 71, 96, 183n56, 193n3, 198n49
Grice, W. L., 98, 194n8, 198n49
Griffin, Cyrus, 162n52
Griffin, Joel, 17–18, 22–23, 75, 78, 81–82, 89, 92, 106, 159n27, 162n52, 187n22
Gudmestad, Robert H., 40, 166n44

Hadden, Sally E., 98
Haddock, J. R., 65, 179n32

Hahn, Steven, 8, 127
Hamilton, Franklin M., 212n38
Harris, J. D., 60–61
Haygood, Atticus, 188n36
Haygood School, 136, 204n23
Haygood Seminary, 136, 204n23
Hempstead County, Arkansas, 119, 203n22, 204n23
Herman, Judith, 84–85
Hibbler, Jerry, 205n34
Hightower, J. P., 126, 207n55
Hill, Benjamin "Ben," 18, 112, 142, 195n19, 213n50, 214n54, 214n55; Benjamin Hill Church, 214n55
Hill, James, 123
Hill, L. N., 62, 180n36
Hollinshead, Andrew, 112
Hollinshead, William H., 37, 38–39, 51
Hollis, J. J., 212n39
Holloway, H. B., 83, 98
Holly Springs, Mississippi, 121, 123–29, 132, 134, 204n28, 206n40, 206n42, 207n54
Holly Springs Normal School, 124
Hollywood, Mississippi, 21, 126, 161n47
Hollywood CME Church, 208n56
Holsey, Lucius, 9–10, 86, 88–89, 94, 111–12, 116, 125, 130–31, 137–46, 150, 156, 187–89, 192, 202, 206, 209, 212–15
Hood, J. W., 92
Houser, D. M., 71
Houser, Louis M., 62, 64, 71, 178n14, 179n22
Houston County, Georgia, 7, 8, 15, 17–18, 20, 22–24, 26–27, 29, 33, 39, 40–42, 48–49, 51–52, 56, 58–59, 61–66, 68–69, 71, 72, 75–78, 81–82, 89, 91–93, 96–97
Howard, Oliver Otis, 69
Hughes, Washington, 65, 179n32
Hulsey, E. M., 78
Hunt, Lang, 205n34
Hunter, Eliza Minnis, 91
Hunter, Jesse, 91

Indian Springs, Georgia, 27, 31
"internal colonialism," 140, 144
Israel CME Church, 85

Jackson High School, 125, 131. *See* Lane College
Jenkins, Charles, 13, 15, 18
Jervis, John A., 101
Jewett, George, 33–34, 36
Johnson, Andrew, 13–14, 69, 99
Johnson, Herschel, 158n4
Johnson, James, 13
Johnson, Nicholas, 105
Johnson, R. J., 139
Johnson, Sylvester, 140
Johnson, Warren, 65, 179n22
Jones, Charles Colcock, 50–51

Keen, Matthew, 115
Ku Klux Klan (KKK), 7, 16, 93, 96, 98, 104, 136
Ku Klux Klan Act, 100

Lamar, Henry G., 166n39
Lane, Isaac, 9, 86, 125, 136, 140, 150, 201n87, 206n37, 212n34, 214n56, 215n60
Lane, Jennie, 136
Lane College, 3, 125, 131, 136, 150, 214n56, 215n60
Leake, Ida, 207n55
Leake, R. D., 126, 207n55
Lepler, Jessica M., 37
Lewis, Dennis, 74
life estate, 37–38
literacy test, 129, 133, 135, 208n65, 210n15
LittleJohn, M. G., 122
Lodge, Henry Cabot "Force Bill," 134–35, 210n22
Losey, Daniel, 61–67, 70–71, 74
Love, James, 179n30
Lowe, J. W., 82
"Lydia," 71
Lynch, J. R., 101–2, 151, 196n30, 215n4
lynching, 10, 136, 141, 188n34

Macon, 22, 30–34, 36–37, 39–43, 47–49, 54, 93–94, 105, 108, 165n29, 166n39, 180n38, 192n73, 198n51; churches, 39, 48–49, 90, 94

Macon Guards, 162n52
Marshall County, Mississippi, 121, 123–24, 204n28, 206n38, 206n40, 208n67, 211n26
Martin, Bonnie, 37
Matkin-Rawn, Story, 108, 117
Matthews, Donald, 51
Matthews, J. W., 82, 105
Matthews, William A., 81
Meade, George, 18, 23, 78, 82
Methodist Episcopal Church (MEC), 123, 127, 190n60
Methodist Episcopal Church South (MEC, S), 21, 37, 39, 48–57, 59, 86–90, 95, 110–11, 124–25, 127, 130, 137–38, 140–46, 161n44, 188n36, 189n43, 190n60, 206n37, 212n36, 214n53, 214n56
Miles, William, 86, 92, 122–23, 131, 140, 188n38, 212n34, 213n48
Mississippi Constitution (1890), 129, 130, 135, 210n15
Mississippi Industrial College, 123, 215n60
Mississippi Plan, 105
Montgomery, Isaiah, 135, 211n23
Montgomery, William, 9, 127
Moore, B. M., 126, 207n55
Moore, Romulus, 162n56
Mound Bayou, Mississippi, 117, 135
Mulberry Street Methodist, 33, 39, **43**

National Association of Colored Women (NACW), 132
New Alabama, 27–31, 33–34, 47
New Hope School, 181n42
Nicademus, Kansas, 117
Nordhoff, Charles, 116, 177, 203n17
Northup, Solomon, 42

Ocmulgee Bank, 34, 36, 166n39
Ocmulgee River, 31–32, 34
O'Dell, Denton, 135, 208n67, 211n26
O'Donovan, Susan E., 5, 177n6
Ormond, George, 23, 68, 72–73, 75, 89, 92, 97–98, 106, 108–9, 115, 118–19, 181n42, 194n8
Ozane, Urbain, 121

Pace, Redding, 98
Paine, Robert, 86
Paine Institute (Paine College), 125, 130, 141, 143–46
Painter, Nell, 10, 117
Panic of 1837, 34, 39, 166n41, 170n94
Panola County, Mississippi, 69, 120–23, 127, 135, 205n34, 206n35, 206n38, 206n40, 208n67, 211n26
"Paper Wars," 138
paternalism, 21, 140
Patterson, J. H., 207n52
Patton, Silas P., 126, 207n55
Perry Methodist Church, 50, 52, 55
Peters, George Bodie, 115, 202n6
Phillips, C. H., 136, 212n38, 213n46, 214n52
Phillips County, Arkansas, 118, 119, 204n23
Pierce, Robert, 88–90, 94, 111–12, 140–42, 190, 201n86, 213n50
"Pig law," 135
Piles, J. H., 122
Planters Bank (Fort Valley), 106, 132
Pledger, W. A., 116
Plessy v. Ferguson (1896), 129, 133
Pollard, E. A., 32
Pomperoy, Samuel Clarke, 79
Pope, John, 14, 158n5
Porter, James, 81
Postea, J. G., 179n30
Postell, William F., 64, 78
property bank, 37
Primus, Isaac L., 23, 73

Quintard, Charles T., 77

railroads, 7, 26, 31–33, 39, 41, 60–61, 72–73, 81, 107, 110, 117, 126, 132, 134, 136, 162n1, 166n43, 177n11, 183n62, 195n25, 196n26, 205n30; Central, 33, 41, 60–61, 72, 177n11, 183n62; Central Illinois, 205n30; Fort Valley Depot, 150; Illinois Central, 126; Louisville, New Orleans and Texas (LNO&T), 126, 205n30; Macon and Brunswick, 72–73; Sardis, Pontotoc and Birmingham, 120; Sardis and Delta,

205n30; Southwestern, 25, 39, 41, 57, 72, 109, 132
Reconstruction Act of 1867, 78, 105, 158n9
Reidy, Joseph, 5, 38, 41, 154n6
Republican Party, 14, 17, 24, 26, 55–56, 58, 73, 82, 84, 96, 99, 101–2, 105, 113, 122, 142, 162, 175, 184n67, 185n5, 186n6, 190n90, 193n4, 195n20, 205n34
Richardson, C. H., 106, 113
Robinson, Fortune, 55
Robinson, Jeremiah, 65
Rodgers, Shep, 75
Ruger, Thomas, 61, 158
Russell, Nancy, 63
Russell, William H., 63
Rust College, 124, 127, 131
Rutherford, William, 113

Sabbath schools: Fort Valley, 53, 59, 68, 76, 181n42; Mississippi, 128, 161n46; Perry, 181n42
Samuels, Richard, 119, 203
Sardis, Mississippi, 120–24, 127–29, 131, 210n12
Sardis CME Church, 126, 207n55
Satcher, Buford, 205n34
Scurlock, Little John (L. J.), 102, 188n41
Second Creek War, 31
Second Great Awakening, 47–48
Settle, Josiah T., 122
Shegog, Peter, 205n34
Sherman, William T., 69
Silbey, C. C., 70
Simmons, A., 89, 92, 106
Simmons, John C., 55
Sims, James M., 81
Skiles, James, 99
Slappey, George, 115
slave missions: Fort Valley, 20; Perry, 52
Smith, James M., 97, 104, 107, 114
Southern Homestead Act, 69, 117, 182n49
Southern Rights Guard, 105, 110
Special Field Order, 69
Staley, Jim, 52
Stephens, Alexander, 142, 158n4, 214n54

St. Francis County, Arkansas, 119, 204n23
Stone Mountain, Georgia, 27
Sumner, Charles, 113, 175n45
Swift, William T., 64, 66, 78

Taylor, Caesar, 52, 65, 91, 110
Taylor County, 15, 22, 23, 67
Terry, Alfred H., 79–81
Thomas, George H., 190n60
Thompson, C. Mildred, 4, 5, 12, 155n6
Thompson, James Maurice, 157n1
Tift, Nelson, 78, 185n5
Tillson, Davis, 68–70, 108, 177, 181n44, 199n67
Toombs, Robert, 112, 213n50
trauma, 9, 62, 74, 147, 149; Black Church, 84–85, 156n17; theory, 84–85
Treaty of Indian Springs 1825, 26–28
Trelease, Allen, 100, 105

Usher, J. H., 180n38, 209n9
Ushers Chapel, 68, 143, 172n12, 181n41; beginning, 49–56

Vanderhorst, Richard, 86, 92, 102, 111, 140
Vardaman, James K., 210n18
Vesey, Denmark, 49
Vincent, Josiah, 65

Wallace, Adeline, 67–68, 181n41
Wallace, George, 79, 81, 99, 102, 106, 193n4
Wallace, S. B., 85
Walton, Overton Harrison (O. H.), 158n12, 161n51
Warren, Eli, 24, 26–27, 162n1, 170n94
Watkins, Beverly, 203n19
Watkins, Mack, 71
Watkins, Ruth, 10
Wells, Ida B., 123–24, 137
Wesley, John, 87
Wesleyan College, 33, 166n39
Wheeler, Edward L., 84
Williams, Henry, 208n65, 210n15
William v. Mississippi (1898), 129
Wilson, Henry, 101, 184n67

Wilson, John, 205n34
Winn, T., 80
Wood, Eliza, 136
Woodman, Harold, 33
Woodward, John, 73
Wooten, C. A., 80
Wynn, T. L., 88

Yellow Fever of 1878, 123–24, 206n42

Zass, Cereal, 64

ABOUT THE AUTHOR

Photo courtesy of the author

ALICIA K. JACKSON is associate professor of history at Covenant College. She earned her PhD from the University of Mississippi and is a contributor to *Southern Religion, Southern Culture: Essays Honoring Charles Reagan Wilson* (University Press of Mississippi, 2018). She is also the author of "The New Negro Movement in Shreveport," in *New Orleans and Urban Louisiana, Part C, 1920 to Present, Volume 14, New Orleans and Urban Louisiana*, edited by Samuel Shepherd (University of Louisiana at Lafayette Press, 2006).

www.ingramcontent.com/pod-product-compliance
Lightning Source LLC
Chambersburg PA
CBHW030621230426

43661CB00053B/2091